Teacher Education, Learning Innovation and Accountability

Series Editor

Claire Wyatt-Smith, Institute for Learning Sciences and Teacher Education,
Australian Catholic University, Brisbane, QLD, Australia

This book series offers research-informed discussion and analysis of teacher preparation, certification and continuing professional learning and the related practice and policy drivers for change and reform. The series fosters and disseminates research about teaching as a profession of choice while offering a unique link to the realities of pre-service experience in workforce preparation. It takes account of research on teacher formation that opens up issues not routinely connected: what teachers need to know and be able to do, and who they are, namely the person of the teacher and their capabilities in contributing to students' personal development and wellbeing. This goal provides a current, practical and international view of the future of initial teacher education programs.

Antonio Bautista García-Vera

Editor

Photographic Elicitation and Narration in Teachers Education and Development

 Springer

Editor
Antonio Bautista García-Vera 
Education Faculty
Complutense University
Madrid, Spain

ISSN 2524-5562   ISSN 2524-5570 (electronic)
Teacher Education, Learning Innovation and Accountability
ISBN 978-3-031-20166-0   ISBN 978-3-031-20164-6 (eBook)
https://doi.org/10.1007/978-3-031-20164-6

Preface

The essay is a collective book, (thirteen chapters), which presents new research and experiences that implement the use of photography in teacher professional development. The research uses visual methodological tools, such as photo-elicitation and photo-voice, and the photographic narration; however, there remains a lack of clarity about what they mean, how they are used, and whether they are effective in providing valuable information about teachers' everyday world. Through different proposals and examples, and the presentation of photographs, the reader will understand the value of photography to facilitate inquiry and reflection on practice. All this synthesizes the major contribution of the book. An interesting field to diversity of readers: Researchers, Postgraduate students, Undergraduate students, Practitioners, and international professionals associations.

What is it about photography that earns it its place in the pre-service and in-service training of teachers discussed in this essay? Well, among other virtues, it is a representational system that provides three levels of information: denotation or material information, connotation or semantic information, and punctum or emotional information. The first two are included in Panofsky's iconography (1995) and in Barthes's visual semiotics (1989). Denotation is linked to the level that represents the what or/and the who that give content to the image, and connotation refers to the meaning given to the image captured in a photograph. It was Barthes (1989) who expressed the need to contemplate the emotion transmitted by an image, making it the third level of information transmitted by a photograph. He called it punctum, meaning the wound, the prick or pain experienced and represented in a photograph taken by its author, or reported to those who observe it.

While the first refers to physical or material information external to humans, the last two symbolically convey their tacit and intimate ideas and feelings. All three are necessary and sufficiently representative, and therefore communicate our experiential life. Given these basic levels of information, in this essay we will also discuss the two sub-levels into which Van Leeuwen (2008) later divided the symbolic level: the iconographic symbolism of a photograph, referring to the external meanings of its author stemming from agreements and sociocultural conventions; and the icono-logical symbolism, that includes the creator's own meanings represented in symbols arising from his or her emotions and ideas.

The nature of this language, or symbolic system of representation facilitated by photography, has sparked our curiosity and interest in knowing how it can mediate the relationship between teachers, their school and their community and improve their pre-service and in-service education. In the following pages, we take for granted that any changes and improvements in the competence of our teachers stems from reflecting on and questioning their own teaching skills. Nevertheless, both histori-cally and culturally, the context where such reflection takes place and the tools used to mediate that relationship have an effect on the direction taken by the intended professional improvement. Thus, an analysis of the institutional and research context allows us to modulate different space-time and organizational situations that will assign different functions to resources and different roles to the various elements that make up teacher training, where photography will be the main tool in these teacher development environments.

This book has been organized into three content clusters intended to contribute to the further development of hot topics and issues in teacher education. The first cluster consists of four chapters that address open topics, such as what content or photographic know-how should be included in the much debated media literacy of teachers or, more specifically, photography as an element of teacher training and research. We also discuss the way in which cameras and photographic language facilitate teachers' reflections and their access to the theories and beliefs that underlie and guide their classroom and school practice, giving them the knowledge they need to change their approach practice and, consequently, improve their teaching skills. In this first cluster we will also study the different ways in which photography can develop the practical dimension of pre-service teacher education in skills that will not only improve their competence as teachers, but will also develop their artistic talents.

Chapter five includes a semantic review of photo-elicitation and the similarities and differences between this and photovoice. We show that they are two procedures based on photographic representation and communication that come from different traditions. Both Collier (1957) and Harper (2002), in the field of anthropology, claim that the essence of photo-elicitation is the incorporation of photographs in research interviews. Wang and Burris (1997), however, coined the term photovoice to refer to the use of photography to identify the opinions of users on their community and how it can be improved. Thus, while photo-elicitation is used as a data collection technique in research that revolves around interviews with a single person, photo-voice has been used in groups in the context of social training and intervention or community change. The essence of procedures developed to evoke and represent contradictions and inconsistencies in teaching, based on photographs taken by the teachers themselves or by any other observer of life in classrooms and schools, have prompted us to combine both photo-elicitation traditions in teacher training, since they bring together both training and research.

In the sixth chapter, therefore, we argue that photo-elicitation is a flexible process open to the variety and complexity of purposes and emerging investigative and training situations in any educational institution. One of the contributions of this essay is to define the purpose of photo-elicitation in the training and in-service development of teachers. Photo-elicitation can be viewed as a cooking pot that receives and holds different elements or ingredients that are combined to prepare a nourishing, or nutritional, training dish. In the case of photo-elicitation, one of the ingredients is the camera used by one of the participants to capture moments of school life which, depending on the particular purpose of the training process, are important to reveal. The second element is the author of the image discussed at each session, who can be one of the trainee teachers, any other member of the educational community, such as a pupil, another faculty member, or a family member or guest observer, or even the person shown in the photograph. The third ingredient is the participants' description, interpretation, assessment, or questioning of the moment contained in the photograph.

The final basic element of a photo-elicitation session is the order in which the members of the group speak, taking into account their dual role as either the creator of an image with a communicative intent, or as an analyst or critic, each interpreting the elements of photography from their cultural frameworks. Therefore, in this element, we have to consider the nature and purpose of the comments made by the participants, which may be to gather more information to better understand what has been previously described, or to determine the reasons for some of the actions included in the photographs, or to question or challenge the validity of the decision made by someone faced by a dilemma reflected in the image. In this way, photo-elicitation in teacher training involves the revelation of theories and beliefs, the intentions behind our own actions, the interpretations made by others that sometimes raise issues that compel us to become aware of the contradictions and inconsistencies in the objective we or any other school colleague pursue in our teaching activities, and that need to be resolved by introducing changes that improve our teaching skills.

In this book, we will see that the function of photography in these sessions is to help participants evoke the meanings, ideas and emotions that, for them, are symbolically contained in the elements that make up that image. In this respect, photography is primarily the vehicle of the connotative and punctum levels of the image, and secondarily of the denotative level that provide the descriptions of what is materially captured in the space of an instant. Thus, the seventh chapter analyses the tutor-student relationships in a practicum aimed at bringing together mutual training—the pre-service training undergone by students during their work experience and the in-service training of teacher-tutors. This second cluster ends with a study on the use of photo-elicitation in virtual teaching communities, specifically: is it possible to transfer the face-to-face essence of photo-elicitation to a virtual environment? What type of changes, or adjustments, must be made to photograph-mediated elements and procedures?

The photographic narrative that forms the content of the third and last cluster of the book is seen as the assembly of a group of still images in a chronological or argumentative sequence (Freeman, 2010). It can also be understood as a dialogue between photographs, or as the fusion of several moments or instants of an episode, task or experience captured in photographs, where the teachers or authors describe textually or verbally their reasons or motives for taking that particular photograph (the result of their private mental inquiry) and how they come together and develop to form the audio-visual story (Chatman, 1992). The narrative introduces the time dimension into the spatial description and analysis provided by photo-elicitation, extending the discussion and debate beyond the content of each photograph, understood, in this sense, as a snapshot of life open to the past and to the future.

The chapters in this cluster explain the lines of research into the relevance of the use of the photographic story as a procedure to promote inquiry and narrative among teachers. For this purpose, we will discuss the modalities and types of narrative structures that call for enquiry among teachers, and which, in turn, contribute relevant meanings and arguments to photographic stories. These include essays and photomontage aimed at documenting and encouraging debate on professional development and, consequently, on improving the quality of the educational institution. Also, by way of example, the inquisitiveness of the self-portrait involves questioning the motivations that led a teacher to take it, and will thus contain their preconceptions and implicit theories about their job. Inquiry encouraged by a photo story enriches the evaluation of the customs or ways of life of the neighbourhood, or of organizational routines and rules on the use and function of corridors, playgrounds or other elements of the school that have been narrated.

In the last two chapters, special situations of teacher training based on photographic narration are described. These are special because of their out-of-school survival contexts in which they occur; one, in places of pain, such as hospitals or childhood spaces and times that cannot be re-lived; and, the other, among the stones and sand of Saharawi refugee camps. If practical teacher training considers the teacher to be an artist, both texts discuss how to prepare him or her as such through photographic narratives, some of which are multimodal. Thus, in the twelfth chapter, the artist's book is presented as the document shaped by photographic auto-ethnographies, or photo-autobiographies, compiled by in-service or trainee teachers in difficult situations that they can only tackle personally as artists, and, perhaps in the future, as professionals. As the author says, these books are important to encourage teacher to engage in reflection, because there is nothing like training in creation to connect us with the other, because complex and subtle photographic auto-ethnographies ask and at the same time partly answer, generating uncertainty that helps teachers, or trainee teachers, to seek rather than find.

In the last chapter of this essay, the difficulty emerges from the context and survival situations in which the Saharawi people live and, consequently, the vital need to prepare them to ensure their future existence. A teacher training centre trains teachers in risk situations and ways of life in two contexts; one, in the occupied territories and, another, in the village of Tindouf where Algeria allows these people to live as refugees. In both situations, photography is important for these teachers, either to show educational content, such as how to identify and deactivate an anti-personnel mine, or how to improve teaching processes or the organization of schedules and spaces designed and used by teachers. In both contexts, the photographic narrative that goes hand in hand with the verbal language of the Sahrawi teachers is the soul of the survival training programmes. These initiatives map pathways between stones and sand for the young, growing population, and encourage teachers to observe, inquire and deliberate using ideas translated into images that will gradually make them safer, more artistically sensitive desert gardeners and, therefore, better teachers.

Finally, the texts that are the source of data in some chapters have, in turn, breathed life back into many digital cameras consigned to drawers or other dark, silent spaces following the advent of smartphones in technologically advanced societies. And there they remain, disinterestedly waiting for a teacher to take them to their schools to redefine their profession.

Madrid, Spain

Antonio Bautista García-Vera
bautista@ucm.es

References

Barthes, R. (1989). *La cámara lúcida*. Paidós.

Chatman, S. (1992). *Historia y discurso. Estructura narrativa en la novela y en el cine*. Taurus.

Collier, J. (1957). Photography in Anthropology: A Report on two experiments. *American Anthropologist, 59*(5), 843–859.

Freeman, M. (2010). *La narración fotográfica*. Blume.

Harper, D. (2002). Talking about pictures: A case for photo-elicitation. *Visual Studies, 17*(1), 13–26.

Panofsky, E. (1995). *El significado de las artes visuales*. Alianza.

Van Leeuwen, T. (2008). Semiotics and Iconograhy. In T. Van Leeuwen & C. Jewitt (Eds.), *Handbook of visual analysis* (pp. 92–118). Sage.

Wang, C., & Burris, M. A. (1997). Photovoice: Concept, methodology and use for participatory needs assessment. *Health Education and Behavior, 24*(3), 369–387.

Contents

Part I
Photography as a System of Representation and Meaning in Teacher Training

Chapter 1
Photography in the Media Literacy of Teachers: What Impression Do We Give?

Alfonso Gutiérrez Martín

Introduction

Baudelaire, the nineteenth century French poet and art critic who scorned early efforts at photography, claiming it would corrupt art, could never have imagined the current state of the art and importance of photography in today's world. "It is time, then, for it to return to its true duty, which is to be the servant of the sciences and arts — but the very humble servant, like printing or shorthand, which have neither created nor supplemented literature." He went on to warn, "But if [photography is] allowed to encroach upon the domain of the impalpable and the imaginary, upon anything whose value depends solely upon the addition of something of a man's soul, then it will be so much the worse for us" (in Baudelaire, 2017: 231–233).

Many years of technological development later, we could conclude that the main role of photography and imagery in general continues to be that of a servant, albeit "a very humble servant" of the sciences and the arts, and in terms of teacher training, also of education in these fields.

In all these years, photography and the language of imagery, despite their importance and ubiquity, do not seem to have merited a leading position in school curricula or teacher training. In teaching, photography is used mainly for delivering presentations and as a teaching aid in various subjects. In teacher training, aside from technical education, it is only used to analyse the didactic potential of imagery and its function at the service of other arts and sciences. Visual literacy, media education, photography as art, are largely ignored in both basic education and teacher training.

A. Gutiérrez Martín (✉)
University of Valladolid, Segovia, Spain
e-mail: alfonso.gutierrez.martin@uva.es

A. Bautista García-Vera (ed.), *Photographic Elicitation and Narration in Teachers Education and Development*, Teacher Education, Learning Innovation and Accountability, https://doi.org/10.1007/978-3-031-20164-6_1

Media Literacy in Teacher Training

Before discussing any possible relationship between photography and education, it is important to highlight the need to introduce audio-visual and media literacy education in basic teacher training.

Since the introduction of Educational Technology in the last century, both photography and other new informational and audio-visual technologies have found their way into the sphere of education as potential facilitators of learning; as tools rather than as a subject of study and reflection. Perhaps due more to external social pressure than the commitment of education professionals and experts, new technological devices have been incorporated into the classroom as other markets, such as that of domestic appliances or business, have become saturated. In other words, cameras, video recorders and computers, for example, were introduced into educational centres once they had already been widely known and used in other settings, such as business or the home. Although these products, unlike whiteboards or overhead projectors, are not specifically manufactured for the classroom, in Educational Technology their more teaching-related characteristics and advantages have been highlighted to justify, albeit "a posteriori", their acquisition and use.

Audio-visual devices and computers undoubtedly have considerable educational potential, and although they were not designed for education, specific educational and instructive programmes have been developed for both television and computers, and classroom activities can be programmed to take advantage of the benefits of each new device in the teaching–learning processes.

Teacher training in the use of these new media resources has always included courses on how to operate them before going on to describe their potential use as a teaching tool. As the complexity and number of devices have increased with digitization, teacher training has prioritised the technological or instrumental dimension over educational aspects (Bautista, 2014). Several experts have warned of this bias, pointing out that the most important thing for teachers is not to know how to use these devices, but when and why to use them, always trying to optimize their possible educational advantages and minimize their drawbacks.

If the role of media in education could be limited to their use as a teaching tool, it would be logical to focus teacher training in ICT and digital media on their technological and didactic dimensions. We know, however, that the educational potential of digital media, their ability to influence the opinions, beliefs and attitudes of users, is currently more important than any role we can assign them as teaching tools in formal education.

As early as 1980, UNICEF recognized, with some optimism, the potential of digital media as agents of informal education. They dubbed them "the third channel", after formal and non-formal education, and defined them as "all the available instruments and information, communication, and social action channels that can be used to help transmit basic knowledge and inform and educate the population regarding social issues" (UNICEF, 1990).

With the advent of the Internet, this third channel has overflowed and flooded schools and other educational institutions. Our students are almost permanently subject to a barrage of increasingly visual information that is shared on social networks and different virtual communities. It is becoming increasingly difficult to identify the values and ideas inevitably implicit in viral messages, in YouTube videos, and in web pages due to the amount of information (infoxication) and the lack of control. In the last century, educommunication was required to develop skills in the critical appraisal of mass media; it is now also needed to join virtual communities, to create and interpret messages responsibly, to learn to value and read not only verbal language, but also multimedia documents, and, in short, to be twenty-first century citizens with all our rights and duties.

If media education is a prerequisite for anyone who is part of the Information Society, it should also be a mandatory subject in teacher training in ICT and digital media. With regard to ICT and media training, from a purely educational, as opposed to instructive, point of view, digital media or digital literacy in teachers is today far more important and necessary than the acquisition of the technological and teaching skills which are prioritised in pre-service and in-service training programmes.

The tendency to prioritize technological and instructive aspects over training in ICT could be a logical consequence of a neoliberal approach, where results matter more than processes, and where these results must be quantitatively measurable. As we have already pointed out in Gutiérrez and Torrego (2018), governments and educational institutions appear to have reached an overall consensus with regard to competence-based education. Teachers at different levels, textbook authors, and educational authorities work together to formulate basic education and teacher training in terms of competencies. In this respect, the Institute of Educational Technology and Teacher Training (INTEF, in its Spanish acronym) published its meticulous 2017 Common Framework for the Digital Competence of Educators (INTEF, 2017).

UNESCO had previously published its "ICT Competency Framework for Teachers", a document that, according to its authors, was created to inform education policy makers, teacher trainers, vocational trainers and in-service teachers about the role of ICT in education reform (UNESCO, 2011).

Although we believe it is essential for teachers to develop clearly definable and assessable ICT skills, in this chapter we are calling for teacher media literacy, so we warn the reader that current competence-based models focus on the technical and operational aspects of media devices more than media literacy education. Potter and McDougall (2017: 85), for example, question both US and European competency frameworks for media literacy, and ask whether this competency model does not ignore two important dimensions that underlie all media literacy education: cultural studies and social literacy.

After publishing its aforementioned ICT competency for teachers, UNESCO went on to release a new document on media and information literacy (Wilson et al., 2011) for teachers, or what every teacher should know about media literacy and how to teach it. This new document, however, was not as influential as the publication on

ICT competency for teachers—hardly surprising in a country where neither audio-visual literacy nor educommunication have been given the importance they deserve in the digital age.

One of the main objectives of media literacy education is to raise awareness among the general public, mostly ICT users, of how the media influence their education, how the images they offer us gradually shape the way we see the world around us and the people in it. In the case of teachers and educators, understanding the educational potential of the media will encourage them to assess their educational potential inside and outside the classroom in awareness campaigns, values education, citizenship education, etc.

Teachers, particularly those that include the media and ICT in their subject content, will also be responsible for the media literacy of their students and for media education. Like languages or mathematics, which have their own teaching methods (Gutiérrez & Torrego, 2018), media education should be included in teacher training programmes in new technologies.

The foregoing authors propose a model for teacher training in ICT and digital media consisting of five general subject blocks that cover the training of different teachers and educators: (1) Multiple literacy in the digital age; (2) Media and digital environments as agents of informal education; (3) Integration of digital media and technologies in the curriculum as teaching tools; (4) Integration of ICT and media in the curriculum as a study subject. Media education in formal education; and (5) Media education in university education and pre-service teacher training.

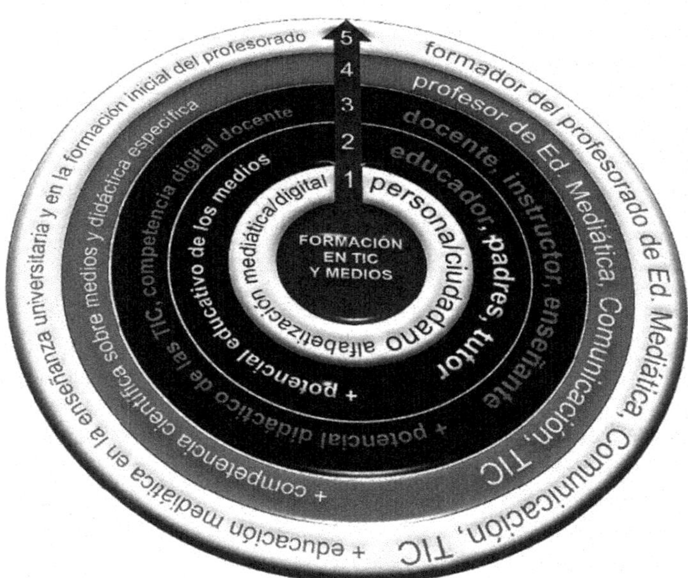

The three basic dimensions of ICT and media training of all teachers, irrespective of their level or subject specialty, are depicted in the first three concentric circles of the graph of this model. In the first place, the competence all teachers should have as members of the Information Society, i.e. media and digital literacy, but which cannot be taken for granted, particularly among older teachers.

In the last two decades of the twentieth century, a series of key concepts of critical media literacy education in schools were developed in Canada (Duncan et al., 1989), based on the approach put forward by Len Masterman (Masterman, 1985; Masterman & Thompson, 1980).

These key concepts (media constructions, representations, institutions and audiences), which formed the basis for the golden age of media education in various anglosphere countries in the 1990s, could also be valid today if the new literacies, "trans-literacies" or "multiliteracies" are taught from a critical perspective instead of focussing on the characteristics of digital technology or the needs of the market.

The time is right, since according to Ollé et al. (2004), in the first years of this millennium, when the hegemony of Mass Media 1.0 gave way to that of the so-called "participatory" media 2.0, critical pedagogy experienced a worldwide boom based on new utopia (such as "Another world is possible"), on the new approach to social and educational theories (Habermas, Chomsky, Freire), and on new transformative educational practices (such as learning communities or democratic schools).

We agree with Jolls and Wilson (2014) that "new media" neither change the essence of media education, nor modify its growing importance for social development. However, we would point out that although these new media, particularly digital photography and video, have not changed the essence of media education, they have changed its content and practices to the extent that we need to establish and clarify the basic principles or essence of liberating media literacy currently obscured by the glamour of digital technologies.

These key concepts inherited from digital media education of the last century would, according to Gutiérrez (2008), give rise to five basic contents that are also applicable to digital photography and new media:

- The photographs and documents released by the media are not mere reflections of the reality they represent, not windows on the world, not pieces of reality embodied in a medium—they are constructions, ways of representing a reality.
- Media companies are complicated networks with considerable commercial and ideological interests that are reflected in the products they create and the way these are distributed.
- Audiences are considered as "products" that are offered to advertisers and data management companies for commercial purposes.
- The media act as educators of their audience, transmitting an ideology and making a decisive contribution to the creation of a particular cultural identity or type of society.

The media literacy of any individual, therefore, involves becoming aware of the potential of the media as agents of informal education. Therefore, we need to add the teacher's need to become aware of the educational potential of the media and ICTs to the second circle of our graph. The teacher, being an educator, must have a greater understanding of the educational potential of the media than would be expected of other individuals, greater than that of first level literacy expected of any other person or student.

Third, we need to add the specific training undergone by the teacher as an educator: understanding the educational potential of each new medium—in our case of photography—and its possible advantages and disadvantages as a tool to facilitate the teaching–learning processes in the instructive and practical dimensions of education.

Levels four and five, as can be seen in the graph, are not applicable to any teacher at any level, but only to those who teach ICT or media-related subjects, such as Photography, Computer Science, Communication or Media Education (level 4), or teachers in training in these subjects (level 5).

Photography in the Development of Media Literacy: A Bit of History

As discussed above, we consider media education to be part of basic literacy, applicable to both students and teachers at any level. In this section, when we refer to the development of media literacy, we mean not only students in compulsory education, but any other person, and in particular teachers, who in many cases find themselves responsible for their own media literacy and that of their students.

According to authors such as Fedorov (2008), media literacy education began in France during the 1920s with the cinema club movement and its clear educational intent. This initiative, launched by the *Offices regionaux du cinema educateur*, coincided with the introduction of photography, cine films, and the gramophone in schools by Freinet and his wife Elise, who carried on the tradition of the "new school" and incorporated into their class the most modern techniques of their time, such as typesetting, photographic and video cameras, cine films, and the tape recorder.

Freinet, whom Fedorov (2008) considers one of the founders of media literacy education, explained that photography and cine films were not simply means of entertainment or teaching resources, but "the new way of thinking and personal expression" (Freinet, 1963: 12). This is why this pioneering French teacher believed that schools should teach the language of audio-visual media in the same way as basic principles of art were taught.

However, these and similar experiences in Europe with state-of-the-art photography or cine films in the first half of the twentieth century can be considered isolated events or individual initiatives that almost always involved the introduction of cine films into the classroom, such as the case of the British Film Institute in the United Kingdom. Media literacy was not introduced into formal education until the 1950s and 1960s. Until then, educational institutions had ignored cameras and the media, and newspapers, comics and other elements of popular culture were banned from the classroom—hardly surprising if we bear in mind that today new media such as telephones and other mobile devices are not allowed in the classroom.

In the second half of the twentieth century, the ubiquity and influence of television made it inevitable that not only the pioneers of audio-visual education, but also formal education systems would consider its introduction into school curricula. This introduction of mass media, film, press, radio and television can be approached from two basic perspectives:

- The contents of films, television programmes and popular culture were considered to have a major (usually negative) influence on education.
- Audio-visual language, television, cameras (photographic and video), and other audio-visual media, together with the written press and radio, could be considered to facilitate the teaching–learning processes.

The distinction between educating "for" or teaching "about" the media, on the one hand, and educating or teaching "with" the media, on the other, is still a useful dichotomy in the study of the curricular integration of new technologies in formal education, and in no way suggests that one can occur without the other. Photography, mass media, ICTs, or any other technology cannot be considered mere classroom learning tools that can be used without taking into account their social, ideological and economic implications. According to McLuhan (1964), every medium has its message, and that message must be analysed and critically investigated in media literacy education. Media literacy education is also inseparable from the use of the media themselves as resources. It would be absurd, for example, to address the importance of photography in social networks without taking into account how students use their mobile cameras.

With regard to the different approaches to media education throughout history, and therefore the introduction of photography and visual language, we would simply recall that early media studies were "counter-media", a strategy that has been dubbed "the inoculation approach" (Gutiérrez, 1997; Kellner & Share, 2008). Later, in the middle of the twentieth century, media education shifted from a fundamentally protective approach against the supposed negative influence of the media, to a "discriminatory" approach, where education was assigned the task of distinguishing between "good" and "bad" products using aesthetic and ideological criteria. It was up to educators to help students distinguish between "Culture" with a capital "C" and so-called popular culture, of much lower rank. From a descriptive perspective, applied to photography as a denotative interpretation of the image, students analysed the form and content of media products without going into the ideology behind in the content, or the ideology of the authors. Technology is assumed to be transparent, its inherent message is not assessed, and media studies, as we have said, focus on a description and formal analysis of the products. The study of both media products and their uses and of the technologies and devices themselves involves analysing their characteristics from supposedly a aseptic perspective; the world of photography, television or the Internet is studied, for example, in the same way as the skeletal system of mammals.

In the study of photography, aesthetic approaches based on the consideration of media products as popular art adapted to the characteristics of new media have prevailed. According to De Abreu et al. (2017: 1), the artistic or aesthetic approach currently promotes media education and media literacy through creation and production, while placing special emphasis on enjoying the media. The greatest danger in this empowerment of individuals to value the aesthetic qualities of photography and to use the camera as a form of personal expression, lies in its tendency to focus too much on what products are like or how they are made, while overlooking the ideological, awareness-raising role of media companies and the role of photographic representations in the social construction of knowledge.

Using the iceberg metaphor that Ferguson (1998) developed to defend a critical approach to media education, we could say that analysing the media using aesthetic, descriptive and technological approaches, together with the denotative interpretation of photographs, focusses on what is visible, while what is truly important is hidden under the surface of the water: "the vast bulk beneath the water is the intellectual, historical, and analytical base". Many educators are unaware of these rationales or principles, while others choose to ignore them in favour of an alleged and impossible ideological and political impartiality.

Audio-visual and media literacy has evolved in parallel with the appearance of new media and new communication resources. As Frau-Meigs (2017: 114) points out, "media literacy is shifting from the critical reception and analysis of mass media of the 1950s, to the reflective practices on media and social networks of the digital age". The very concept and definitions of media education, digital literacy, information literacy, digital competence, audio-visual education, etc. have also been adapted to today's world. UNESCO now recognises that "the empowerment of people through media and information literacy (MIL) is an important requirement for fostering equitable access to information and knowledge and promoting free independent and pluralistic media and information systems"; and defines MIL "as a composite of the competences (knowledge, skills and attitudes) necessary for life and work today. MIL considers all forms of media and other information providers such as libraries, archive, museums and Internet irrespective of technologies used" (https://goo.gl/1hNyZT).

In this chapter on teacher training, we cannot ignore what UNESCO goes on to say about MIL: "A particular focus will be on training teachers to sensitize them to the importance of MIL in the education process, enable them to integrate MIL into their teaching and provide them with appropriate pedagogical methods, curricula and resources".

Photography and Education in the Digital Age

Just as Baudelaire in 1859 could never have imagined the role that photography would play as a means of expression in interpersonal communication and as a visual art in the twentieth century, a few decades ago it would have been hard for us to imagine that the mobile phone camera would be the most widely-used technology today, with functions as diverse as making simple annotations, recording data and events, announcing one's presence in a particular place at a particular time, communicating and exchange information, and its role in personal expression and artistic creation.

The mobile phone is undoubtedly the most widely used technological device today, and proves more than anything else McLuhan's notion of media as an extension of man (McLuhan, 1964). For many users, the loss of their mobile would be nothing less than an "amputation". The ubiquity of mobiles and Internet hyperconnectivity has led to a boom in instant messaging and visual communication, and with it, a renaissance in photography and still images.

Statistics let us see this boom in photographic images in numbers: The number of photos uploaded to networks went from 70 million a day in 2016 to 95 in 2017. In 2017, 46,200 images were published every minute, and 250 million users used Instagram stories every day (according to data from the "Statista" portal). It is easy to assume that these figures will already have multiplied by the time you read this book.

The history of humanity has been marked by milestones that have led to a significant change in the evolution of the world and of mankind, such as writing and the invention of the printing press. The development of digitization is perhaps the event that has had the most impactful and diverse influence on the cultural evolution of mankind. This technology has led to the creation of interconnected communication networks (Internet) and the habitual use of the photographic image to record, store and share information.

The importance of media such as photography, cinema or television in the twentieth century already compelled us to question the excessive bias of literacy towards verbal language. Early computers and networks contributed decisively to the dissemination of alphanumeric information, but technological developments at the turn of the century have also allowed still and moving images to circulate on networks and even surpass verbal language in some settings. The integration of languages means that most of the documents that we usually consume and produce today are multimedia. There are a growing number of mobile applications that make it easier to edit documents and add text to images, and a growing number of users communicate using multimedia documents. As a general rule applicable to the photographs produced by young people, we could say that, as Castañeda (2015: 29) shows in the case of memes, "visual aesthetics matters less than open communication, and that is a notion that must be taken into account when designing visual messages, because effectiveness has nothing to do with aesthetics". Young people, despite the fact that their formal education has been almost exclusively focused on verbal literacy, today communicate with images, but without a basic knowledge of photography or audio-visual literacy.

This is paradoxical, and the fact that visual, audio-visual or multimodal language has not joined verbal language in the basic literacy of the twenty-first century student can only be explained by the inertia and rigidity of educational institutions. Audio-visual language has already permeated the lives of several generations, and we have learned to interpret the basic signs. Obviously, nowadays no one runs away when they see the image of a train advancing towards the camera. The degree of iconicity of visual as opposed to verbal representations means that we can all achieve a basic level of understanding without the need for instruction or teaching. This "natural" or spontaneous visual literacy, however, like the ability to understand and speak orally we acquire as children, does not cover the needs of today's visual civilization.

Furthermore, the traditional, solely verbal literacy taught in compulsory schooling, though intentional and systematic, is also insufficient in today's world. In this so-called era of convergence (Jenkins, 2006), many authors have called for a comprehensive, integrated model of basic training or multiple literacy that integrates languages and knowledge, and for the convergence of real and virtual learning environments (Tyner et al., 2015).

The ubiquity of cameras in mobile devices has led to the rise of photography on social networks, and the rise of image-based communication. This increase in the production and consumption of images is, for some, "a revolution as deep and essential as that of Gutenberg or, even the invention of writing, albeit using still or moving images".

Every day—Millán Muñoz (2016) reminds us—we see as many photos or images as a person living a century ago saw in their entire life. This undoubtedly has educational repercussions, and we should ask ourselves—as does the aforementioned author (ibid.)—if all these thousands of images we consume are not changing the way we think, feel, act, want, speak, or feel moved. Millán goes on to ask: "And are they not changing the way we relate to other human beings? Or could they even, if the pace of technological change continues unabated, as appears to be the case, in some way change our brain, chemistry or cerebral neurology over the coming decades and centuries?"

Photography in Teacher Training

Logically, the ubiquity and widespread use of cameras will give photography centre stage in the pre-service and in-service training of teachers. This book describes the variety of different uses of photography in the teaching profession. We will see how photographic narrative can be used to reflect on and analyse teaching situations and practices, how photo-elicitation can recreate what happened in a situation beyond the immediate action, and bring to light the conflicts and ethical dilemmas found in the classroom (Bautista, 2017).

Photography is undoubtedly a useful tool in improving teaching skills, and is, as discussed above, a very versatile and easily accessible resource in teaching–learning processes. And if, added to this, we consider the importance of this medium in the daily lives of our students, we will see that it is essential to train teachers in photography, ICTs and media in general, and how all these can be used in education.

We have talked about photography and education in the digital age, and of image studies as an essential part of basic literacy for the twenty-first century. This basic literacy is not only needed at an early age, but is part of the in-service training of education professionals who, for the most part, have not received media education in either their compulsory education or in their professional training. As mentioned above, it is part of the audio-visual and media literacy of all teachers to be at least as familiar with photography and other media as any other person (level 1 of the graph).

Teaching teachers how to teach also involves studying photography as a resource. One of the greatest advantages of images as teaching–learning tools has always been the ability to present and represent realities that are not easily accessible to human perception. The use of photography and images as a teaching resource should go hand in hand with media literacy education that shows how images are not real, and how the representations they convey to us and that we convey with them can be biased. This is particularly necessary in today's post-truth era, with fake news, deepfakes, virtual reality, augmented reality, etc.

The image as a teaching tool also acquires a new dimension in the digital age, where it is no longer merely used to facilitate understanding, but where both students and teachers can take photographs related to the learning content, present their work in a visual language, and habitually use photography as a means of expression. Creating images of curricular contents can at the same time be a part of media education and visual language learning. According to Rabadán (2015), teaching literacy through participatory photography should be understood as a way of "empowering communicationally".

It makes no sense to conceive the curricular integration of photography as a tool without addressing the study of audio-visual language, just as it make no sense to study photography or video separately, but rather as part of a comprehensive approach to digital and media literacy. Nor does it make sense to design media education strategies for our classrooms that include photography and other technologies without taking into account the presence, importance, and features of cameras in the daily lives of students and educators.

Teachers must be aware of the new functions of photography that have arisen from the current ubiquity of cameras. As mentioned previously, photography is not only used to record something beautiful or remarkable—for artistic expression—but has replaced text in activities such as collecting ephemeral information or as a notebook. We see that now "take note" on bulletin boards has become "take a photo" Photography is also constantly used as a record of events, particularly "selfies", and as a way of showing that we have been in a particular place. This evidence is shared instantly on social networks.

Some time ago, it was said that "if you're not on the Internet you might as well not exist", in terms of sales and presenting products to potential clients. This now appears to have become personal, especially in the case of young people. Attending a concert or any other event only acquires its full meaning when a photo of it is shared on the Internet. It is not enough to say it in a text message, it must be demonstrated with a photograph taken at that very moment.

Immediacy is, in my opinion, the main characteristic of photography in the digital age—immediacy in seeing the photo—a feature of digital cameras—and the possibility of sharing it immediately. This has become commonplace due to the integration of a camera in mobile devices that, in turn, operate as a small (or not so small) computer connected to the Internet.

Working with cameras in a mobile multimedia device increases the versatility and functions of photography in the daily lives of our students. Cameras can also be used as a record in academic settings, and the teacher should, therefore, know how to make the most of the educational potential of photography.

Visual search and image recognition applications, some of which are integrated into our Internet search engines, are now easy to find. It will be increasingly common to take a photograph of an object, a monument, a person, etc. and to immediately obtain access to written and visual information available on the Internet about what is represented in the photograph. The camera has also replaced the scanner and character recognition software. What's more, a photograph of a text in a certain language already gives you access to a translation in different languages; just like a picture of a maths problem can show you the solution on the Internet. All these functions of photography are part of the daily lives of today's students. Features such as facial recognition, already available in mobiles, can spark a classroom discussion on the potential of this ubiquitous technology to control our actions.

Immediacy and versatility, two characteristics of photography in the twenty-first century, should also ideally be present in the development of educational systems and the corresponding teacher training. Ideally, the changes brought about by the prevalence of visual language in today's communication practices will lead to immediate changes in educational policies and basic education programmes. However, if we can define versatility as the ability to adapt quickly and easily to different functions, it is clear that, unlike digital photography, neither basic education nor teacher training have been able to adapt to new forms of expression.

If classroom teaching continues to move further and further away from the way young people create meaning and communicate, if we limit ourselves to forbidding them from taking photos and bringing mobiles to class, what impression will they have of education? How can we raise awareness of these inconsistencies among teachers? These and other questions will be addressed in the following chapters of this book.

References

Baudelaire, C. (2017). *Salones y otros escritos sobre arte*. Antonio Machado Libros.

Bautista, A. (2014, April 23). Instruir, pero también formar. *El País*. https://elpais.com/elpais/2013/04/03/opinion/1364997141_478189.html

Bautista, A. (2017, Julio–diciembre). La foto-elicitación en la formación permanente de maestros de educación primaria. *Alteridad, 12*(2202–214). https://doi.org/10.17163/alt.v12n2.2017.06

Castañeda, W. (2015, enero–junio). Los memes y el diseño: contraste entre mensajes verbales y estetizantes. *Revista KEPES, 12*(11), 9–33. https://bit.ly/2EtYySD. https://doi.org/10.17151/kepes.2015.12.11.2

De Abreu, B. S. Mihailidis, P., Lee, A. Y. L., Melki, J., & McDougall, J. (2017). Arc of research and central issues in media literacy education. In B. S. De Abreu, P. Mihailidis, A. Y. L. Lee, J. Melki, & J. McDougall (Eds.), *International handbook of media literacy education*. Routledge.

Duncan, B., et al. (1989). *Media literacy resource guide*. Ontario Ministry of Education and the Association for Media Literacy. Queen's Printer for Ontario.

Fedorov, A. (2008). Media education around the world: Brief history. *Acta Didactica Napocensia, 1*(2). http://dppd.ubbcluj.ro/adn/article_1_2_7.pdf

Ferguson, R. (1998). *Representing "race": Ideology, identity and the media.* Oxford University.

Frau-Meigs, D. (2017). Taking the digital social turn for online freedoms and education 3.0. In S. Wainsbord & H. Tumber (Eds.), *The Routledge companion to media and human rights.* Routledge.

Freinet, C. (1963). *Les techniques audiovisuelles* (144 p.). Bibliotheque de l'ecole moderne.

Gutiérrez, A. (1997). *Educación multimedia y nuevas tecnologías.* Ediciones de la Torre.

Gutiérrez, A. (2008). Educar para los medios en la era digital. Media education in the digital age. *Comunicar. Revista Científica de Educomunicación, XVI*(31), 451–456.

Gutiérrez, A., & Torrego, A. (2018). Educación Mediática y su Didáctica. Una Propuesta para la Formación del Profesorado en TIC y Medios. *Revista Interuniversitaria de Formación del Profesorado (RIFOP), 32*(91), 15–27. https://dialnet.unirioja.es/servlet/articulo?codigo=644 1409

INTEF. (2017). *Marco Común de Competencia Digital Docente 2017.* MECD. https://bit.ly/1Y8 8rd6

Jenkins, H. (2006). *Convergence culture: Where old and new media collide.* New York University.

Jolls, T., & Wilson, C. (2014). The core concepts: Fundamental to media literacy yesterday, today and tomorrow. *Journal of Media Literacy Education, 6*(2), 68–78.

Kellner, D., & Share, J. (2008). Critical media education, radical democracy and the reconstruction of education. *Educação & Sociedade, 29*(104), 687–715. https://doi.org/10.1590/S0101-733020 08000300004

Masterman, L. (1985). *Teaching the media.* Comedia Publishing Group.

Masterman, L., & Thompson, J. L. (1980). *Teaching about television.* Macmillan.

McLuhan, M. (1964). *Understanding media: The extensions of man.* Mentor.

Millán Muñoz, J. (2016, Agosto 15). ¿Cuántas fotos se hacen en el mundo? *Mundiario.* https://goo.gl/qZ2Hsm

Ollé, M. F., Simó, A. A., Carol, M. R. V., & Sánchez, E. D. (2004). *Dialogar y transformar: Pedagogía crítica del siglo XXI* (Vol. 2). Grao.

Potter, J., & McDougall, J. (2017). *Digital media, culture and education: Theorising third space literacies.* Palgrave Macmillan/Springer.

Rabadán, A. V. (2015). Media literacy through photography and participation. A conceptual approach. *Journal of New Approaches in Educational Research,* [S.l.], *4*(1), 32–39. https://doi.org/10.7821/naer.2015.1.96. https://naerjournal.ua.es/article/view/96

Tyner, K., Gutiérrez-Martín, A., & Torrego-González, A. (2015). "Multialfabetización" sin muros en la era de la convergencia. La competencia digital y la cultura del hacer como un revulsivo para una educación continua. *Profesorado, 19*(2), 42–56.

UNESCO. (2011). *ICT competency framework for teachers* (Version 2.0). UNESCO. https://bit.ly/1cx3SPW

UNICEF. (1990, September 26–30). *Children and development in the 1990s: A UNICEF sourcebook, on the occasion of the World Summit for Children.*

Wilson, C., Grizzle, A., Tuazon, R., Akyempong, K., & Cheung, C. K. (2011). *Media and information literacy curriculum for teachers.* The United Nations Educational, Scientific and Cultural Organization.

Chapter 2
Photography as an Element of Reflection in Teacher Training and Research

Rosa María Esteban Moreno

Introduction

When Niépce created his first photographic or heliographic procedure in 1824, little did he know how far his invention would go. He called his idea "heliography" (sun and writing or drawing). Daguerre continued Niépce's research and invented the daguerreotype, and in 1839, Bayard discovered how to obtain positive images on paper. In 1906, Gabriel Lippman received the Nobel Prize for discovering how to obtain photographs directly in colour on the same plate, the precursor of holography (Kurtz, 2001).

By the end of the eighteenth century, photography had democratised printed images at a time when it is believed that only 29% of adults could read (Burke, 1991). In 1885, the Kodak Company began marketing its first cameras, with a long roll of film, under the slogan "You press the button, we do the rest", following which the Brownie, which cost just one dollar, was designed for children (Ramírez Alvarado, 2011). Digital photography ushered in a radical change in terms of the quality of the photograph versus the quantity that can be taken with this type of photography, with unlimited use and repetition. In its early years, photography was associated with the bourgeoisie—the only sector of society that could afford it—and was promoted by liberal, pro-capitalism groups. As a result, photography came to be associated with rise and fall of various ideological movements.

According to Dondis (2003), the invention of the photographic camera ushered in a new perspective on communication and with it, a new approach to education; in other words, photography has changed the way we perceive and communicate. Even Schnaith (2011) claims that photography elevates the importance of visual images to a universal code of communication, similar to language. With the introduction

R. M. Esteban Moreno (✉)
Autonomous University, Madrid, Spain
e-mail: rosamaria.esteban@uam.es

A. Bautista García-Vera (ed.), *Photographic Elicitation and Narration in Teachers Education and Development*, Teacher Education, Learning Innovation and Accountability, https://doi.org/10.1007/978-3-031-20164-6_2

of different technologies, imagery is used in all discourses, personal experiences, information on events, communicating, teaching, etc., but it is seldom used as the protagonist of the information instead of the adjuvant of written or spoken information. Marzal Felici (2007), highlights the importance of photography: "we all too often forget that photography is the basis – gnoseological and technological - of all contemporary forms of expression and audio-visual communication" (p. 19).

The advent of the digital age saw the introduction of devices such as video recorders and mobile phones that some thought would be the death of photography. And true enough, photography as it was known to the first promoters of this language is far removed from how we know it today, but it can still be a fundamental element in teacher training and research. For the children of the digital age—"digital natives"—the speed of images, both in games, films, and all kinds of video clips, would appear to have rendered the still image obsolete; nevertheless, it survives.

Photography is an essential part of our everyday life: that desire to immortalize the moment and bring back memories of a past event, a place visited, or a programmed experience. However, it is seldom used in education, specifically teacher training, even though everyone uses it. Unlike old cameras, where we had to make a detailed study of the image before taking the photo in order to avoid wasting a shot, today's digital mobile photography allows us to take an unlimited number of photographs that can easily be erased and taken again. This has increased the potential of photography and led to the creation of massive digital photo libraries (Pantoja Chaves, 2010).

In fact, the photographic image has become so generalized that it is used to express any type of idea, report on any event, or share any type of experience, and is also used for partisan interests. The almost unhealthy obsession among adolescents of constantly exposing their personal life on social networks using photographs or selfies that are taken to mark their role in society cannot be ignored, and is an example of the informative function of photography (Holzbrecher, 2015). It would be interesting to explore the perspective of students and children by studying the photographs that interest them.

We are witnessing a struggle between those in favour of the use imagery and those opposed to it, rather like what Umberto Eco (1994) called the apocalyptic and integrated intellectuals, where the former consider that overestimating the value of imagery results in seeing the image without understanding it, thereby devaluating conceptual language, while the integrated intellectuals adore cybernetic culture and are enthralled by the digital revolution and audio-visual communication systems. Umberto Eco, who published his book for the first time in Italian in 1964, was 50 years ahead of his time when he talked about the ubiquity of communication systems and the existence of more mobiles connected to the internet than people in the world. According to Hootsuite (2018), there are currently 8,485 million devices connected to the internet worldwide, the mobile phone has changed the way we use the internet, and 55% of emails are opened from a mobile phone. In percentage terms, the number of devices is equivalent to 112% of the total population in the world, that is, an average of 1.65 devices per user.

Eco distinguishes between those who trust in the evolution of mass media—the integrated intellectuals who experience this situation and believe that users participate and are taken into consideration—and the apocalyptic intellectuals, who think that the mass media destroy the characteristics of society and create a citizenry who follow sheep-like after slogans designed to keep them entertained without thinking. Therefore, the integrated intellectuals advocate the access of all citizens to culture, and the apocalyptic intellectuals believe it will destroy the human being as such. In the context of ith these opposing views, here we intend to demonstrate the value of the photograph, hitherto scarcely used in education, as a tool for reflection in teacher training. Trainee teachers use photographs in their reports when they want to illustrate the setting in which they work, but they do not use it to show the different aspects that photography can illustrate: use of space, student groups, teaching model, use of imagery in primary education, the emotional component of photographs, etc.

In all academic fields, photographic image can give information that is not initially evident, and that can be missed if it is replaced by diagrams or drawings (Mustelier & Díaz, 2017). Nevertheless, the photographic image can play a very important role in the transmission, conservation and visualization of all kinds of activities; it can document social situations (Pantoja Chaves, 2010) and fulfil the function of memory to recall events that allow for deliberate reflection and the prolonged exercise of this reflection over time, instead of the compulsion to react immediately to a scene from a film or television.

The image has emerged in different fields of study, such as history, where the phenomenon of the image and its uses in visual communication has become the means of conserving and expanding the visual memory of humanity. Photography, therefore, enshrines memory, and helps all fields of study to construction a visual discourse, "illustrating complex concepts or as a bridge to language" (Holzbrecher, 2015, p. 384).

It is important to consider photography as an element of reflection in educational history, such as historic photographs of schools in the past, and our disbelief that a teacher had 70 children in a single classroom, and could rely solely on his or her own methodological strategies. These photographs should serve as an excuse to learn about the methods of yesterday, to investigate the keys to the success of these methodologies that produced educated citizens in all social strata who participated in the society of their time. This is the capacity of the image to preserve, transmit and organize information, and thus contribute to memory (Díaz Barrado, 2004).

We can also reflect on what has really changed and what remains, as if we were wholly unaffected by the passage of time. Have deep-rooted changes occurred since the encyclopaedia gave way to the textbook, and since writing with a pen gave way to writing with a ballpoint or a digital device? When did the image lose its essence as a communicator? If we go back in time, before the written word, people obtained their cultural education from the images and words used by minstrels—travelling artists who memorized and orally recited traditional stories—and troubadours, who composed and performed their plays to both educate and entertainment their audience. Thanks to their extensive training in trivium (grammar, logic and rhetoric) and quadrivium (arithmetic, geometry, music and astronomy), they gained access to European courts and their texts spoke of love and medieval knights. Both minstrels and troubadours were popular between the twelfth and fourteenth century (Quiñonero Hernández, 1997).

A study of text books shows that the text occupies all the space, and the image is a mere ornament, incapable in itself of accommodating a conceptual language. This was true until the advent of digital photography, in which the texts refers to the image and the viewer is not compelled to look at the text and image at the same time (Pantoja Chaves, 2010).

Looking at a photograph can generate concepts and make us reflect on bygone times and the historical journey of education. Photographs are essential for understanding, and should always be linked to written language. It is important to consider that there are written descriptions of what schools and teaching methods were like in the past, but there is no doubt that this description is far more complete when it is accompanied by an image.

A Note on Photography Today

Today's use of the digital image has taken photography out of the passive role of accompanying text to transform it into a gateway to communication with other sounds, graphics and images. The intention is to galvanize society into taking action, taking sides, and even eliciting both critical and emotional reactions.

The press has begun to give priority to the photographic image over the moving image. This is because a photograph promotes interactivity, as can be seen in the daily edition of the Washington Post (2019). Photographs are used in the same way on television, where news programmes publish a series of photographs to highlight the information, as in the case of missing children or important events.

None of us will ever forget some of the images that impacted society, such as the naked girl from the Vietnam War in 1972 that showed the effects of napalm and that even contributed towards ending the war. Neither can we forget the image taken in 1993 of the starving Sudanese boy Kong Nyong sitting on the outskirts of his village with a vulture lurking nearby, or the image of Aylan, the Syrian boy of Kurdish origin who in September 2015 was found drowned on a beach in Turkey together with his brother and mother—this photograph of the drama of emigration caused a major impact worldwide. Other examples are the recent photograph of the 26-year-old teacher Laura Luelmo, murdered in Huelva in December 2018, showing a person full of vitality who should never have been murdered and who would never have wanted to be the protagonist of that news bulletin, or the shocking rescue of Julen in January 2019, which was followed by everyone in Spain and around the world.

However, the way an image in perceived is determined by cultural factors, and it can have different meanings depending on who sees it and where. Therefore, the Sudanese child represented poverty and the vulture that stalked him can symbolize capitalism. In Aylan's case, although photographs of shipwrecked immigrants are nothing new, the image of a drowned white boy lying on a beach shocked the whole of Europe. Or take the case of Julen, the two-year-old child everyone could identify with: a life lost too young; an example of the solidarity of all involved in the fifteen days of rescue; or the scale of the irregularities committed in Spain to save money and defraud the State, without understanding that such actions affect us all.

Photography in Teacher Training

The establishment of the European Higher Education Area following the Bologna Declaration of 1999 involved a major commitment to the role of Information and Communication Technologies in the future of teaching. Photography is part of many of the courses taught in Fine Arts degrees, starting in the first year, but little is known about the use of photography as a conceptual language in other degree courses. However, this technique can be useful in the initial training of teachers at all educational levels, and also in in-service teacher education.

As shown in a comparative study by Alba et al. (1994) on the situation of technology in undergraduate teaching, the still image, such as photography, is included in some educational technology teaching guides, although it is given less importance than other elements, such as applied technology, moving images, or computer programs, and even the direct use of cameras by students. Given that teacher training addresses situations that stimulate higher mental processes, such as reflection, reasoning, participation, etc. (Bautista García-Vera, 2013), photography can be very effective in activating these mental processes in students both during their undergraduate training and later in their teaching practice. They can go from seeing the photograph as an additive to a text to making it the protagonist of what they want to study and learn in depth.

ICTs are clearly an important tool for teaching, research and knowledge transfer (Morgado-Aguirre et al., 2015). However, according to Bautista García-Vera (2007), in the case of university lecturers they have not been used to acquire these skills, a factor that influences the scant use of such media by this professional group. The same authors found that when present in undergraduate teaching, in the Vygostskian sense, ICTs are mainly used to reproduce information and not to create documents with students or to promote the psychological interrelation between them in their training function (Vygotsky, 1979). Therefore, it is hard to find photography being used beyond subjects taught in Art and Educational Technology, and even less so for the purpose of training and research for future teachers.

Photographs help in deduction, interpretation and imagination, so subjects and their sociocultural belonging become involved in the cognitive processes that are set in motion by observing an image (Ramírez Alvarado, 2011). They are never an end in themselves. but rather a means of communication (González Granados, 2008), while photography encloses a world that transcends the camera and the printing of images (Fandiño Lizarraga, 2013). According to Brown (2009, p. 14), photography is important because of "the veracity of the appearance of things". Photography can be fundamental in helping teachers engage in detailed, thoughtful reflection on what goes on in their classrooms, the use made of space, the work done by their pupils, the relevance given to certain contents, or the classroom rules, shared responsibility and activities. It can even help in creating a collective memory and promote parent-teacher relationships.

We rarely reflect in depth on the image we transmit to the educational community, in other words, to children, parents and even colleagues and ourselves, and these elements are rarely studied by the teachers of today and tomorrow.

Based on the notion that photographs provide evidence, proof, and certify an experience, we could say that "every photographic image is, in a certain way, self-authenticating" (Schaeffer, 1990, p. 61), it helps us verify our actions by forever freezing that exact, fleeting moment. "Human beings think not only with language, but also with visual images, with gestures and with sound models" (Eisner, 1992, p. 15). Harper (2002) argues that images evoke deeper elements of consciousness than words alone. This does not mean that he considers the importance of photographs without words, but that, ideally, these two forms of representation should be combined.

Based on the premises put forward in this chapter, and given that photography is not a subject of study in undergraduate teacher training, we believe it should play a leading role in reflection without being linked to a specific specialist subject, but as a tool for analysis and inquiry before action, during action, and after action. If communities of practice can be formed in educational centres and schools, special emphasis will be placed on joint reflection on certain aspects which, though peripheral, are no less important.

Communities of practice can involve not only teachers, but also students and other members and agents of the educational community in debate or discussions about certain elements that conform educational centres. Dialogue, based on photographic images that capture a specific moment in time and that include not only material elements but also people, can help shape debate that reveal our preconceptions, our training and experience. These are all elements that configure how we perceive reality, but discussing them with others can help us consolidate our ideas or rethink elements that we had not previously considered.

Photographs could be taken of the space reserved for students, teachers and parents in the school, and spark debate on which routines, situations or relationships are considered suitable and which should be changed or remodelled. It often happens that certain elements that strike an outside as being strange will have gone completely unnoticed by those who pass by them every day.

When students are given a voice, they are also capable of analysing the corridors, classrooms and other elements of the school, and of discussing how they would like them to be, what is missing or what is superfluous, and why. However, they are rarely given the opportunity to express themselves, and with this, the schools misses an opportunity of making them feel an active part of school life and equally responsible for caring for and improving their surroundings. This means that school facilities are not perceived and experienced as places we have to inhabit, but are identified with the tastes and preferences of those who make use of them.

Photographs can be used for the purpose of debate during both the theoretical and practical stages of undergraduate pre-school and primary school teacher training. This would allow photography to become an important part of this training, instead of being used merely to illustrate class work or the final practicum report. Thus, in the initial stages of teacher training, on a weekly basis, undergraduate students could be encouraged to bring photographs of schools to class to discuss them with their classmates. This will give them insight into their weak points and compel them to engage in activities and projects that can remedy these situations, habits and space–time relationships that can be improved.

The project can be productive and creative or reproductive. In the first case, the students work with their own photographs, in the second, they reflect on photographs obtained from other sources, but not taken by them. They can engage in the same activities every week during their practicum under the supervision of their university tutor, discussing photographs with other colleagues in the same situation who are tutored by the same professor. Any situation related to life at their school can be discussed in these meetings, giving the student the opportunity to become aware of them and analyse them on the basis of their theoretical training or on their own life experience. During the debate, participants can suggest changes, which should then be reflected in subsequent photographs, once the change has been implemented. Another idea is to keep a visual record—a sort of practicum diary—not for the purpose of reporting what has happened every day, but to highlight whatever drew their attention for a specific reason, presenting it as an object of perception, analysis, reflection and debate, giving prominence to the photograph when it is accompanied by a text or verbal narration.

Trying to identify possible solutions or changes that can be made to the situations detected contributes to both reflective training and active investigation. These must then be implemented by the student, so that the group can analyse whether it led to any effective change. Some of these reflections, the result of the work developed with trainee teachers in the subjects I teach, may involve the following topics:

- Distribution in the classroom and its space, such as: workplaces (isolated tables for individual work, tables in small groups, in large groups, distributed in a U-shape, in pairs, etc.); distribution of work areas (corners, library with cushions on the floor, pets, plants, terrariums, minerals, small laboratory, experiments, etc.); use of the classroom walls (they become an element of training, a reminder of rules, activities, announcements of events, exhibition of school work, etc.)
- Use of material resources and working conditions: classroom material (computers, tablets, video projector, digital whiteboard, mobile phones, work platforms, educational games, abacus, painting material, writing, recycled material, etc.); elements that affect students' work, such as lighting, temperature, sound insulation, etc.
- Classroom and recess methodology: individual or group activities (in pairs, in small groups, large groups, interactive groups, assemblies, etc.); characteristics of the students (homogeneity, heterogeneity, special needs students working with others in the classroom or alone or with a specialist teacher, etc.); recreational

activities (groups doing the same activity, talking groups, traditional games, football, separation by gender, by age, by social background, etc.)

- The school's commitment to sustainability: energy sources, recycling bins, use of paper in the classroom, use of recycling items, etc.

Each of the foregoing elements can be the object of group reflection among trainee teachers, because they can stimulate discussions on classroom methodology, distribution of space, organization of classes, etc. Each of the elements presented in each section can indicate the processes followed in the classroom, and can help participants reflect on how they are carried out. For example: the presence of separate tables may mean that the students engage in personal work, but it can also indicate individualized work, which is not the same; or the presence in the classroom of children with special needs can mean inclusion, or merely integration.

Photography can also help us to go beyond the school itself and compare our own personal experiences with those of other schools in Spain or abroad, analysing whether these teaching situations can be transferred to other locations, or whether they require conditions that cannot be met in our setting. This is because photographs allow participants to explore their own lives, and inquire after and initiate conversations with others (Bautista García-Vera, 2013). Sometimes, a very limited view centred on the school itself does not allow us to evaluate and learn from everything around us, and does not allow us to be aware of elements in our setting that can be used to teach both children and teachers alike. Therefore, photographs can also be taken outside the school and submitted for debate.

Communities of practice, as described by Wenger (2001), can plan to meet weekly, twice-weekly, monthly or twice-monthly in their school. These meetings can take place in person or online, taking advantage of modern technology to involve the educational community in their ongoing debates: students, teachers, parents and other social and cultural actors. This will give them the opportunity to participate in the interpretation made and put forward their own interpretation and suggestions for change.

It is important to remember that still photographs allow us to analyse in greater detail images that may be part of a continuous sequence. Capturing the moment gives us the chance to stop time and become aware of that which surrounds us but does not become part of our daily analysis. This might be an excuse to talk about topics that otherwise would not have been the subject of debate.

In this regard, as will be seen in the following chapters that focus on photo-elicitation and narrative photography, the still image helps teachers and their students develop sensitivity to aesthetics and an interest their surroundings (Ramírez Alvarado, 2014). This intuitive representation system, therefore, can promote self-awareness to both pre-service and in-service teachers. This knowledge can help teachers deal with unforeseen events that may arise in their teaching practice by developing a fundamental skill: the ability to observe, to look in detail at everything in their classroom and school. This will allow them to gather information and combine it with information they receive through the eyes of their pupils, enabling them to find the best ethical solution to the dilemma.

References

Alba, C., Bautista, A., & Nafria, E. (1994). Situación actual de la Tecnología Educativa a través del análisis de los programas de las asignaturas que se imparten actualmente en las Universidades españolas. In J. de Pablos (Ed.), *La tecnología educativa en España* (pp. 101–128). Universidad de Sevilla.

Bautista García-Vera, A. (2007). Estudio del equipamiento, organización y utilización de las nuevas tecnologías hecha por el profesorado de universidades presenciales de España. *Revista Interuniversitaria de Formación del Profesorado, 21*(1), 111–126.

Bautista García-Vera, A. (2013). Indagación narrativa visual en la práctica educativa. *Educación y Futuro, 29*, 69–79.

Brown, R. (2009). Photography. Ongoing moments and strawberry fields, the active presence of absent things. Conference paper at the *International Visual Sociology Association, Annual Conference*. University of Cumbria.

Burke, P. (1991). *La cultura popular en la Europa moderna*. Alianza.

Díaz Barrado, M. P. (2004). Imágenes para la memoria. La fotografía en soporte digital. *Pasado y Memoria, 3*, 5–45.

Dondis, D. (2003). *La sintaxis dela imagen*. GG Diseño.

Eco, U. (1994). *Apocalípticos e integrados*. Editorial Lumen.

Eisner, E. (1992). Reflexiones acerca de la alfabetización. *Arte, Individuo y Sociedad, 4*, 9–22.

Fandiño Lizarraga, R. (2013). Los principios de la fotografía para primer grado de Educación Secundaria en Colombia. *Revista De Didácticas Específicas, 9*, 69–89.

González Granados, P. (2008). A través de sus ojos. Etnografía visual en un centro educativo de la periferia urbana. *Periferia. Revista de Recerca i formació en antropología, 9*, 1–26.

Harper, D. (2002). Talking about pictures: A case for photo elicitation. *Visual Studies, 17*(1), 14–26.

Holzbrecher, A. (2015). La fotografía en la educación mediática: su papel en la labor educativa (extra) académica. *Profesorado. Revista de curriculum y formación del profesorado, 19*(1), 381–394. http://www.ugr.es/local/recfpro/rev191COL6.pdf

Hootsuite. (2018). *Digital in 2018*. https://marketing4ecommerce.net/moviles-conectados-a-int ernet/

Kurtz, G. F. (2001). Origen de un medio gráfico y un arte. Antecedentes, inicio y desarrollo de la fotografía en España. In *Summa Artis. Historia General del Arte. Vol. XLVII. La fotografía en España: de los orígenes al siglo XXI*. Espasa Calpe.

Marzal Felici, J. (2007). *Cómo se lee una fotografía: interpretaciones de la mirada*. Cátedra.

Morgado-Aguirre, B., López-Martín, E., & Conesa-Tejada, S. (2015). El uso de las TIC en la enseñanza universitaria de la fotografía. Primeros resultados del proyecto de innovación docente de la Universidad de Murcia. *Arte, Individuo y Sociedad, 27*(2), 295–319. https://doi.org/10.5209/rev_ARIS.2015.v27.n2.45150

Mustelier Portuondo, V. E., & Díaz López, J. R. (2017). La fotografía como recurso didáctico para mejorar la comprensión de las prácticas de laboratorio de Física III. *Didasc@lia: Didáctica y Educación, VIII*(6), 195–200.

Pantoja Chaves, A. (2010). La fotografía como recurso para la didáctica de la Historia. *Tejuelo, 9*, 179–194.

Quiñonero Hernández, J. (1997). *Mester de Juglaría*. Editorial Octaedro.

Ramírez Alvarado, M. M. (2011). El valor de la fotografía como objeto de estudio y en las investigaciones sobre comunicación: reflexiones teóricas. *Discursos Fotográficos, 7*(11), 55–76.

Ramírez Alvarado, M. M. (2014). Aprendiendo a mirar. Imagen fotográfica y alfabetización audiovisual. *Prisma Social. Revista de Investigación Social, 11*, 383–398.

Schaeffer, J. M. (1990). *La imagen precaria: del dispositivo fotográfico*. Cátedra.

Schnaith, N. (2011). *Lo visible y lo invisible en la imagen fotográfica*. La Oficina.

Vygotski, L. S. (1979). *El desarrollo de los procesos mentales superiores*. Crítica.

Washington Post. (2019). http://www.washingtonpost.com/wp_srv/photo/index.html

Wenger, E. (2001). *Comunidades de práctica. Aprendizaje, significado e identidad*. Paidós.

Chapter 3
Photography as a System
for Representing the Teacher's Theories
and Beliefs

Ana María de las Heras Cuenca and Laura Rayón Rumayor

Introduction

In this chapter, we give teachers a practical overview of how photography can be used to create a record of images representing the theories and beliefs that shape their method of teaching. We emphasis the value of discussing classroom situations using the photographs taken by the teachers themselves. We analyse which semiotic elements of the photographic language need to be considered when we express ourselves with images. In other words, the language of the image, like all language, has the ability to create meaningful actions.

We begin by briefly explaining how photography has become an interesting resource for educational research and training by providing a multimodal tool for expressing our feelings, narrating our experiences, and showing our particular world view. This is particularly useful for educational inquiry, as it facilitates access to subjective views and focuses the student's attention. Recent studies into the theories and beliefs of teachers have discussed the use of photography as a way of allowing them to speak through their camera. This investigative approach has rarely been used in the field of in-service teacher training; however, it is interesting due to the contributions made by photography to our identification and understanding of the teacher's practical knowledge. These contributions will be identified at the beginning of the chapter. We will dwell on one of the issues that emerge from these studies, and that defines the purpose of this chapter: if photography has its own language that facilitates the communication of messages and ideas, it would be interesting to reflect on how this language can enable teachers to capture what they experience in

A. M. de las Heras Cuenca (✉) · L. Rayón Rumayor
Complutense University, Madrid, Spain
e-mail: delasheras@edu.ucm.es

L. Rayón Rumayor
e-mail: larayon@ucm.es

A. Bautista García-Vera (ed.), *Photographic Elicitation and Narration in Teachers Education and Development*, Teacher Education, Learning Innovation and Accountability, https://doi.org/10.1007/978-3-031-20164-6_3

their classrooms and, in this way, explain more effectively the theories and beliefs that shape their methodology.

Representing the Teacher's Practical Knowledge Through Photography

In recent years, interest in the use of photography for recording data for educational research has increased. Audio-visual media have transcended positivism and have given rise to other rich, interesting approaches to research in different areas of the social sciences (Mannay, 2017). Today, photography is conceived as a valuable educational research tool because it gives access to a series of data that can hardly be expressed with words (Burke & Grosvenor, 2004). Authors such as Schwartz (1994) highlight the value of photography as a tool for narrating experiences, evoking feelings, and revealing the participants' beliefs and points of view. In this way, photography complements verbal narration by facilitating an understanding of the reality and the actions of the subjects. Photography is conceptualized by Ardèvol (2006) as *self-records*, defined as the presentation and collection of data by a social actor who shows us information about their culture or their social group through their subjective experience. This new perspective places the teacher in the role of creator of cultural records and documents, a person who not only illustrates a reality, but who is understood on the basis of the meanings they contribute as creators of these productions (Ball & Smith, 1992; Thompson, 2008). This way of understanding the role of the camera in inquiry and education shows that photography is a symbolic tool, one that is capable of generating meanings through the voices and worlds of teachers who use them in the democratic work process in which they take part as creators and key narrators of reality (Harper, 2002; Pink, 2007, 2009). In the words of Ardèvol (2006, p. 32) "the study of visual forms of social practices in modern societies should allow us to go beyond simply pointing out their importance - it should allow us to describe, understand and explain each specific practice".

On the basis of these arguments, various studies have been performed with teachers in which photography plays a key role in in-service teacher training (Bautista, 2017; Bautista et al., 2018; Hamilton, 2015; Mukeredzi & Nyachowe, 2018; Ruto-Korir & Lubbe-De Beer, 2012; Stockall & Davis, 2011; Taylor, 2016). In these studies, teachers photograph important situations in their classroom that are later presented to a working team together with the reasons that prompted them to take the photograph. This creates a space for dialogue and discussion about the teacher's practice that gives insight into the beliefs and theories that shape their method of teaching. In other words, photo-elicitation involves telling a story from a photograph, and with it, interpreting and giving meaning to the actions, objects or events shown in the photograph (Harper, 2002). This allows us to see "through eyes of the teacher" and access their particular interpretation of the image. In these studies, photography is used in teacher training to first record important situations arising in their classroom, and later to prompt discussion on these situations. In addition, the following advantages of photography have been identified, showing its importance in in-service teacher training:

i. Photographs give insight into the teacher's experience: using a photograph taken in an interactive situation in the classroom, teachers can use photo-elicitation to highlight professional dilemmas and conflicts arising during their classes (Bautista, 2017). This study was conducted with two primary school teachers who analysed and discussed the situation shown in the photographs. The resulting dialogue prompted questions that allowed the teachers to stop to think about the decisions they made and reflect on their experience. This process gradually allowed these teachers to become aware of the theories, beliefs and values that underlie their method of teaching.

> The experiential image in the context of in-service teacher training is the mental image that teachers make of the events experienced in their classroom and their work environment. These mental images, the result of experience to some extent, give substance to the theories and beliefs of male and female teachers, and can therefore be used to relive the events they represent when they are thought about outside the classroom. (Bautista, 2017, pp. 205–206)

ii. Photographs give access to tacit knowledge, thereby facilitating deeper insight in reality as it is experienced and interpreted by the teacher. This idea is clearly presented by Ruto-Korir and Lubbe-De Beer's (2012) study in four kindergarten teachers, and by Taylor's (2016) study in adult education. These papers analyse the value of photography and photo-elicitation and their contributions to teacher training by reflecting on the practice itself. These two studies show that it would have been difficult to access this type of information with other investigative methods. Photography makes it possible because, unlike other data records, it provides us with a more intuitive language with which to access thoughts and generate discussion that allows us to talk about our emotional and rational thinking to obtain more complex, richer information on school life (Bautista, 2011). Photographs, therefore, give us a deeper understanding by revealing issues that are either part of our subconscious or are part of the school's hidden agenda (Prosser, 2010).

iii. Photo elicitation facilitates collaboration between teachers and researchers (Ruto-Korir & Lubbe-De Beer, 2012), and allows them to establish the democratic procedures that are so essential for accessing knowledge in education and for improving teaching practices. For Tardif (2004), it is crucial to involve teachers as co-researchers in order to know and understand the knowledge on which they base their teaching practice.

> If we assume that teachers are competent actors - active subjects - we must acknowledge that the classroom is not only a space for the application of theoretical know-how, but also a space for the production of specific know-how that comes from teaching practice. In other words, the teacher's job should be thought of as a specific practical space for the production, transformation and mobilization of know-how, and with it, theories, knowledge and the know-how specific to the teaching profession. This perspective

is equivalent to making the teacher - like the university lecturer or the educational
researcher - a scholar or actor who always develops and possesses theories, knowledge
and know-how about his own activity. (Tardif, 2004, p. 172)

iv. The use of photography and photo elicitation to transform beliefs and teaching
practice has been another major findings in various studies, such as that of
Bautista (2017), who shows how two teachers with extensive experience start
to change different aspects of their practice as a result of the process of enquiry
involved in photo elicitation. Stockall and Davis (2011) draw similar conclusions
in their work with trainee teachers. In an earlier study (Bautista et al., 2018), we
showed the analysis of the first 26 photographs taken by four teachers in which
they identify the most relevant theories and beliefs that guided their actions in
problematic situations. The photo elicitation sessions became a forum for debate
in which the teachers themselves question some of their professional beliefs
and suggest new ways of responding to the problems experienced. In this study,
we were able to show the richness of the collective and deliberative dialogue
generated by photo elicitation of the situations captured in the photographs. This
dialogue prompted participants to come up with alternative actions to resolve,
and in some cases change, certain dilemmas and conflicts. Similar findings were
reported by Mukeredzi and Nyachowe (2018) in a longitudinal, 20-year study
in newly qualified teachers to analyse the evolution of professional theories.
Among the most relevant results, the authors observed how practical thinking
became transformed as theory and practice shaped a more coherent discourse. By
studying teachers who are just starting their professional careers, these authors
show how photo elicitation helped shape their professional identity.

v. Photographs provide users with a different language to express their thoughts
and narrate a richer story. This can also help teachers achieve audio-visual
literacy, as understood by Bautista (2007). The study by Bautista et al. (2018)
shows the evocative and expressive power of photographic language when they
present the teachers' mental image and analyse how this cognitive representation materializes in the photographs. This confirms the importance of rhetorical
figures, particularly metonymy, to understand the semiotic process of conceptualization and signification of objects and events experienced in classrooms
and their photographic representation. Bautista (2017), meanwhile, has shown
how metaphor and hyperbole were the prominent rhetorical figures used by
two teachers to evoke situations and emotions they had experienced in their
photographs. This, as Hamilton (2015) also observes, shows the value of the
expressive resources typically found in the language of photography. It reveals
how the use of multimodal languages and the expression of metaphorical ideas
allow teachers to showcase their knowledge of teaching and its practice, and
how this has favourable implications for their professional development.

In the rest of this chapter we will develop the latter aspect in detail in order to show
the different ways in which the language of photography helps represent and evoke
elements of practical knowledge. Specifically, we identify the potential of rhetorical

figures and photographs taken using meta-representations, and the connotative possibilities offered by different types of framing and angulation selected to organize the space of the representations.

Photographic Representation and Elicitation of Teachers' Theories and Beliefs

We conceive photography as a visual sign, and like any sign that facilitates communication, it uses a series of codes that enhance the transmission of messages. The communicative potential of imagery is now studied in various fields, but we are interested in highlighting how semiotics allow us to understand the power of signification inherent in images. Contrary to the positivist approach to photography, we believe that these signs are culturally and subjectively conditioned, and their representation cannot be separated from the interpretation inherent in each photograph. According to Barthes (1990), imagery is intention and interaction between the object shown, the author and the audience. Therefore, it forms a link between the reality, the person taking the photograph, and the spectator, highlighting the need to pay attention to the semiotic signification that occurs when visualising and interpreting the image. Therefore, we grasp the idea of Dubois, who says that "the photographic image, we tried to show, is not a neutral mirror but a tool for transposition, analysis, interpretation, even transformation of what is real, in the same way as, for example, language, and like it, is culturally encoded" (Dubois, 1986, p. 20).

Peirce's (1986) study of signs has been interpreted from the perspective of visual semiotics, and his contributions are included in books by authors such as Dubois (1986) and Eco (1974) when analysing the signification of photographic messages. We would like to elaborate on the second trichotomy of Peirce's signs, which explains the existence of three types of signs that have been associated with the signification of photography:

i.   The photograph can be an icon that expresses quality, verisimilitude between what is shown and the message created with the intention of being a true reflection of reality.

ii. The image can be a symbol, i.e. a set of codes that evokes a reality through association of ideas, which "is analysed as an interpretation-transformation of what is real, as an arbitrary, cultural, ideological and perceptually encoded creation" (Dubois, 1986, p. 51).

iii. The image can be an index, insofar as its significance is linked to experience and, therefore, it acquires significance from the more subjective and personal ideas with which we establish a real connection through the represented object. "Any visual index communicates something to me by means of a more or less blind impulse, based on a system of conventions or a system of learned experiences" (Eco, 1974, p. 219).

The difference established between the sign and its signification leads us to mention the two planes of analysis of photographs: denotation and connotation. These have already been mentioned by Barthes (1977), who claims that an image can transmit signification on two planes—the literal and what he calls concealed messages, both of which are necessary for reading and understanding the image.

Now, we will show how visual rhetoric and the different elements that make up the image can be used in photographic representations. These give particular meanings to the image, and can therefore be used by teachers to take a look at reality and capture it in an photograph that tells us about their experience and the conceptual references used to analyse and interpret this experience. We illustrate the ideas put forward with some photographs taken in schools by a principal and three teachers that show the beliefs and professional theories that guide their teaching practice. These four teachers took part in the study *Narraciones visuales basadas en imágenes experienciales en la formación del profesorado* [Visual narratives based on experiential images in teacher training] (R&D + i project, reference EDU2014-57103-R).

The Rhetoric of Imagery

Rhetorical figures have the advantage of enhancing the meaning and expressiveness of a photograph. They are creative resources used to communicate meanings (López Fernández-Cao, 1998; Moliné, 2000) and allow us to provide information about our internal representations and world views (Lakoff & Johnson, 2009). The potential of rhetorical figures lies in the many different ways they can transmit messages, and they play a particularly important role in accessing subjective interpretations of an event or reality. This idea is well expressed by Lakoff and Johnson (2009):

> Metaphorical imagination is a crucial skill for creating relationships and communicating the nature of experiences that are not common. This skill largely consists of the ability to shape one's own vision of the world and adjust it to the way in which each individual categorizes their experiences. (p. 276)

We focus here on the possibilities offered by five rhetorical figures: metonymy, synecdoche, metaphor, antithesis and irony, due to their considerable expressive and symbolic value. They also played an important role in our aforementioned research project.

Metonymy consists of the substitution of one term for another with which it establishes a causal relationship or of the association between an object and its purpose. It is a useful rhetorical figure for accessing theories and beliefs that determine a teaching activity or an event by means of a photograph of an object or place that teachers consider representative of their practice.

This is the case of Fig. 3.1, in which the school principal reflects on the excessive use of textbooks by some primary education teachers, criticizing their inherently academic approach. Photo elicitation revealed educational innovation-related teaching theories the analyse the situation experienced in the school.

> This undermines issues we are later asked to teach, such as values, or anything else. For example, working with an external association or from the city council, many teachers answer: *We can't because we can't waste time.* This, for them, is a waste of time. I am worried about all that.

As we can see in the discourse elicited from the photograph, the image serves as a reference to the context and the knowledge of the teacher, for whom textbooks evoke educational practices based on a technical curricular approach.

Synecdoche is a type of metonymy that establishes a relationship between the part and the whole. In other words, a part is photographed to represent a complete entity. What is interesting about this rhetorical figure is what is highlighted, that part on which we focus and that signifies the construction of the photographic message. The photograph shown in Fig. 3.2 evokes a theory about the need for continuing professional training to improve teaching practices. In this situation, a school principal spoke about the difficulties she is experiencing with some colleagues who have an individualistic and traditional teaching style. To illustrate this concern, she took a photograph of part of the door to the classroom of a teacher known for her innovative teaching style.

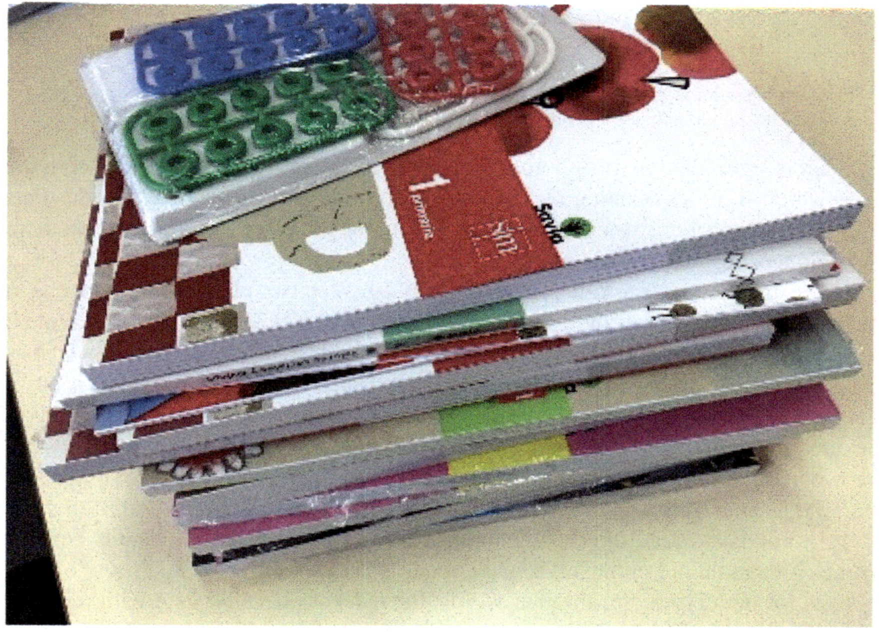

Fig. 3.1 Textbooks (taken by head teacher SI)

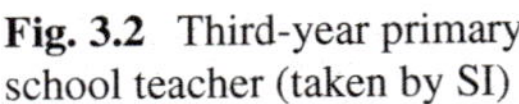

Fig. 3.2 Third-year primary school teacher (taken by SI)

This girl has a lot of training, and she is always on the go. She wrote to tell me that she's going to do a course this weekend … Great, I told her, let me know how you get on.

What is significant in this photograph is the idea of showing the glass inset in the door, which signifies opening by allowing us to observe what happens inside. This highlights the teacher's teaching style while evoking the place, the classroom, where the main teacher in this story works.

The visual metaphor establishes an analogy between two elements, that is, due to the presence of similar attributes in both objects, people, etc. Therefore, one element is used in the place of another to acquire or highlight its qualities. This often consists in associating a real term with an imaginary or abstract term with which it has a certain similarity. According to Moliné (2000), metaphor *transports* the meaning of one idea to another, in such a way that our mind establishes a comparison between the two. An example of this in our study is shown in Fig. 3.3. At the start of the school year, the teacher took a photograph of her suitcase to talk about her return to work after the holidays. According to her, this period was not only one of leisure, but also a time to rekindle her enthusiasm and collect ideas and materials and think of new projects for her classroom. In other words, the teacher packs her bag with renewed strength and new learning. This is an example of Lakoff and Johnson's (2009) notion of the personal nature of metaphors.

> Just as we seek out metaphors to highlight and make coherent what we have in common with someone else, so we seek out personal metaphors to highlight and make coherent our own pasts, our present activities, and our dreams, hopes, and goals as well. (pp. 277–278)

In this example, the photograph presents a belief in the need to stop and look at the effects of lessons taught in the classroom, and how that requires taking time to enjoy, analyse the progress made during the school year, and continue to develop new lessons. In other words, it shows the need for down-time that allows the teacher to reflect on and improve their practice.

Antithesis is a tool that allows us to show how one image contrasts with another that has the opposite meaning, or how two opposite or contrary ideas can be contained in a single image. The importance of this rhetorical figure lie in its capacity to give us access to valuable knowledge about the teacher's thinking, since it reveals the assessments made and the position taken by the teacher when faced with a practical dilemma, identifying what they view as positive and correct versus what is incorrect or unwanted. In our study, teachers expressed a variety of beliefs in connection with

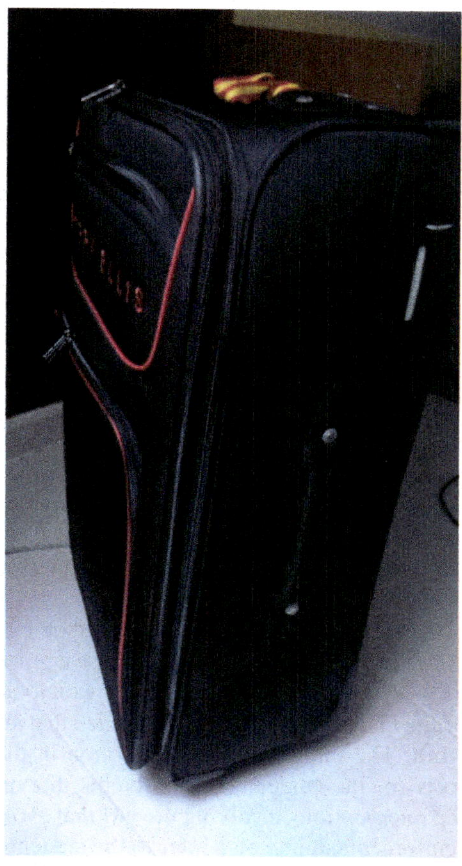

Fig. 3.3 The suitcase (taken by teacher PI)

Fig. 3.4 White hearts and coloured hearts (taken by teacher PI)

classroom conflicts, describing pupils' behaviour and the situation the teacher wants to achieve. They also allow us to reflect on teaching, identifying underlying beliefs and theories and examining it to identify what teachers do and what they would like to do. Another interesting use of antithesis involves an exercise in reflection and observation in which two antagonistic situations are represented in order to show the evolution or transformation of an event over time. Figure 3.4 shows this latter use of antithesis, where one of the teachers shows how the use of interventions based on behavioural theories have changed students' attitudes and shows how their relationships have improved.

This is shown by objects that represent a behaviour modification technique she used during the school year. The teacher modifies the behaviour of the students by using coloured hearts which the students can use each day to thank a classmate for a good deed. The technique consists of writing the name of the boy or girl and the good deed done, and hanging the heart on a board. The white hearts seen in the image are used when a classmate wants to report a conflictive situation or has felt hurt by another student. The image shows how the teacher draws attention to the difference in quantity between some hearts and others, thereby illustrating the change in student behaviour.

Irony magnifies an object or a person by means of exaggeration, and is therefore a rhetorical figure that seeks to cause a greater impact on the spectator. An image of exaggeration is shown in Fig. 3.5, which highlights the difference between the size of the chair and the girl to symbolise that she has fallen a year behind in her school work. The image evokes an emotion in the form of the empathy that the teacher feels for the student. The problems that arise prompted the teacher to talk about the interventions involving the girl that evoked behavioural theories such as positive reinforcement, and also refer to the student's motivation.

Fig. 3.5 Student's back
(taken by teacher CA)

We can see how this rhetorical figure is useful for showing situations that disrupt the logical order of things and how teachers perceive them. This gives rise to significances that reveal their world view, how they interpret the reality that exists in their classrooms.

Meta-Representations

Another form of representation that is particularly interesting in the field of teacher training is the meta-representation—a written production that allows us to capture complex or abstract processes. An example of such images can be a sheet of paper from an exam, student notebooks, and report cards. These objects allow the teacher to represent different learning processes that involve both theoretical and proprietary teaching. Figures 3.6 and 3.7 explain this concept. They show the interactive notebooks made by students as an example of their teaching style and the theories and beliefs on which it is based.

Fig. 3.6 Photographs of interactive notebooks (taken by teacher PI)

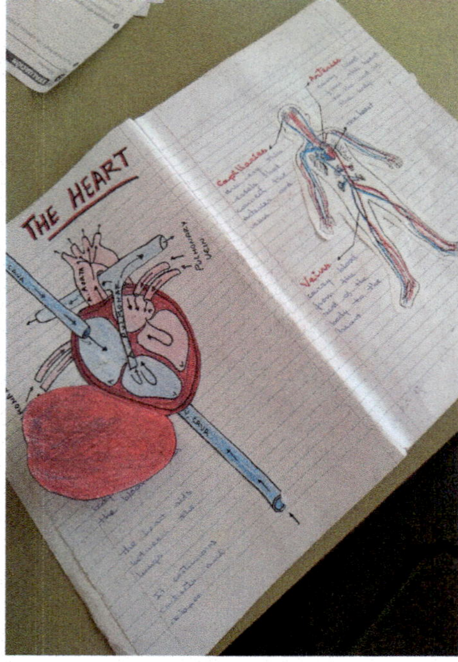

Fig. 3.7 Photographs of interactive notebooks (taken by teacher PI)

> They stick all the pieces in, then it's a kind of lift-the-flap book. The same with this one, you lift the flaps. This one was of invertebrate animals, here it is, this is the outline of the whole subject (..) And they know that they put the blood in on one side, and it comes out the other. At least that's how they see it. Because they do, they draw it, they colour it, they paste it in, and they draw it and so they remember the idea … and the truth is that they get into it, they love it, they love it (…) This is the outline. Instead of having an outline with little arrows, this is the outline. These are all the groups of invertebrates and then they lift the flap and underneath they write the characteristics of each group, for example the heart came out very well […] and then I also put them on the blackboard… I label them … I label them, I take time to label them, to draw them on the board.

With this type of photograph, which evokes different teaching theories, such as meaningful and observational learning and stories, beliefs in the usefulness of different teaching tasks, such as manual activities, drawing or schematization emerge. These images allowed the teacher to think about and confirm the effectiveness of her learning enhancement strategies.

Spatial Organization: Camera Angle and Shot

The frame or shot in the world of photography involves selecting a fragment of the scene that allows us to identify what we are interested in capturing. This act of selection and exclusion determines the photographic message, and highlights the significance of the scene in terms of what is shown and what is excluded (Gauthier, 1996; Sontag, 2003).

According to visual semiotic analysis, the frame shows the existence of a relationship between the type of shot and the physical distance between what is represented and the photographer. This is closely related to the concept of *social distance* and the type of relationships that the photograph is intended to represent (Hall, 1966; Kress & Van Leeuwen, 2006). This distance, they point out, has to do with the type of relationship that the photographer establishes with the object, person or context represented. The message of the photograph can focus more on showing a context or a specific action, or the meanings can be intended to provide information about a specific person or an object represented. Table 3.1 summarizes the meaning that Fernández Ibáñez (1986), Hall (1966) and Kress and Van Leeuwen (2006) give to each type of shot. As can be seen, the closer the photographer is to the person or object photographed, the closer and more intimate are the personal discourses evoked, making the photograph more expressive and giving it a greater symbolic value.

Teachers can use long shots (for example, the wide and establishing shot) to illustrate teaching situations where the story of the action is emphasized; for example, situations that evoke professional theories on student learning by photographing the classroom, the narration of educational experiences that reveal their teaching style, while the atmosphere and relationships between their students can be illustrated in different spaces, such as the classroom or the playground, among others. Short shots, in contrast, (such as close-ups or detail shots) offer endless possibilities of showing personal, intimate ideas and opinions and expressing feelings. These shots highlight

Table 3.1 Photographic significance of different planes

Hall (1966) and Kress and Van Leeuwen (2006)			Type of photographic plane	Function
Intimate distance		We see only the face or head Singles out part of the scene	Extreme close-up Detail shot	Expressive, symbolic Emotional and intimate
Close personal distance		We only see the head and shoulders	Close-up	Confidentiality, privacy Emotion
Far personal distance		We see from the waist to the head	Medium shot	Dialogue Emotion
Close social distance		We see the whole body	Full shot Complete view	Narrative
Far social distance	The surroundings are more interesting than the subject	We see the person in their surroundings	Wide shot Descriptive	Descriptive

the importance of the object or person represented, giving them prominence in the narration that accompanies the photograph. In the case in hand, short shots can build stories aimed at revealing a more personal dimension of the teacher, creating more subjectively weighted messages related to the events shown. This happens because the teacher's eye is focused on a specific aspect that he or she wants to draw attention to. Therefore, these types of shots can be used to represent feelings, such as joy, sadness and the concerns caused by conflictive situations or professional dilemmas. In this type of photograph we typically find beliefs that reveal the teacher's point of view on the conflicts that occur in school, and are also useful for eliciting theories and beliefs relating to scenarios and teaching practice that not are instructive in nature.

The camera angle shows the point from where the photographer looks at the reality represented. It is considered one of the most expressive imaging tools for creating connotations. According to Balázs (1957),

> The camera angle is the film maker's most intense means of characterization; only by using unusual and unexpected configurations created using surprising shots can old and familiar objects strike us as new (...) Camera placement and angle can make objects hateful, kind, terrifying or ridiculous. (p. 11)

Some of the most common and the most useful angles for the subject at hand are the eye level angle, the high angle and the low angle. In the normal angle, the camera is positioned parallel to the ground so that the photograph is taken at eye level of the person represented or at the same height as the object. This angle is usually used by people with no audio-visual literacy. It does not give the representation any significant connotations, or simply shows a point of view of equality, or implication with the object photographed (Kress & Van Leeuwen, 2006). The other two types of angle, however, are more expressive because they give the person or object represented certain attributes. "Seeing from top to bottom or from bottom to top is equivalent to feeling unconsciously taller or smaller, and correlatively, feeling reality as dominated or dominant" (Fernández Ibánez, 1986, p. 65). Similarly, experts in visual semiotics have studied how the use of the camera evokes the power relations between the subjects represented and the photographer or the person who visualizes the image (Kress & Van Leeuwen, 2006). In the high angle, the camera is tilted slightly towards the ground at the time the picture is taken. The meanings conveyed by the author of the image using the high angle are inferiority, innocence, weakness, fragility. It is also used to portray a person we consider harmless, or even to ridicule the subject. When the photographer represents a person or object by tilting the camera slightly upwards, this is the low angle. This gives the image connotations of uplifting and magnifying the subject or object.

For teachers, camera angle is an interesting tool for expressing evaluations and opinions with their photographs. They can use the high angle to show aspects that are not to their liking or to criticise events, and the low angle to achieve the opposite. This is the case of the photograph shown in Fig. 3.1, where the high angle clearly reinforces the teacher's message: to criticise over-reliance on instructive teaching methods. The high angle can also be used when beliefs involving conflictive situations emerge, and can be used to imply criticism and dislike of a particular situation. This shot is also useful for showing aspects of the teacher's practical knowledge, such as when they analyse injustices suffered by their students.

Figures 3.8 and 3.9, taken by one of the teachers, illustrate how the type of shot and camera angle used give a particular meaning to the photographs, In these cases, the representation fulfils a different communicative function while conveying the different extent to which the teacher is involved with each of the events narrated.

This photograph is an eye-level, wide angle shot that narrates the task set for that day: the students were asked to apply their knowledge to everyday objects and show the results.

> I gave them the idea: I want you to present me with a simple machine that is one of the three types of machine we have studied. I don't care if you make the machine yourselves, or bring a simple machine that you have at home. One of them simply brought a pair of scissors and described it … this is the fulcrum, this is effort arm, this is the load arm…

In this way, the teacher reveals the theories, such as meaningful learning, that are part of her daily practice. The message is not one of judgement—it is not primarily intended to portray the students represented, but rather to report the activities carried out in the classroom that morning. The subject of this photograph can be compared to Fig. 3.9, which shows a close up of the hands of a child who bites his nails.

The teacher uses this image to tell the story of the arrival of a new child to her class. She says that she had certain misgivings about the student, prompted by her initial understanding of his family situation.

> He doesn't live with his parents but with his uncle and aunt, and I thought, oh no, this child is going to be a potential problem

During the session, the teacher narrated an emotional story based on her concerns. She explained the child's precarious home situation, where beliefs involving the

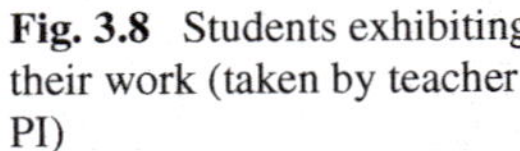

Fig. 3.8 Students exhibiting their work (taken by teacher PI)

extent to which the influence of his family and sociocultural environment in which this child lived would determine his behaviour and involvement in academic tasks. However, the most significant aspect involves the moment when the photograph was taken, saying:

> The boy stayed, I sat him next to me like this, and then I started to think, I was watching him, and I saw that he was a good little boy, and then I felt guilty, and said to myself What an awful person I am, what a bad person! I mean, a child is not like a football card - now I get it, now I don't want it, now I swop it. And I saw him, and I realized that he had bitten all his nails. When a child bites … well, when a person bites their nails, it's due to anxiety, … that's why I took the picture, I felt terrible, absolutely awful

The close up, reinforced by the high angle of the shot of the student's hands, is significant in that it show the emotions, at times contradictory, expressed by the teacher. In any event, these elements help draw our attention, to become involved in this situation, and highlight the element that acted as the *photographic punctum* (Barthes, 1990): the child's hands.

In conclusion, based on what we have seen in the chapter, knowledge of photographic language is particularly interesting in the case of these teachers, as it allowed them to convey the dilemmas they face in their work and show their thoughts about these problems. They reveal to us the foundations on which their practical knowledge

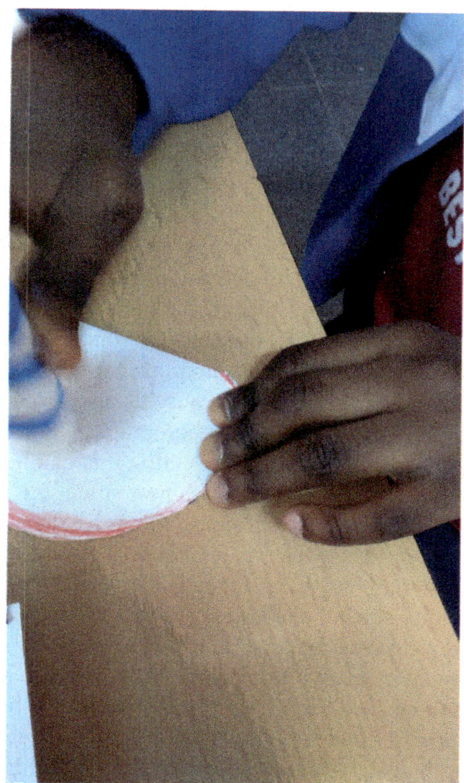

Fig. 3.9 Bitten nails (taken by teacher PI)

is built. Cao and Pérez (2000) have already shown the importance of understanding the language of imagery when they discuss how this language allows us to become critical readers of audio-visual messages.

> The point of view, the focus, the shot, the composition, the stereotype they define or fight against, the symbols and rhetorical elements they use must be analysed and deconstructed in order to be able to fully capture them. (p. 56)

This becomes particularly relevant when we place teachers in the role of co-researchers and creators of visual productions that allow them to become aware of the theories and beliefs that shape and determine their teaching practice. Thus, we see how rhetorical figures and meta-representations allow teachers to evoke abstract ideas and concepts that are difficult to represent and express. Rhetorical figures in particular show a more complex degree of communication—one that correlates ideas, concepts or realities that gradually reveal the teacher's experience and how it is built on the bases of different ideas and beliefs acquired by experience. These ideas and beliefs emerge when teachers explain the reasons for taking a particular photograph. This is why rhetorical figures are valuable tools for allowing the theories and beliefs of teachers to come to the surface during photo elicitation. This process allows teachers to become aware of the knowledge that shapes their teaching practice.

With regard to shots, we have shown how those that establish the greatest distance between the person or object represented have a more descriptive and narrative communicative intention. These photographs can show the theories and beliefs that emerge in classroom interventions. This was illustrated in Fig. 3.8, where the teacher explains the learning theories that underlie her daily practice. But shots can also capture group situations that show the relationships between the elements of the group, such as conflicts that, primarily, describe this dilemma and how it is analysed. On the other hand, placing the camera closer to the people or entities represented allow the photographs to show professional dilemmas in which the teacher is emotionally involved. These representations are useful for showing situations involving specific issues or dilemmas that cause teachers to question what happened, such as the case of the teacher who took photographs 7 and 1. In the photo elicitation sessions, these images lead to deeper reflection that can help teachers question their own teaching practices and come up with new strategies.

Different camera angles allows teachers to critically evaluate the situation represented. This gives greater insight into how they interpret the situations presented and how they feel about them. Therefore, a low angle can facilitate reaffirmation of the reality shown, elicit a feeling of satisfaction and surprise. A high angle, meanwhile, as we have seen, can be used to criticise a situation that worries and displeases the teacher, or, as shown in Fig. 3.9, it can also prompt the narrator to question his or her motives and reveal how their beliefs have been transformed.

In short, photography as a tool for in-service teacher education is conceived as an index, as presented by Peirce (1986). It is a sign built on the basis of our own experience. In our case, we have seen that it allows teachers to become aware of all the elements that determine their points of view and actions. Imagery can help teachers observe reality, become aware of the elements that conform their practical knowledge, question this knowledge, and gradually extend their theoretical repertoire by identifying practices that require other conceptual references. That is to say, like any communicative act, the image can reveal the teacher's educational know-how, and knowledge, in education, can touch our emotions and appeal to our feelings. It is a knowledge that determines us personally and professionally and, when we expand our conceptual references, can sometimes transform us.

References

Ardèvol, E. (2006). *La búsqueda de una mirada*. Editorial UOC.

Balázs, B. (1957). *El Film. Evolución y esencia de un arte nuevo*. Losange.

Ball, M., & Smith, G. (1992). *Analyzing visual data*. Sage.

Barthes, R. (1977). *Image music text*. Fontana Press.

Barthes, R. (1990). *La cámara lúcida. Notas sobre la fotografía*. Paidós.

Bautista, A. (2007). Alfabetización tecnológica multimodal e intercultural. *Revista de Educación, 343*, 589–600.

Bautista, A. (2011). Miradas de la antropología audiovisual al estudio de las funciones de las herramientas simbólicas y materiales en educación intercultural. In A. Bautista & H. M. Velasco (Coords.), *Antropología audiovisual: medios e investigación en educación* (pp. 112–136). Trotta.

Bautista, A. (2017). La foto-elicitación en la formación permanente de maestros de educación primaria. *Alteridad, revista de educación, 12*(2), 202–214. https://doi.org/10.17163/alt.v12n2.2017.06

Bautista, A., Rayón, L., & de las Heras, A. M. (2018). Imágenes experienciales y foto-elicitación en la formación del profesorado. *Educatio Siglo XXI, 36*(2), 135–161.https://doi.org/10.6018/j/333001

Burke, C., & Grosvenor, I. (2004). *The school I'd like.* Routledge Falmer.

Dubois, P. (1986). *El acto fotográfico. De la Representación a la Recepción.* Paidós.

Eco, U. (1974). *La estructura ausente: Introducción a la semiótica.* Lumen.

Fernández Ibáñez, J. J. (1986). *Didáctica de la imagen: Educación de la sensibilidad visual.* I.C.E. Deusto. Ttarttalo, S.A.

Gauthier, G. (1996). *Veinte lecciones sobre imagen y sentido.* Cátedra.

Hall, E. (1966). *The hidden dimension.* Doubleday.

Hamilton, E. R. (2015). Picture this: Multimodal representations of prospective teachers' metaphors about teachers and teaching. *Teaching and Teacher Education, 55*, 33–44. https://doi.org/10.1016/j.tate.2015.12.007

Harper, D. (2002). Talking about pictures: A case for photo elicitation. *Visual Studies, 17*, 13–26.

Kress, G., & Van Leeuwen, T. (2006). *Reading images. The grammar of visual design.* Routledge.

Lakoff, G., & Johnson, M. (2009). *Metáforas de la vida cotidiana* (8th ed.). Cátedra.

López Fernández-Cao, M. (1998). La retórica visual como análisis posible en la didáctica del arte y de la imagen. *Arte, Individuo y Sociedad, 10*, 39–62.

López Fernández-Cao, M., & Gauli Pérez, J. C. (2000). El cuerpo imaginado. *Revista Complutense de Educación, 11*(2), 43–57.

Mannay, D. (2017). *Métodos visuales, narrativos y creativos en investigación cualitativa.* Narcea.

Moliné, M. (2000). *La fuerza de la publicidad: Saber hacer buena publicidad, saber administrar su fuerza.* MCGraw-Hill.

Mukeredzi, T. G., & Nyachowe, M. S. (2018). The content and evolution of practical theories of teaching: Experiences of professionally unqualified teachers in Rural Zimbabwe Secondary Schools. *Sage Open.* https://doi.org/10.1177/2158244018785410

Peirce, Ch. S. (1986). *La ciencia de la semiótica.* Nueva Visión.

Pink, S. (2007). *Doing visual ethnography: Images, media and representations in research* (2nd ed.). Sage.

Pink, S. (2009). *Doing sensory ethnography.* Sage.

Prosser, J. (2010). Visual methods and the visual culture of schools. *Visual Studies, 22*, 13–30. https://doi.org/10.1080/14725860601167143

Ruto-Korir, R., & Lubbe-De Beer, C. (2012). The potential for using visual elicitation in understanding preschool teachers' beliefs of appropriate educational practices. *South African Journal of Education, 32*(4), 393–405. https://doi.org/10.15700/saje.v32n4a661

Schwartz, D. (1994). Visual ethnography: Using photographs in qualitative research. *Qualitative Sociology, 12*(2), 119–154.

Sontag, S. (2003). *Ante el dolor de los demás.* Alfaguara.

Stockall, N., & Davis, S. (2011). Uncovering pre-service teacher beliefs about young children: A photographic elicitation methodology. *Issues in Educational Research, 21*(2), 192–209. http://www.iier.org.au/iier21/stockall.html

Tardif, M. (2004). *Los saberes del docente y su desarrollo profesional.* Narcea.

Taylor, E. W. (2016). Using still photography in making meaning of adult educators' teaching beliefs. *Studies in the Education of Adults, 34*(2), 123–139. https://doi.org/10.1080/02660830.2002.11661466

Tompson, P. (2008). *Doing visual research with children and young people.* Routledge.

Chapter 4
Photography in the Formative Dimension of the Practicum

María Rosario Limón Mendizabal, Mercedes Blasco Torrejón, and Antonio Bautista García-Vera

Introduction

The preceding chapters have analysed the value of photography itself and what it contributes as a system of representation in teaching. To finalise the first section of this teacher training essay we need to identify the role photography has played in the practicum of the two undergraduate degrees in teaching; specifically, in their formative dimension. This topic is related to Chap. 7, where we analyse the role of photography in photo-elicitation as a means of improving the mutual training of tutors and practicum students.

This topic is important, given the requirement that every educational system must adapt to the challenges of modern society by preparing individuals to live in the age of information and uncertainty. Teaching strategies need to evolve to adapt to these changes. Teacher must be skilled in terms of content, group work, communication, preparing projects with colleagues and students, analysing data to compare their results with those of other studies, and in terms of emotional intelligence, to train reflective, critical and responsible students who can cope with real life problems. This requires a different type of education professional, one with a critical approach who is capable of rethinking both the contents and the methodology used to transmit them.

All this highlights the importance of the early training of tomorrow's teachers. At this point, we need to mention the importance of shared inquiry that enables

M. R. Limón Mendizabal (✉) · M. Blasco Torrejón · A. Bautista García-Vera
Complutense University, Madrid, Spain
e-mail: mrlimonm@ucm.es

M. Blasco Torrejón
e-mail: cherche@ucm.es

A. Bautista García-Vera
e-mail: bautista@ucm.es

© The Author(s) 2023

A. Bautista García-Vera (ed.), *Photographic Elicitation and Narration in Teachers Education and Development*, Teacher Education, Learning Innovation and Accountability, https://doi.org/10.1007/978-3-031-20164-6_4

pre-service teachers to be reflective and to bring a spirit of enquiry to any real problems observed in the school that their theoretical training has not prepared them for. Practicum students work under the supervision of the classroom teacher, who is also engaged in his or her in-service education through a process of analysis and systematic reflection on their own practice, rethinking, if necessary, the actions taken to solve any problems that emerge, and remaining in contact with other teachers with whom they can interact, pool experiences, and compare research results in order to improve their teaching practice.

According to Martínez Martín (2016, p. 11) "Proposals to improve initial teacher training in our country - in which part of the university and faculty teaching staff are involved - cannot be understood or developed independently of a joint proposal to improve teacher training: Initial training and in-service education are part of an ongoing process - that of the teacher's professional development".

In other words, in the practicum classroom it is possible to combine both types of training, and these will be consolidated when the problems that arise transition from a phase of doubt and hesitation to a constructive, creative phase of constant rethinking of what is rational, of what their methodology is becoming, in order to arrive at a solution (Dewey, 1909). In this regard, a real formative process can only take place when spaces are created in the classrooms for inquiry and questioning about what is being done, where the teacher will take on the role of tutor for practicum students, protagonists in this process, to encourage them to argue, listen, disagree and express themselves freely (González, 2000). This is because, according to Rogers (1995), education must be student-centred and transversal, in accordance with their cognitive, cultural, affective, spiritual and existential life.

In their classroom, most future teachers will act in the same way they saw their teacher act during their practicum, and it is essential for them to have acquired the ability to make decisions based on observation and debate. It is not about training teachers to take certain knowledge to the classroom or to use certain tools, in other words, teaching them only how to teach the contents of the different curricular subjects. Rather, it is about training inquisitive teachers, capable of self-criticism and of always seeking solutions to the problems they encounter, even if this means breaking away from their habitual or planned course of action. We need to create a system of relationships in the classroom in which knowledge is shared between teacher and students (Coll & Solé, 2001) in the student–teacher-curriculum triangle (Astolfi, 1997).

With this in mind, we will end this introduction by describing the framework of analysis used in the following sections, in which we present the formative dimension of practicum training in general and that of the practicum included in undergraduate degrees in Pre-School Education and Primary Education taught at the UCM in particular. The practicum is a subject that places pre-service teachers in direct contact with schools, with classroom tutors engaged in in-service education, and with university tutors. This setting is conducive to research using the camera and, more specifically, the images it provides. It is also a chance for reflecting on the actions of the agents involved, so that practicum students can acquire the skills they need to understand and resolve emerging problems in their classroom or their school. Therefore, we must first of all describe the role of photography in the formative dimension of the practicum, that is, the extent to which it is used, and above all, the levels of the formative framework in which the use of the essence of photography is limited or facilitated as a system of representation and communication, as described in the preceding chapters.

The Practicum: Formative Dimension

If the practicum is a fundamental factor in teacher training, *formation* is an essential part of this work experience. Formation refers to the educational dimension that addresses three important issues. The first is the need to activate the student's higher mental processes, such as observation, analysis, reflection, reasoning, deliberation and criticism. The second is to promote the development of emotions (joy, sadness, etc.), sensations and feelings (love, hate, etc.). Finally, the third is to introduce students to the values accepted by the educational community, such as respect, solidarity, honesty, freedom and participation; and to virtues, such as the possibility of being excited by the colour of the sunlight at a particular time of day, or by the murmur of the waves as one looks out to sea, or by the smell of perfume when walking through a park, or by the misery, sadness or melancholy a certain person sitting on a pavement might feel. In this regard, formation refers to situations aimed at setting in motion thoughts about taking a stand when faced by ethical dilemmas, or by events that challenge ideas and values, that question beliefs and feelings. It also refers to the analysis of procedures used to reach agreements and solutions (Sánchez Cánovas, 2013).

In this way, formation emphasises the purposes of education that are related to the affective, social and ethical world of humans. Including formation in the Practicum gives content to Peters's (1979, p. 311) interpretation of teaching as an intentional activity that reports an achievement or learning about something to someone who is learning "for example, a belief, an attitude, a skill". The basis of this formative content of the Practicum can also be found in the educational aims that justify the organic laws of the last decades. For example, the three fundamental principles enshrined in the Organic Law on Education (LOE) 2/2006 of May 3, and that appear in its preamble, are:

> The first is the requirement to provide quality education … To ensure that all citizens achieve the maximum possible development of all their individual and social, intellectual, cultural and emotional capabilities … At the same time, they must be guaranteed effective equality of opportunities.
> The second principle is the need for all components of the educational community to work together to achieve this ambitious goal … But the responsibility for the educational success of all students not only falls on the individual students, but also on their families, teachers, schools …

The third principle that inspires this Law is a firm commitment to the educational objectives established by the European Union for the coming years … Promoting lifelong learning implies, above all, providing young people with a complete education, … that allows them to develop the values that sustain the practice of democratic citizenship, community living, and social cohesion.

We can see that the first of the three includes the intellectual and affective components of practicum training described in previous paragraphs. The last two principles include the values students must be taught that are included in the educational stages described in this Organic Law, such as participation, democratic citizenship, etc. In this regard, the European Council has also underlined on several occasions the key role of formation in the future growth and long-term technological progress of the European Union. According to the Commission of the European Communities (2007), this can only be achieved by fully developing the innovation potential of European citizens, together with a respect for diversity and the promotion of intercultural dialogue in schools.

So, what formative training do teachers need to enable them to create situations in classrooms and educational centres in which students can learn these mental processes, emotions and values? Stenhouse (1984), among other authors, suggested that to achieve this, teachers should be artists and planners and should research the lessons they teach; seen from another perspective, teachers can only teach the foregoing skills when they themselves have learnt how to *form their students,* This is because formative practices, as described by Macintyre (2001), need and, therefore, seek experiential learning, something that is acquired by humans when they experience situations where the objects to be learned are present. Thus, emotions and attitudes, or values such as justice, solidarity, freedom, respect, participation, etc., are learned when participating in and experiencing the situations of love or sadness, honesty, collaboration and respect required by the three principles underlying the LOE. Therefore, for teachers to be able to help students to learn freedom, solidarity, democracy, etc., and to establish channels for family involvement, they must know how to organize teaching situations where freedom, solidarity, and collaboration are present, practiced and, therefore, experienced.

Photography in the Formative Dimension of the Practicum

To understand the importance of photography in the practicum, in the foregoing paragraphs we showed the formative essence of the practicum. This is configured or materialized in classroom practice by teaching situations where, among other things, observation and analysis of reality are part of this essence. This is because they are mental processes that feed other mental activities, such as reflection, deliberation, etc., since cannot inquire or deliberate in a vacuum—only on previously perceived information. Accordingly, practicum formative situations must primarily include those that promote observation and analysis; for example, asking the pre-service teachers what elements, situations, places in the school and classroom, etc., they find most interesting, and then asking them to explain why. These are exercises that help students notice places they do not usually see when they give in to the inertia of their routine, habits and customs, and that are not always relevant in the space–time contexts where they are applied.

Nevertheless, in order to give these observations and analyses of the reality of the school formative significance, practicum students must be given references of the content to be perceived and studied. For example, one of those proposed in the teaching innovation projects developed by the co-authors of this chapter are: "In your school, discover events, actions or relationships that, from your point of view, help the students build a better world, based, among other things, on the values of equity, respect, solidarity, participation and development cooperation".

This is where the camera enters the scene, because in the hands of a human being it takes on the function of a social and cultural microscope. Basically, in addition to controlling other elements such as the diaphragm, the shutter, the type of lens and the zoom, the viewfinder allows the practicum student and their tutor, if applicable, to select a particular space in the entire educational universe and, consequently, capture what happens there at a given moment, leaving out any other experiences or events taking place in that school. The viewfinder, therefore, helps to perceive, to look selectively and, once the content of the shot has been chosen, to analyse it.

The function of the image does not end with mere observation and analysis, because the outcome of the photographic study is a valid nutrient for the assessment of its content. The stillness provided by this iconic information medium helps pre-service teachers participate in and experience the foregoing situations of perception, analysis and evaluation of the educational reality of their school. This is because, among other arguments, in order to analyse or study and evaluate the situation photographed, its component elements must be compared and contrasted, and to do this, the contents thus confronted must be temporary.

The above arguments, partly the result of reports of our experience in the development of the educational innovation projects PIE2016-23 and PIE2017-41 in the Complutense University (Bautista, 2016, 2017a), are echoed by Dubois's (1994) perspective of photography as a way of thinking that introduces users to a new relationship with signs, with space, with reality, with the subject, and with being and doing. Images provide essential information on the interpretive referents of the meanings or sense given to the reality represented by the participants—pre-service teachers. Photographs, therefore, are part of the content of their own reflection on school life, they are taken with the aim of stimulating interpretations, feelings and responses (Hurworth, 2003). In other words, they allow them to acquire another perspective that goes beyond what they thought was happening or what was meant. After that series of interpretations about a specific situation, they will come to a provisional conclusion about its essence.

If photography facilitates observation, analysis, reflection and deliberation on the elements of reality, and reconceptualizes meanings and thought and action processes, then it is valid tool for the formative dimension of the practicum. That is to say, it is a tool that can help practicum students activate their higher mental processes, to experience emotions and affects, and, finally, to introduce them to the values accepted by the community where their practicum school is located.

Case Study: Photography in the Practicum of Teaching Degrees Taught at the Universidad Complutense De Madrid

Continuing with the subject of this chapter, we will now analyse a specific example of the teaching practicum offered in the Complutense University of Madrid. As mentioned above, each practicum is a space for pre-service teachers to relate the theoretical framework of teaching, learning or human development with life in classrooms and schools (Bautista, 2009). However, as discussed in the preceding section, for these areas to enrich each other, the pre-service teacher must have access to moments of observation and personal inquiry, along with others of deliberation, questioning and exchange of points of view between tutors and practicum students.

At the same time, albeit it in another technical and social field, the advances made in technology in recent decades has made the camera available to everyone. In fact, photographic images are increasingly present in everyday life, and as a result they are used more and more in educational contexts as a teaching and learning tool (Barr, 2013). If we combine this with the arguments presented in the previous section, we can see that photography is a creative tool that encourages communication and reflection, and as such is suitable for use in the teaching practicum. Accordingly, photography can gradually be incorporated into practicum situations in order to promote observation, reflection and debate on a certain content or cognitive or emotional event in the practicum that is significant for the students.

One way of approaching an analysis of the role of photography in the teaching practicum is to describe the competencies teachers have to acquire and the activities included. The Recommendation of the European Parliament and of the Council of 18 December 2006 identifies eight key competences for lifelong learning that are common to all undergraduate courses. In this document, key competences are those that all educators need for their personal fulfilment, active citizenship, social cohesion and employability in a knowledge society Specifically: (1) Communication in the mother tongue. (2) Communication in foreign languages. (3) Mathematical competence and basic competences in science and technology. (4) Digital competence. (5) Learning to learn. (6) Social and civic competences. (7) Sense of initiative and entrepreneurship. (8) Cultural awareness and expression.

The Complutense University has adapted this competence framework to the theoretical and practical know-how that will allow pre-school and primary teachers to master the situations they will encounter in their future professional life. This has been summarised in five competences: professional, pedagogical, subject, intercultural and linguistic. In terms of methodology, the University has designed a procedure that helps practicum students acquire each of these five competences and, at the same time, requires them to use the formative processes described in the preceding section, namely: observation, implementation (consisting of analysis and deliberation) and evaluation.

Specifically, the following recommendations are made to pre-school and primary education undergraduates doing their practicum training.

On Professional Competence

Observation: In this competence, practicum students are asked to analyse the classroom relationships established by the teacher for the purpose of promoting comprehensive personal development. As mentioned above, classroom communication is essential to achieve this goal. In this regard, we must bear in mind that photography communicates through visual symbols without requiring a written or spoken language. Photography is a moment in time of an event. The stillness of the photograph allows analyses and deliberations to emerge that culminate in knowledge. Therefore, it is important to promote the use of photography as a means of communication that can elicit narratives, provoke brainstorming, express emotions, feelings, concerns, know-how, and to improve digital competence and create spaces for interaction between schools and families.

Implementation or implementation of what is observed: During their practicum, undergraduate teachers are asked to contribute to creating a coexistence based on equal rights and the practice of social justice, tolerance, the exercise of freedom, peace, and respect for nature. All these values are abstractions that have no material manifestation; however, they need to be represented in some way in order to give fluidity to the corresponding analysis, debate and working plan. One of the easiest ways of achieving this is by using visual devices, or rhetorical figures, such as visual antithesis or metonymy.

Evaluation: Practicum students are asked to share with the practicum site tutor their own reflections on the development of the teacher's professional competence. Chapter 6 describes, among other things, photography-based procedures that facilitate the representation of beliefs and theories that motivate teaching practices, as well as the visual materialization of the contradictions between different theories, or the inconsistencies regarding the aims of a teacher and their teaching practices.

On Pedagogical Competence

Observation: To perceive this competence, the student is asked to reflect on how school tutors plan their classes and provide teaching instructions to enable their students to learn. They are also asked to analyse in detail of how they manage the class and the strategies that best promote coexistence, and to observe the available resources, including ICTs, that facilitate the teaching–learning process. Photography, unlike other media such as video, focuses the observation of details of classroom practice through the camera's viewfinder. After identifying some such details that the practicum student believes to be important, they are immortalized by releasing the shutter, and the resulting image can then be quietly analysed.

Implementation: In order to inform the tutor of what they have seen, or of the effect their teaching has on their students' learning, on the value of the relationships that must be established between them as part of the planned teaching situation, the practicum student must to show the tutor indicators of the degree of interest and participation that he or she has aroused in their students. Both the organization of spaces and materials and the significances and emotions assigned to teaching situations can be represented, and therefore, communicated to the tutor through photographs.

Evaluation: It is precisely these photographs that will help the practicum student to compare the principles of his or her pedagogical approach with that of the practicum site tutor.

On Subject Competence

Observation: In order to follow the guidelines they are given for observing the tutor's skill in designing and developing lessons, practicum students must be fully acquainted with the subjects taught. In turn, they are told that the subsequent evaluation of the way they implement tasks using materials and other methodological strategies will be based on the information resulting from these observations.

Because of the wide range of subjects taught, it is impossible to give a detailed analysis of the use of photography in each; however, practicum students are encouraged to review relevant studies. For example, Bazalgette (1991) makes analyses the use of the camera in the teaching of Natural Sciences, History, Geography, Language, etc.

On Intercultural Competence

Observation: In the Complutense University's 2018–2019 Practicum Guide for undergraduate teachers, the students are asked to identify the different cultures represented in their school and in their classroom, and to analyse how the school caters for this diversity on an educational level. They are also asked to compare these observations with their university training, and to later discuss with the practicum site tutor how such ethnic diversity can be used to enrich intercultural education situations.

Implementation: A photograph is the materialization of a human being's perspective of an aspect of life. Each perspective of life is the result of interpreting life within the particular cultural framework built by each human during their lifetime. Thus, photography is a good representation system for training practicum teachers to work in multicultural environments, because it facilitates the observation and communication of different, sometimes contrasting, points of view on education. In this regard, it can change preconceived ideas of "others" and create a climate of respect and understanding between cultures. The speed at which photography has advanced as a result of digital technology is improving intercultural communication and relations and, consequently, mutual understanding.

Evaluation: In this section, students are asked to perform a self-evaluation and an evaluation of the entire process with the classroom tutor. Photographic language can rapidly communicate profoundly different world views. A group of photographs taken by these diverse students can be combined to create a mosaic of contrasting points of view on which to organize and develop the analysis and evaluation of what has been experienced in relation to their previous theoretical and experiential references. In practicum sites with a high ratio of immigrants, asking primary school students to bring photographs of their family and their culture (Bautista, 2017b) promotes the intercultural understanding necessary for coexistence. These photographic situations will help practicum students to consider and examine the relationship between the activity carried out in the classroom and their university training.

On Linguistic Competence

Observation: Practicum students are asked to recognise their own needs and establish priorities regarding the use of language in teaching communication. They are also asked to choose resources that will improve their own communication skills. As mentioned in the general introduction, photography is a useful communication-stimulating tool that future teachers can use to elicit three types of information. For example, the denotative level of the image is an excellent reference point for eliciting the description of physical contexts, while the connotative and affective (punctum) levels allow them to communicate through rhetorical figures—internal elements that, though invisible, can elicit affects, beliefs or values.

Implementation: Practicum students are urged to take advantage of conversations among their practicum site colleagues to improve their knowledge of professional language. Likewise, they are required to use the appropriate linguistic register for each context. It is in this requirement that photography plays the role of an auxiliary representation system, and future teachers will need to learn the language of photography and add it to their communication skills.

Evaluation: For the purposes of evaluation, students are asked to work with the practicum site tutor to assess the extent to which their own progress with language facilitates their relationship with the class, and their mastery of the language specific to each subject. They must base their assessment on information recorded, among other things, in photographs taken of teaching situations arising in the classroom. In this regard, photography helps more than video to determine the progress made, because it can be assessed by comparing two moments or positions. This comparison is best achieved using two photographs that can be studied in detail. Video, however, shows continuous movement, and therefore two particular moments cannot be compared unless the image is paused, played, and then paused again, etc.

Our analysis and discussion of the Complutense University of Madrid's basic practicum guidelines shows the possibility of introducing a new element, namely, the use of cameras in the work of undergraduate teachers. Authors such as Pérez-Campanero and Sánchez (1996) describe the practicum as a paradigm that determines how school life is viewed. The proposed change will only occur when participants see and experience school life in another way, namely, in the case study analysed, through the lens of a camera and through the images that immortalize the activities that take place.

This change, we believe, can turn the practicum into more than just another subject in the curriculum, and the practicum student as more than just a hindrance. Instead, the practicum should be considered an opportunity for the school and the classroom tutor to be, together with the camera, a living and dynamic element of the entire process that will culminate in the student becoming not only a teacher, but an artist.

References

Astolfi, J. P. (1997). *El error, un medio para enseñar.* Díada.

Barr, R. (2013). Memory constraints on infant learning from picture books, television, and touchscreens. *Child Development Perspectives, 7*(4), 205–210.

Bautista, A. (Coord.). (2009). *Practicum y Campus virtual.* Da Vinci. Colección Redes.

Bautista, A. (Dir.). (2016). *La formación del alumnado del* Grado *de Maestro de Educación Primaria mediante sesiones de fotoelicitación en el Practicum* [Proyecto de Innovación docente, PIE2016-23]. Universidad Complutense.

Bautista, A. (Dir.). (2017a). Incorporación de la narración audiovisual, soportadaen la foto-elicitación y centrada en la diversidad sociocultural de los escolares, en el Practicum de los grados de maestro [Proyecto de Innovación docente, PIE2017-41]. Universidad Complutense.

Bautista, A. (2017b). Comunicación entre familias a través de sesiones de foto-elicitación en un colegio diverso culturalmente. *Revista de curriculum y formación del profesorado, 21*(3), 327–348.

Bazalgette, C. (1991). *Los medios audiovisuales en la educación primaria.* Morata.

Comisión de las Comunidades Europeas. (2007, May 10). *Comunicación sobre una Agenda Europea para la Cultura en un Mundo en vías de Globalización.* https://eur-lex.europa.eu/legal-content/ES/TXT/PDF/?uri=CELEX:52007DC0242&from=GA

Coll, C., & Solé, E. (2001). Ensenar y aprender en el contexto del aula. In C. Coll, J. Palacios, & A. Marchesi (Eds), *Desarrollo psicológico y educación, 2. Psicología de la educación escolar* (pp. 357–386). Alianza.

Dewey, J. (1909). *How we think.* D.C. Heath.

Dubois, P. (1994). *El acto fotográfico.* Paidós Comunicación/20.

González, V. (2000). La educación de valores en el curriculum universitario: Un enfoque psicopedagógico para su estudio. *Educación Media Superior, 14,* 74–82.

Guía de Prácticas del Grado en Maestro en Educación Infantil. Curso 2018–2019. Practicum. Facultad de Educación: Universidad Complutense de Madrid.

Guía de Prácticas del Grado en Maestro en Educación Primaria. Curso 2018–2019. Practicum. Facultad de Educación: Universidad Complutense de Madrid.

Hernández, F. (2010). *Espigadoras de la cultura visual*. Octaedro.

Hurworth, R. (2003). Photo-interviewing for research. *Social Research Update* (40). http://www.soc.surrey.ac.uk/sru/sru40.html

Ley Orgánica de Educación (LOE). 2/2006, de 3 de mayo.

Macintyre, A. (2001). *Tras la virtud*. Crítica.

Martínez, M. (2016). La formación inicial de los Maestros: Una responsabilidad compartida. *Bordón, 68*(2), 9–16.

Pérez-Campanero, Mª P., & Sánchez, A. (1996). *Guía para un alumno en prácticas*. Colección Guías I.F.O.R.

Peters, R. S. (1979). *Filosofía de la educación*. FCE.

Recomendación del Parlamento Europeo y del Consejo. (2006). Sobre las competencias clave para el aprendizaje permanente. Diario Oficial de la Unión Europea del 30 de diciembre de 2006.

Rogers, C. (1995). *El camino del Ser*. Kairós.

Sánchez Cánovas, J. F. (2013). Participación educativa y mediación escolar. Una nueva concepción en la escuela del siglo XXI. *Aposta Revista de Ciencias Sociales*, n° 59. http://www.apostadigital.com/revistav3/hemeroteca/jfcanovas2.pdf

Stenhouse, L. (1984). *Investigación y desarrollo del currículum*. Morata.

Part II
Photo-Elicitation in Teacher Professional Development

Chapter 5
Photovoice and Photo-Elicitation: Similarities, Differences, Incorporation and Contribution in In-Service Teacher Training

María Jesús Romera Iruela

Introduction

Teaching involves an on-going process of inquiry into our own teaching practice in order to resolve the educational problems encountered and to optimise our methodology through innovation and improvement. Teachers also need to update their theoretical and practical knowledge to keep abreast of new developments that emerge from research into the spheres of knowledge that affect their broad and complex pedagogy. Hence the need for in-service training, an activity that allows teachers to grow both personally and professionally, and to provide their students with comprehensive, integrated education that is relevant to their sociocultural reality.

The meaning of in-service training is changing, and varies between countries, as the international review carried out by Villegas-Reimers (2003) has shown. In most developed countries, this type of education includes all training activities engaged in by primary and secondary teachers and school principals after obtaining their undergraduate degree. The training is aimed mainly, or exclusively, at improving their professional knowledge, skills and attitudes so that they can educate children more effectively (Bolam in Villegas-Reimers, 2003, p. 55). In Spain and other countries, in-service education takes place at different educational levels. One of the fundamental factors involved in achieving quality education is the ethical and professional strength of teachers and professors, in other words, the possession of strong values and professional resources (Braslavsky, 2005). This, in turn, means that these elements need to be present in both their undergraduate education and in the activities undertaken to update and perfect their in-service education.

In 2015, schools boards at the regional (autonomous community) and national level in Spain embarked on a systematic study of the teachers of the twenty-first

M. J. Romera Iruela (✉)
Complutense University, Madrid, Spain
e-mail: mjromera@ucm.es

A. Bautista García-Vera (ed.), *Photographic Elicitation and Narration in Teachers Education and Development*, Teacher Education, Learning Innovation and Accountability, https://doi.org/10.1007/978-3-031-20164-6_5

century. The study identified several challenges faced by teachers in their in-service education, some of which have also been reported by other authors. Of these, the following have particular relevance in this chapter: the ability to detect their training needs, the need to enhance in-service education, the need to update their scientific and didactic knowledge to meet the needs of their students, and the need to use information and communication technologies as teaching aids, together with the resources needed to improve their teaching activity (pp 17–18). The study was followed by a forum *"Educar para el siglo XXI. Desafíos y propuestas sobre la profesión docente"* [Educate for the XXI century. Challenges and proposals for teachers] sponsored by the Ministry of Education and Vocational Training, which is taking place at the time of writing, in which participants outlined proposals to reform teacher training. From our perspective, the tradition of engaging in action research is a valuable part of teacher training, both at the undergraduate level and in all aspects of in-service education. Both these stages can be linked by means of participatory action research during the practicum, leading to innovation.

In recent decades, new processes linking photography with narrative and dialogue, namely, photo-voice and photo-elicitation, have gradually been incorporated in research activities and the practicum stage in various fields, including education. In this chapter, we will study and compare approaches, and explore their potential as a tool in in-service education for teacher.

Conceptualization and Methodological Delimitation of Photovoice

The literature on photo-voice unanimously dates the origin of this practice to the works of Wang and Burris on health promotion. In 1997, these authors published an article in which they described the concept, methodology, and use of photo-voice in participatory needs evaluation. Later, Wang (2006) noted that both authors had created this methodology, and defined its use in participatory action research (p. 148). Both authors describe this method as a subtle, flexible process that can be adapted to participatory objectives, groups or communities and any problems or issues that need to be addressed. Photovoice has been defined as "a process by which people can identify, represent and enhance their community through a specific photographic technique" (Wang & Burris, 1997, p. 369). It does not merely involve the use of photographs to talk about or teach something; instead, the photographs must make it possible to know the point of view of the participants who take them on a problem or community issue, in other words, their experience or individual knowledge and also social, through dialogue, with the aim of conveying their views to social and political leaders who can introduce changes and improvements. The visual image thus becomes a means for people in certain situations of vulnerability to communicate their needs, problems or perspectives on the social issues that affect them. These opinions are contextualized and discussed by the participants and can stimulate social action to improve community welfare. Photovoice, as a practice based on the production of knowledge has three main objectives:

- To enable people to record and reflect their community's strengths and concerns,
- To promote critical dialogue and knowledge about important community issues through large and small group discussion of photographs,
- To reach policymakers (Wang & Burris, 1997, p. 369).

In the definition put forward by these authors, photovoice, as a participatory method, is intended to elicit living folk wisdom, observation, and community stories in visual and oral terms. Photography is the vehicle for the emergence of the political voice. The concept of photovoice was developed from the following sources:

- The theoretical literature on education for critical consciousness, particularly the work of Paulo Freire.
- Feminist theory.
- A community-based approach to documentary photography.
- Health promotion principles (Wang, 2006, p. 148; Wang & Burris, 1997, p. 369).

Wang (2006) has described this methodology as a nine-step strategy; the order of the first two is interchangeable:

- Select and recruit a target audience of policy makers or community leaders.
- Recruit a group of photovoice participants, ideally consisting of between 7 and 10 individuals.
- Introduce the photovoice methodology to participants, and facilitate a group discussion about cameras, power and ethics.
- Obtain informed consent. This should include: a statement of project activities and significance, specific potential risks and benefits, the voluntary nature of participation and freedom to withdraw at any time for any reason, and the understanding that no photographs identifying specific individuals will be released without separate written consent of not only the photographer but also the identified individuals. This must be put in writing. In the case of minors, informed consent must be obtained from their parents or guardians. This also applies to youth participants.
- Pose an initial theme or themes for taking pictures.
- Distribute cameras to participants and review how to use the camera.
- Provide time for participants to take pictures.
- Meet to discuss photographs and identify themes. This discussion is divided into three stages: selecting photographs, contextualizing or storytelling, and codifying issues, themes, or theories. These stages are carried out in each round of photographs taken by the participants. The number of photovoice rounds will depend on various factors, such as facilitators' and participants' preferences, overall project scope and budget, and other practical considerations.
- Plan with participants a format to share photographs and stories with policy makers or community leaders, for example, a PowerPoint slide presentation or a exhibition (pp. 149–152).

By way of synthesis, the methodology involves providing participants with cameras so that they can photograph their everyday realities. Images teach concepts and can influence policy. This is why community members ought to participate in creating and defining the images that shape healthful public policy (p. 148).

According to Rabadán and Contreras (2014), participatory photography is known internationally as photovoice. With regard to photovoice terminology, Doval (2015) has shown that it is referred to by different names in the academic literature, and is sometimes confused with photo-elicitation. It is not uncommon for both to merge - a phenomenon that will be discussed later in this chapter. The author goes on to say that "there continues to be a lack of consistency in the identification of methodology in studies using photovoice" (p. 246) a consideration present in the scientific literature. Likewise, it is common to find it referred to both as a method and a technique.

The potentialities of photovoice as described in several of the forgoing studies, particularly Wang and Burris (1997), are fundamentally the following:

- To provide a glimpse of the reality experienced by groups of people or communities as a means of facilitating transformation.
- To people who have not learnt to read and write, it is a way of visually representing their reality, and thus giving them a voice.
- To show different behavioural and social contexts, such as settings, moments and ideas, of which the community is unaware.
- To include participants from different practicum fields who are not professionals or who are not outsiders in these fields.
- To provide benefits to people and their social networks.
- To determine the community's needs, resources and assets.
- To identify shortcomings in the theories underlying social programmes or policies by highlighting the evidence obtained from the participatory approach.
- To evaluate, based on a needs analysis, the beliefs or philosophies that drive different programmes, and the approaches, goals and values that sustain them.
- To motivate change in the goals, objectives, beliefs and theories found in social practices.
- To promote problem-solving, organization and social action in favour of personal and community well-being.

Although photovoice has several advantage, it is also important to bear in mind its disadvantages:

- The potential risk to participants derived from the political intent of the photograph and the critical nature of the dialogue for action.
- The personal judgement of the photographer, and with it, their intent, may made it difficult to identify elements that have been omitted.
- The broader stratification of classes can be reproduced by controlling resources.
- The complexity and difficulty of analysing the photographs.
- Methodological ideals may not tally with reality.
- In addition to the foregoing limitations, we believe the fundamental limitation of photovoice is that participatory dialogue and consensus does not guarantee

that the voice obtained expresses reality as it. This, therefore, can undermine the effectiveness of programmes or practices that require everyone to participate. This is an epistemological limitation.

In the last two decades, photovoice has been used in art, in community development and social action, health, gender studies and education. It has been found to be especially useful in children, adolescents and young people, in addition to the most vulnerable populations. Doval (2015) identified the themes that have been addressed in our field: education in general and in particular, teaching and learning strategies, educational and intellectual disability, autism, education in orphanages, right to education, coeducation, inclusive education, literacy, perception of school spaces, and university education (p. 220). Photovoice is rarely used in Spain, and few studies have been published so far. In this respect, according to Rabadán and Contreras (2014), "using participatory photography as an educational experience can be quite a challenge" (p. 153).

Having outlined the conceptualization of photovoice, we will now do the same with photo-elicitation.

Conceptual and Methodological Overview of Photo-Elicitation

The origin of photo-elicitation is generally considered to be article on mental health published by John Collier in 1957, who mentioned the term when comparing interviews based on photographs with traditional interviews, used as controls. In this study, he showed the advantages of the photo-interview in terms of the nature of the information provided. He continued to investigate this type of open interview, using it in various anthropological investigations that led to other publications. Harper (2002) gave a widely cited definition of photo elicitation, described the history of its development in anthropology and sociology, where it originates, and evaluated its current use and future potential. Very briefly, "Photo elicitation is based on the simple idea of inserting a photograph into a research interview" (p. 13). He had previously suggested that photo elicitation "be regarded as a postmodern dialogue based on the authority of the subject rather than the researcher" (p. 15). Harper found that anthropological studies that rely primarily on photo elicitation are few and far between, and that it has played a greater role in visual sociology, although it was given marginal importance compared to mainstream research methodology. Nevertheless, it has also penetrated fields such as psychology, education, and organizational studies. In addition, he placed the photographs used in photo elicitation research along a continuum, depending on what they represented, and identified the potentialities of photo-elicitation as (briefly): it evokes different information, feelings and memories than those obtained through traditional empirical research, and thus expands its possibilities; it can reduce areas of misunderstanding in in-depth interviews by bringing researchers and subjects to a common understanding, either by opening their perspectives or by bridging their cultures through research collaboration (pp. 15 and 20–23).

Angulo (2007), based on Harper (2002), describes the nature of photo-elicitation as being "about dialoguing about and with images, recalling what they show, linking with memories, experiences (past and present), sensations, and emotions (p. 1). We believe that although this involves combing two data collection techniques typical of observation and survey methods, in which visual and verbal forms come together, this combination makes sense within research methodology of which is a part, and more specifically, within the framework of the issue investigated and the knowledge to be obtained, which always fall within a certain paradigm that guides such research. It is in the absence of this incorporation where we consider that the confusion and lack of unanimity present in the scientfic literarure lies, when referring to photo elicitation, indistinctly, as a methodology, a method, a technique or a research tool.

The greatest differences between the approaches that have been established in photo-elicitation are found in paradigmatic context of research.

In a study that uses photo-elicitation, a series of decisions have to be made that, according to Lapenta (2011), revolve around the following three questions:

- Who is going to make or select the images to be used in the interviews?
- What is the content of the images going to be?
- Where are the images going to be used and how? (p. 204)

From our perspective, the answer to these questions depends on the paradigm that guides the research, and this will resolve any dilemmas presented by the use of this technique.

Lapenta (2011) has identified four approaches to photo-elicitation that we will briefly describe below, following their systematization:

- *Photo-elicitation* (classic)

This is the first perspective that arose from the theoretical-methodological debate that questioned the principles of traditional structured surveys/interviews, the nature of the interaction between the researcher and the interviewee, and the supposed knowledge that this interaction produced. Photo-elicitation is a variation on an open-ended interview. It is a non-directive procedure that creates a relaxed atmosphere that allows the researcher, according to the object of study, to use images taken or selected of the subject's world that they assume to be meaningful in order to elicit comments, memories and discussions. These photographs or images may also be taken by the researcher while accompanied by one or more informants to guide him or her on their content and how to take them. This approach has been used to test research hypotheses and to compare results and interpretations with other interviews or with studies that may use the same or similar images. The photographs generated by the researcher can produce descriptions and meanings that illuminate issues not initially visible to the researcher, but visible to the interviewees, and enable the researcher to develop new hypotheses and interpretations. New images can be added to stimulate the analysis, and such groups of photographs can help open up the interviewee's perspectives. The epistemological dilemma that arises from this approach, and that has led to the development of others, concerns the following questions: Whose knowledge do the selected photographs really represent? Who were those images really made for? What topics of interest, discourse or aesthetics do they represent?

- *Reflexive photography or photo elicitation autodriven*

Harper first introduced the idea of reflective photography by formulating the hypothesis that in the reflective photographic method the subject shares the definition of the meaning. In this approach, the production or selection of the images is done by the interviewees. Like other forms of photo-elicitation, photographs are used to increase the respondent's engagement in the interview, but they are typically encouraged to delve into the content and meaning of the photographs they have produced. The respondent's responses to the research questions are motivated by the stimulus directly drawn from the photographs they have taken. Thus, the interview is conducted by the informants themselves, who see their behaviour through the processes of selection, observation and interpretation of their photographs. This not only enables the researcher and the respondents to negotiate the interpretations of the images, but also gives the latter a greater voice and authority to interpret their lives and social contexts, and an "action perspective" that helps to make their observations on life and social systems meaningful to outsiders. One advantage of this approach is its ability to reduce the investigator bias that is inherent to the selection of specific images, subjects, and themes used in interviews, thereby producing a body of knowledge that concerns events as perceived by the respondents. Another advantage is that the images chosen can reinforce and deepen the findings of quantitative approaches, and they can also be used in other qualitative research methods, such as focus groups.

- *Photovoice*

This is the third of the photo-elicitation approaches identified by Lapenta (2011), who claims that it enriches image-based interview methods. As this approach has already been discussed in the previous section, we will only add here that it involves community-based image production that is followed by a critical, individual and collective dialogue on the significance and meaning of the images in terms of transforming the community. According to Lapenta, citing Wang, photovoice is unique in that following a similarly participatory approach, it engages all the members of the community to select those photos that most accurately reflect their concerns and assets. These might include those they consider most significant, or simply like best (p. 207). The author adds that this approach distinctly separates photovoice from other methods in that is conceives the photographs as catalysts of participatory stories that emerge from the composed voices, meanings and interpretations elaborated by the members of a small or large group.

- *Collaborative or participatory image production*

This fourth approach to photo-elicitation, referred to by its descriptive name, is another participatory approach that involves, according to Lapenta (2011), following Banks (1995), images generated by the researcher "together" with respondents as a "collaborative representation" which serves to remove obstacles between the observer and the observed. Banks later argued that to some degree all research results are collaborative, and concluded that the very presence of the researcher when using a camera among a group of people is necessarily the result of a series of earlier contacts and negotiations. In collaborative research, these negotiations are a methodological dilemma, since the researcher has to decide how much information to share with respondents about the research agenda. Photographing together provides opportunities to discuss how the researcher sees what he or she photographs, and how informants interpret the researcher's photographs. These interactions can bring researchers closer to understanding their visual knowledge, and provide criteria for evaluating what they and the responders see differently. This reflective process can be used as part of learning to see how others do in a directed way. Researchers, by collaboratively representing everyday experiences, empower responders to produce shared understandings of their past experiences and current practices. The images and audio-visual materials provide data that informants can comment on to produce further knowledge. The production of collaborative images can also empower the interviewees by granting them a role in the selection and framing of images, thereby uncovering their experiences, perspectives and histories (Lapenta, 2011, pp. 204–209). Photo-elicitation can provide trainee teachers with this same educational content, together with others that will be presented in the next chapter.

From the epistemological and paradigmatic perspective, photo-elicitation is belong fundamentally a hermeneutical or interpretative paradigm, because it attempts to grasp the significance and meaning of people's objects, behaviours and actions. However, regardless of this common purpose, photovoice goes one step further because it is rooted and based in the critical paradigm, as indicated in its theoretical basis, and its classic approach in the context of exploratory qualitative studies, lies in the post-positivist framework.

We believe that photo-elicitation, in the context of a comprehensive epistemology, can be used in different ways, among them, Gadamer's hermeneutical approach and the interpretative and constructive perspectives.

Having explained the specific procedure involved in photovoice, and despite the variations that exist when using photo-elicitation in different research processes, we will now give an overview of the stages involved in this procedure. Ndione and Remy (2018) identify two phases in the implementation of photo-elicitation: the photo-essay phase and the interview and elicitation phase. The latter, in some cases, can be followed by classification. The methodology of photo-elicitation can be described thus:

- Identification of the issue under study by the researcher or the team and contact with participants to include them in the project using communication and dialogue.
- Planning of the data collection processes and establishment of the session schedule.
- Training or introduction to the technique of photo-elicitation.
- Obtaining informed consent to take and use the photographs.

- Taking the photographs or compiling them from a source (photo-essay phase) in which the images will be obtained in the amount set by those determined in planning phase within an established time.
- Photographic narration sessions, or the interview and elicitation phase, in which the researcher, or some members of the team, interact with the participant/s to elicit verbally the significance and meaning that the images have for him, her or them, and in some approach, for the researcher. In this way they express their beliefs, theories, concepts or values, while revealing their sensations and feelings. In some types of photo-elicitation, the final phase of the interviews may be followed by further questions aimed at deepening the inquiry by classifying the photographs and the resulting narratives. Ndione and Remy call the final part of this phase "classification". All narrations are recorded.
- Analysis and interpretation of the data obtained, in which the recordings are transcribed, the analysis categories are established, and the information obtained from the narrations is classified using content analysis. This is followed by interpretation of the narrations, in which, according to Warhurst and Black (2015), one of the approaches used is symbolic interpretation based on semiotic.
- Conclusions, reporting and dissemination of results.

In our view, the potential of photo-elicitation, considering all its different approaches described by the foregoing sources, are as follows:

- It enables the expression of tacit knowledge.
- It facilitates a deeper understanding of the phenomena and practices that are investigated, by combining its two linguistic forms.
- It can help to discovery and solve problems.
- It enables participants to question the most consolidated knowledge and open new perspectives and theoretical frameworks.
- It enables participant to identify beliefs or misconceptions.
- It manifests and clarifies possible dilemmas experienced by participants.
- It has the potential to train participants.
- It makes the relationships between researchers and other participants more flexible.
- It encourages collaborative and participatory inquiry.
- It optimizes actions based on improved understanding.

Photo-elicitation has the limitations inherent to each of its paradigms and approaches. However, the main limitations, generally speaking, are the following:

- Difficulty in establishing, relating and integrating categories in the analysis and interpretation of the data.
- The understandings are not put into practice.
- The observations, together with their theories and values, despite their dual representation, may not be consistent with reality, and if this is the case, the practices associated with them will not be effective.

Based on the foregoing description of photo voice and photo-elicitation, we will now discuss their similarities and differences.

Similarities and Differences Between Photovoice and Photo-Elicitation

Despite the terminological diversity and semantic plurality surrounding the different approaches and techniques of photo-elicitation, I believe the paradigmatic perspective provides clarity and allows us to differentiate between its terms.

Photo elicitaton and photovoice have in common the linking of their two constituents techniques, one from the observation method and the other from the survey method; therefore, both use visual and verbal languages. Both involve taking photographs followed by narrative sessions regardless of the number of phases involved in this process. This may explain why photovoice is regarded as a type of photo-elicitation.

The main difference between photovoice and photo-elicitation is that the former is based on the critical paradigm, which provides the framework for its application and distinguishes, fundamentally, its participatory and community-based nature. In other words, photographs are produced by the members of the community who, individually and collectively, express their experiences critically, seeking consensus and the dissemination of their interpretation and significance to political leaders and leaders of society for the purpose of bringing about a change in the community. The latter, photo-elicitation, is mainly based on interpretative paradigm and its different traditions, but can be based on the post-positivist paradigm. Therefore, this paradigmatic difference, with its traditions, determines the approaches of photo elicitation and differences arise above all in the researcher–participants-images triad. From the post-positivist, qualitative approach, the researcher produces photographs and plays an external, directive role; the collaborative role of the participants is limited to the answers they provide, and the photographs play the role of information inputs or objective inventories. These characteristics are found in classic photo-elicitation. The interpretive paradigm, likewise, determines differences in the other two approaches to photo-elicitation, and with respect to the previous ones, which are reflected in the aforementioned triad. First, in reflexive photography, the subject or subjects interviewed take or select the images, the aim being to understand their worlds. The researcher plays a collaborative role with minimal leadership; the interviewees are self-driven. The images, due to their content, are located along a continuum—inventories, contextual images or intimate images (the last two being important), and due to their function, are informative, analytical-reflexive or unitary report, the last two being important. On the other hand, in the *collaborative or participatory image production* approach, images are produced by the researcher/s "together" with the interviewees in order to obtain a shared understanding. The relationships between the researcher/s and the responders are of participation and collaboration to varying degrees. The content and function of the images are the first two of each of the aforementioned continuums.

New approaches to photo-elicitation may emerge in the light of new paradigms, and criticism and transformation may be included in the interpretation. The last aspect will be discussed in chapter six, which deals with the process of eliciting information from photographs—not, in this case, for research purposes (to answer questions or hypotheses), but as part of in-service education described in chapter four.

Having conceptualized, compared and delimited photovoice and photo-elicitation, we will now describe how they have been incorporated into in-service teacher education.

Application and Value of Photovoice and Photo-Elicitation in In-Service Teachers Education

We searched the main educational and multidisciplinary databases available, namely REDINED, ERIC, Dialnet, TESEO, CISNE, Web of Science, Scopus, and Google Scholar to determine the extent to which these methodologies are present in in-service education in the teaching profession. The search was performed using search terms in the natural language of the databases, and combining these languages with the indexing language of each database and with strings containing the following keywords in Spanish: *fotovoz, foto-elicitation, formación permanente, formación en el servicio, desarrollo profesional*, and *profesor*. After eliminating unsuitable results, we finally retrieved 31 documents. Although our search was not exhaustive, we believe it was comprehensive enough to obtain a meaningful overview of the use and potential of these methods in in-service teacher education. This number of documents retrieved shows the gradual incursion of photo-elicitation and photovoice in this field of training. Most studies were published within the last 5 years. The analysis of the use of each procedure in the documents retrieved, based on the author's assignment, yielded the following: photo-elicitation is used in 25 studies, photovoice in 3, and another 3 studies used a combination of both. This shows that photovoice is still rarely used in in-service education in teachers. In the studies in which photovoice was used focussed on empowerment, social criticism, and transformation. Regarding the use of these procedures in Spain, based on the institutional affiliation of the authors or the location of the study, 26% studies were conducted in Spain, with the group authoring this book accounting for 16% of papers.

Our review of the content of the studies obtained revealed a number of different of themes in which photovoice and photo-elicitation were used in in-service education. These themes have been established by means of an assignation that has prioritized exclusivity and are described below.

Many of these studies have investigated the potential of photo-elicitation, and to a lesser extent photovoice, to train adult educators, teachers of deaf children, and pre-school and primary school teachers in issues such as expression and assignment of meaning to their beliefs, the development of critical reflection and dialogue skills in their teaching practice, the understanding and the introduction of changes in their teaching practice, the representation of the mental image of their experiences in the classroom with elicitation, the presence of dilemmas and decision-making in their educational action, the emergence of theories, values and feelings; teacher thinking and the use of digital hybrids (Bautista, 2017; Bautista et al., 2016, 2017, 2018; Taylor, 2002; McCracken, 2015; Parker et al., 2016; Rayón et al., 2017; Ruto-Korir & Lubbe-De Beer, 2012; Wolfenden & Buckler, 2015).

The identity of the teacher and, in particular, mathematics teachers, has been studied using photovoice, photo-elicitation and a combination of both. The studies have analysed the identity of the teacher on the basis of education in social justice, on the basis of the teachers' perspectives providing a proposal of action for their re-professionalization, and the identity of mathematics teachers has been explored from the perspective of visual narrative linked to positioning (Chao, 2012, 2014; Hage, 2016; Santamaría-Goicuría & Stuardo-Concha, 2018).

Teacher training and professional development programmes have been developed with a view to incorporating new approaches and teaching procedures in subjects such as geography, science, mathematics or physical education, and also in under-graduate degrees in engineering and in early education. Likewise, in training in rural schools, outside the teacher training institution (Hunter, 2016, 2017; Mukeredzi, 2016; Mukeredzi & Nyachowe, 2018; Murakami et al., 2018; Parker et al., 2016; Pears et al., 2008; Ring, 2017; Ring-Whalen et al., 2018; Ruiz, 2017).

The presence of social and cultural diversity in schools and higher education centres has led to the implementation of teacher training programmes in critical understanding of these realities and in achieving the goal of inclusive and multicul-tural education (Boucher, 2018; Behari-Leak, 2017; Mount, 2018; Perez et al., 2016; Strickland et al., 2010; Strickland & Marinak, 2016).

Finally, tools combining photography and text have been developed and used, on the one hand, as a in-service education strategy for teaching art, and on the other, to help kindergarten teachers create learning stories using a digital system (Mesías-Lema, 2017; Shida et al., 2017).

In this chapter we have shown that photovoice and photo-elicitation have only recently been incorporated into in-service education and are rarely used in this context. However, bearing in mind existing research and other publications focussing on the use of these technique, we believe that they will be a valuable tool for training teachers at all levels of education, insofar as they will encourage their professional and personal growth by incorporating cognitive, theoretical and practical compo-nents and their corresponding values, These values include, among others: aware-ness of tacit experiential knowledge; expression and reflection on ideas, theories and beliefs, and identification of misconceptions; opening of theoretical frameworks and perspectives; expression and reflection on values and feelings; clarification of dilemmas encountered in teaching practice; development of dialogue together with critical thinking and reflection skills; perception of teaching practice, the progress made in the profession, and the transformations brought about; mastery of action research techniques and performance of teaching projects; broadening the awareness of identity and development of identity.

Photovoice and photo-elicitation have the potential and limitations inherent to the epistemological paradigm of which they are part. In this regard, and to conclude, we believe that a participatory inquiry paradigm, developed by Heron and Reason (1997), is an ideal framework for the application of photovoice and photo-elicitation techniques, and that it could give rise to a new, value-added approach to photo-elicitation for teacher training and education that is truly participatory and community-based.

References

Angulo, J. F. (2007). *El uso de la fotografía en la investigación educativa.* http://www.academia.edu/9120331/El_uso_de_la_fotograf%C3%ADa_en_la_investigaci%C3%B3n_educativa

Bautista, A. (2017). La foto-elicitación en la formación permanente de maestros de educación primaria. *Alteridad, 12*(2), 202–214.

Bautista, A., Rayón, L., & De las Heras, A. M. (2018). Imágenes experienciales y foto-elicitación en la formación del profesorado. *Educatio Siglo XXI, 36*(2), 135–162.

Bautista, A., Rayón, L., Limón, R., Muñoz, Y., & De las Heras, A. M. (2017). La foto-elicitación y los híbridos digitales en el desarrollo profesional de docentes. En *Educación digital y gestión del talento humano en Iberoamérica* (pp. 582–597). CIMTED.

Bautista, A., Rayón, L., Muñoz, Y., De las Heras, A. M., & Herrero, M. (2016). La foto-elicitación en la formación permanente del profesorado. En *Libro de actas CIMIE16 de AMIE* (T10–11). Sevilla: AMIE. http://amieedu.org/actascimie16/

Behari-Leak, K. (2017). New academics, new higher education contexts: A critical perspective on professional development. *Teaching in Higher Education, 22*(5), 485–500.

Boucher, M. L., Jr. (2018). Interrogating whiteness: Using photo-elicitation to empower teachers to talk about race. In J. M. Boucher (Ed.), *Participant empowerment through photo-elicitation in ethnographic education research* (pp. 201–225). Springer. https://doi.org/10.1007/978-3-319-64413-4_10

Braslavsky, C. (2004). *Diez factores para una educación de calidad para todos en el siglo XXI.* Santillana.

Chao, T. (2014). Photo-elicitation/photovoice interviews to study mathematics teacher identity. In J. J Lo, K. R. Leatham, & L. R. VanZoest (Eds.), *Research trends in mathematics teacher education* (pp. 93–113). Springer. https://doi.org/10.1007/978-3-319-02562-9_6

Chao, T. P. (2012). *Looking within: Mathematics teacher identity using photo-elicitation/photovoice.* (Unpublished Dissertation PhD). University of Texas, Austin,

Collier, J. (1957). Photography in anthropology: A report on two experiments. *American Anthropologist, 59*(5), 843–859.

Consejos Escolares Autonómicos y del Estado. (2015). *El profesorado del siglo XXI.* Ministerio de Educación, Cultura y Deporte.

Doval, M. I. (2015). *Una mirada crítica sobre la participación en la escuela a través de fotovoz.* Universidad de Vigo, Orense.

Hage, D. D. (2016). *Re-professionalizing teachers: Earning a seat and a voice at the table (Unpublished Dissertation).* Graduate College of Marshall University.

Harper, D. (2002). Talking about pictures: A case for photo elicitation. *Visual Studies, 17*(1), 13–16.

Heron, J., & Reason, P. (1997). A participatory inquiry paradigm. *Qualitative Inquiry, 3*(3), 274–294.

Hunter, J. (2017). Developing interactive mathematical talk: Investigating student perceptions and accounts of mathematical reasoning in a changing classroom context. *Cambridge Journal of Education, 47*(4), 475–492.

Hunter, N. (2016). *Assessing sense of place and geo-literacy indicators as learning outcomes of an international teacher professional development program* (Unpublished Dissertation PhD.). Portland State University, Portland.

Lapenta, F. (2011). Some theoretical and methodological views on photo-elicitation. In E. Margolis & L. Pauwels (Eds.), *The Sage handbook of visual methods* (pp. 201–213). Sage.

McCracken, W. (Ed.). (2015). *Framing and its role in promoting reflective practice among trainee teachers of deaf children in the UK*. Routledge.

Mesías-Lema, J. M. (2017). Art teacher training: A photo essay. *International Journal of Education through Art, 13*(3), 395–404. https://doi.org/10.1386/eta.13.3.395_1

Mount, L. (2018). Teaching in unfamiliar terrain: Empowering student and teacher learning through a photography assignment. *Teaching Sociology, 46*(1), 54–61. https://doi.org/10.1177/009205 5X17725131

Mukeredzi, T. G. (2016). Teacher professional development outside the lecture room: Voices of professionally unqualified practicing teachers in rural Zimbabwe secondary schools. *Global Education Review, 3*(4), 84–106.

Mukeredzi, T. G., & Nyachowe, M. S. (2018). The content and evolution of practical theories of teaching: Experiences of professionally unqualified teachers in rural Zimbabwe secondary schools. *SAGE Open, 8* (2). https://doi.org/10.1177/2158244018785410

Murakami, C. D., Su-Russell, C., & Manfra, L. (2018). Analyzing teacher narratives in early childhood garden-based education. *Journal of Environmental Education, 49*(1), 18–29.

Ndione, L. C., & Remi, C. (2018). Combining images and words in order to understand the cultural meaning of practices: What photo-elicitation reveals. *Recherche Et Applications En Marketing,* 1–24. https://doi.org/10.1177/2051570718782450

Parker, M., Patton, K., & Sinclair, C. (2016). 'I took this picture because …': Accessing teachers' depictions of change. *Physical Education and Sport Pedagogy, 21*(3), 328–346. https://doi.org/ 10.1080/17408989.2015.1017452

Pears, A. N., Fincher, S., Adams, R., & Daniels, M. (Eds.). (2008). *Stepping stones: Capacity building in engineering education*. New York: Saratoga Springs. https://doi.org/10.1109/FIE. 2008.4720485

Perez, M. S., Guerrero, M. G. R., & Mora, E. (2016). Black feminist photovoice: Fostering critical awareness of diverse families and communities in early childhood teacher education. *Journal of Early Childhood Teacher Education, 37*(1), 41–60. https://doi.org/10.1080/10901027.2015.113 1209

Rabadán, A. V., & Contreras, P. (2014). Noviembre). La fotografía participativa en el contexto socio-educativo con adolescentes. *Comunicación y Hombre, 10*, 143–156.

Rayón, L., De las Heras, A. M., Muñoz, Y., & Bautista, A. (2017). Smartphones as a support for the language of images in continuing professional development. In *The Ninth International Conference on Mobile, Hybrid, and On-line* Learning (pp. 47–50). IARIA.

Ring, E. A. (2017). *Teacher conceptions of integrated STEM education and how they are reflected in integrated STEM curriculum writing and classroom* implementation (Unpublished Dissertation PhD.). University of Minnesota, Minnesota.

Ring-Whalen, E., Dare, E., Roehrig, G., Titu, P., & Crotty, E. (2018). From conception to curricula: The role of science, technology, engineering, and mathematics in integrated STEM units. *International Journal of Education in Mathematics Science and Technology, 6*(4), 343–362. https:// doi.org/10.18404/ijemst.440338

Ruiz, B. (2017). *La foto−elicitación, propuesta formativa para la educación intercultural en el marco del desarrollo sostenible: Propuesta e implementación formativa para el profesorado de la Facultad de Ingeniería de Sistemas de Producción Agropecuaria (FISPA), en el Estado mexicano de Veracruz (Unpublished Master's dissertation)*. Universidad Complutense, Madrid.

Ruto-Korir, R., & Lubbe-De Beer, C. (2012). The potential for using visual elicitation in understanding preschool teachers' beliefs of appropriate educational practices. *South African Journal of Education, 32*(4), 393–405.

Santamaria-Goicuría, I., & Stuardo-Concha, M. (2018). Una mirada a prácticas docentes desde un marco de justicia social. *Revista Internacional De Educacion Para La Justicia Social, 7*(1), 177–196. https://doi.org/10.15366/riejs2018.7.1.009

Shida, K., Sugimoto, H., & Kurata, A. (2017). *A small system to support nursery school teachers making learning stories.* Proceedings of the 5th International Conference on Information and Education Technology (pp. 16–20). ACM. https://doi.org/10.1145/3029387.3029406

Strickland, M. J., Keat, J. B., & Marinak, B. A. (2010). Connecting worlds: Using photo narrations to connect immigrant children, preschool teachers, and immigrant families. *School Community Journal, 20*(1), 81–102.

Strickland, M. J., & Marinak, B. A. (2016). Not just talk, but a "dance"! How kindergarten teachers opened and closed spaces for teacher-child authentic dialogue. *Early Childhood Education Journal, 44*(6), 613–621.

Taylor, E. W. (2002). Using still photography in making meaning of adult educators' teaching beliefs. *Studies in the Education of Adults, 34*(2), 123–139.

Villegas-Reimers, E. (2003). *Teacher professional development: An international review of the literature.* UNESCO.

Wang, C., & Burris, M. A. (1997). Photovoice: Concept, methodology and use for participatory needs assessment. *Health Education and Behavior, 24*(3), 369–387.

Wang, C. C. (2006). Youth participation on photovoice as a strategy for community change. *Journal of Community Practice, 14*(1–2), 147–161.

Warhurst, R., & Black, K. (2015). The use of photo-elicitation interviewing in qualitative HRD research. In M. Saunders & P. Tosey (Eds.), *Handbook of research methods on HRD* (pp. 127–140). Edward Elgar.

Wolfenden, F., & Buckler, A. (2015). Teacher learning in Sudan: Building dialogue around teachers' practices through reflective photography. In S. Miles & A. Howes (Eds.), *Photography in educational research. Critical reflections from diverse contexts* (pp. 79–94). Routledge.

Chapter 6
Structures of the Photo-Elicitation Process and Emergence of Contradictions in Training Teachers

Antonio Bautista García-Vera

Introduction

When we talk of contradictions in teacher training, we refer to the existence of opposing beliefs in the same teacher, or to inconsistent theories in the same teacher, or to inconsistencies between the aim of their teaching activity and a particular activity they set their students. When this happens, the teacher's cognitive and professional balance is disrupted. Teachers' beliefs are linked to their ideas about some educational situation that they consider to be true, even though there is no evidence to distinguish them from those that are not. One of the basic assumptions is that professional development can only take place when teachers systematically change their beliefs and adopt others that are better constructed, or that are supported by rational arguments that give them the status of a theory.

Beliefs and theories, therefore, are conceptual elements in which the teacher is the protagonist and the subject. However, a construct emerged in teacher training in the beginning of the century - professional vision - that solidifies beliefs into educational goals and into the activities carried out by students to achieve these goals. Specifically, the teaching vision refers to the teacher's personal position in respect of the values, ideals or educational goals to be achieved by their students through teaching situations (Kennedy, 2006; Lefstein & Snell, 2011).

The foregoing arguments in respect of teacher's perspective support, in turn, the conceptual line between their contradictions and inconsistencies that will help to specify the elements and mental processes needed to bring about a change in their teaching activities. Therefore, contradictions are the teacher's opposing beliefs or antithetical theories. For example, the belief that the school is a meeting place for families and teachers, while being convinced that parent-teacher associations and

A. Bautista García-Vera (✉)
Complutense University, Madrid, Spain
e-mail: bautista@ucm.es

A. Bautista García-Vera (ed.), *Photographic Elicitation and Narration in Teachers Education and Development*, Teacher Education, Learning Innovation and Accountability, https://doi.org/10.1007/978-3-031-20164-6_6

other social agents are more of a hindrance than a help. Now, the teacher's lack of coherence, in other words inconsistency or incongruity, refer to the lack of logical synchrony between the aims sought for groups of students and the activities they have to engage in to achieve them, such as attempting to promote values of cooperation and solidarity while setting the student individual, competitive tasks.

An important issue in teacher training is the analysis of the structure of the elements and relationship and interventional procedures of photo-elicitation situations that are most likely to prompt manifestation and/or awareness in the teacher of the potential inconsistencies and contradictions in their professional development. This is important, because these incongruities and mental inconsistencies are sometime embedded in their routines, and will be perpetuated unless another person perceives and questions them. The changes made can be taken as an indicator of the teacher's level of awareness that all is not well in their classroom and, therefore, of the need to make a change to restore the possible loss of balance and personal and professional stability and, consequently, to improve their teaching practice.

Photo-Elicitation Situations: Elements and Procedures

Following the concepts put forward in the introduction, the material and human elements involved in photo-elicitation sessions are as important as the organizational and participation procedures in terms of manifesting the teacher's beliefs, theories and practices, and the possible contradictions and inconsistencies between them. We will analyse each of these elements separately.

Elements Involved in Photo-Elicitation Situations

Bearing in mind the conceptual analysis presented in the preceding chapter, photo-elicitation in this chapter is, above all, an educational situation in the framework of professional teacher development that involves a group of elements that can be contemplated, or inventoried, into two groups. One group consists of teachers and other members of the educational community participating in these sessions. Specifically, in addition to the students present or not in the photographs taken for the session and the external observers, such as parents, university lecturers and researchers, the session also includes trainee teachers, who act as both author and informant, or as questioner and critic, of the content of each photograph. In order for them to exercise these functions, they must be given the opportunity to speak at some point in the process; in other words, they must be given the floor. This is another essential element of the photo-elicitation session. Further on, we will suggest that another relevant question is the order in which each participant intervenes, depending on the purpose of a session or on one of the situations included in the previous session.

Panofsky (1972) and Barthes (1994), among others, have argued in favour of accompanying images with verbal or textual language. According to Panofsky (1972), language is essential at the time of denotation, or identification of the content of the image. Denotation, in turn, is important for subsequent interpretation, because it acts as a reference for connotation and emotion. The presence of the spoken word in photo-elicitation situations is also fundamental due to the polysemic nature of the image. Barthes (1994) documented two of the functions of words when used to accompany a photograph. The first, which is meant to give certainty to its referential elements, he called anchorage, which establishes the meanings of the photograph. It is the function that the authors of an image assign to the word when they use it to help participants identify or fix the meaning of the setting and its content and, therefore, to prevent errors in the denotative plane. This is achieved by the information they provide when describing the elements in the photographs. Similarly, at the connotative level, authors can also use anchoring verbal language to prevent external observers from making interpretations that are far removed from the purpose of the image, or they can also use verbal communication to specify their intended meaning.

The second function of words when used to accompany a photograph, according to Barthes (1994), is relay. This he saw as complementary to the image, because it adds new meanings or interpretations not previously given. This is the function that external observers usually give to the word when they intervene to wonder, or question, or express something different about the apparent content of a photograph, or about what is expressed verbally by its author.

The other group of elements is made up of tools, or cultural artifacts in terms of the historical-cultural approach, in their dual material or symbolic dimension. Photo-elicitation situations require a camera and the language of the still image. Knowledge of the latter will allow the creator of a photograph to look at reality, capture it and represent it differently from those who are not familiar with this analogical representation system, since they will perceive it according to the historically configured world view prevalent in their particular socio-cultural context. The symbolic language of photographs obtained using a camera, which consists of elements such as the shot, the camera angle, light, colour and composition, enable those familiar with this language to produce other types of images beyond the stereotyped, traditional and even ancestral depictions typical of a certain culture or society at a certain historical moment. In the hands of a teacher, these elements will convey something different about the school, because this type of language helps breathe life into the camera.

Teachers who have this visual communication competence, unlike those who do not, will maximise the technical possibilities that cameras offer, above all, their representative functionality. This is because in addition to denoting, they will be able to add meaningful and emotional connotations to the image of the chosen situation. For example, the teacher will use the image to educate, question, and also to describe a school activity, because it will establish both an analogy with that particular educational context, and a symbolic or figurative interaction. In this way, the teacher, more than merely informing, will be able to evoke and therefore intervene in and facilitate photo-elicitation situations. This is because photographic language will enable them to represent and manifest their entire teaching experience and the residue that this leaves in their so-called practical knowledge.

The Order of Intervention of Each Protagonist

Our review of the different ways of using photo-elicitation sessions in different fields of knowledge shows, among other things, the organizational flexibility of these situations, insofar as a photograph can be taken or chosen from among several photographs by one of the participants. These session, therefore, are welcomed because they help the protagonists of these elicitation processes analyse situations from the photographic and verbal perspective. Now, we need to analyse the different possibilities in order to identify their essence, because the way the meanings are constructed will, to some extent, depend on the organizational approach followed in each session.

These procedures have been studied by various authors. Fernández (1988), for example, contributed four technical sequences for analysing video recordings of teaching practice. The structures used in processes called video-analysis/discussion are designed to provide information that can improve the teaching practice of one or several teachers. To this end, Fernandez created four sequences, each of which follows the same structure:

Recording → Viewing → Analysis/Discussion → Project.

Each of the aforementioned procedural structures is distinctive for the way in which it gathers information for the video and the nature of that information. Specifically:

Type 1: Video of an earlier survey of a small group of teachers taking part in a training programme in which they discuss the problems or issues to be addressed in the project.
Type 2: Recording of surveys carried out on a large sample of teachers to gather information on the concerns and difficulties they encounter in their teaching practice.
Type 3: Recording of interviews held with a small group of teachers about their urgent needs to improve their teaching.
Type 4: Recording of an in-depth interview with one of the participating teachers committed to professional development.

Fernandez has shown the complexity and diversity of sequences obtained during these training sessions; for example, the foregoing procedures can be broken down into sub-procedures, depending on the role taken by the external expert, or by the colleague of the teacher or group of teachers, or depending on whether or not they appear in the video or have previously viewed the content of the shots. Torre and Murphy (2015), meanwhile, suggest that photo-elicitation involves three related moments: taking the photograph, showing it to a group and, finally, the intervention of the participants to obtain information. None of these authors stop to investigate the effect that the speaking order has on the nature of the information evoked and the interactions generated.

Given our interest in knowing how to facilitate the emergence of contradictions and inconsistencies between the teachers' theories, beliefs and practice, in this chapter we will specify the order in which each participant intervenes in photo-elicitation sessions in order to achieve the goal sought by a particular photograph in a particular situation. This decision is justified by the importance that verbal elements have on the content of a photograph that characterises these situations, as mentioned above. If the word is so essential, therefore, each protagonist must be allowed to speak; but, in what order?

In this chapter, we will deal with this issue by identifying the two aspects involved in deciding the order of intervention in a photo-elicitation situation: one is the purpose of the session, and the other is the person who has taken the specific photograph used in the session. In terms of purpose, we can distinguish between two types of photo-elicitation sessions. The first type is the descriptive-informative session, in which a teacher describes which characteristics of their teaching practice they consider to be ordinary, and which are extraordinary. The second type is, in essence, the formative-interrogative session, in which the classroom and school activities of teachers committed to improving their practice are subject to public scrutiny, which involves a critical inquiry, questioning, and analysis of the motivations behind their actions and the benefit of such actions.

Now, to the foregoing must be added the protagonist or person responsible for staging the photo-elicitation session. Specifically, we need to differentiate between who has requested a certain session for one or two of the above purposes—whether it is a specific teacher interested in exploring their own practice, or whether it is that teacher's working group, acting on the commitment of all its members to improve their teaching practice. The difference between these sessions is that in the first case, the photograph is taken by the teacher, and in the second case it is taken by one of the members of the group—either a colleague or an external observer interested in asking about or questioning certain aspects of the work of a specific teacher undergoing external analysis and evaluation. Authors such as Taylor (2002) even distinguish between situations in the same session where the photograph was taken by the teacher who is the subject of the assessment, and when a photograph of the teacher's work is taken by another person. He refers to the first case as self-photography, and to the second as photo-elicitation.

The essence of each of the four procedures involving the combination of the two dimensions indicated will be discussed on the basis of different studies carried out in the field of teacher in-service education, and specifically, on the basis of the value of the experiences reported when different orders of intervention are used in the different situations where photographs are projected or viewed in a given photo-elicitation session.

Procedure A: Session Requested by One of the Teachers

Most authors on this subject agree that most sessions take place at the request of a teacher committed to improving their teaching practice (Birkeland, 2013; Dockett et al., 2017). The person who has called the session and taken the photographs to show each situation they bring to the table usually speaks first about the content of the photographs. This is based on the "auteur theory" (Mannay, 2017; Rose, 2001), which states that the most relevant thing about a photograph is what its author wants to convey. Following this, if necessary, the rest of the group are asked to respond to the author's concerns and teaching activities, or to explore the value of his or her work from the point of view of others.

Subprocedure Aa: Descriptive-Informative Function of the Photo-Elicitation
                   Session

If the purpose is informative, once the photograph has been shown to the group, the teacher who has taken the photograph is allowed to speak. He or she can then describe their teaching practice in the classroom or school using the elements shown in the image and the relationships between them to support their argument. At this stage, the description of the content will be referential/denotative, and will facilitate the interpretation and, therefore, understanding of the meaning of later events that will also be photographed.

In this type of session, when the photograph is taken by a teacher who is the subject of the session, he or she describes typical situations encountered when working with students in the classroom and, as a sort of therapeutic confession, seeks the agreement and approval of the other participants. This interest manifested by the teacher who first intervenes then becomes the purpose of the photo-elicitation session, and the function of the rest of the participants is to listen, agree and understand the work described by that teacher. External observers will only ask questions if they need to fill in gaps in the description or need further information in order to understand the situation.

Within this function, an interesting situation arises when the photograph used in the elicitation session includes one or more students (Pyle, 2013; Trott, 2013). This is because these students will usually be required to speak later to confirm or refute any statements the teacher might have made during his or her interpretation of the photograph.

Subprocedure Ab: Interrogative-Formative Function of the Photo-Elicitation
                   Session

Though less frequent, the teacher's request may also be motivated by their concern about a circumstance or unforeseen event that has taken place in some part of the school and captured in the photograph (Bautista et al., 2018). The teacher's intervention will first allow them to specify the polysemy of the image while conveying their dilemma, doubt or concern to their colleagues, students and external observers present in the session. These participants will then be able to analyse it from another point of view, and suggest other courses of action or other possible decisions open to the teacher who is the author of the image that has facilitated the verbal evocation of the situation.

As mentioned above, the sponsor or teacher and, therefore, the primary protagonist of a photo-elicitation session, sets the agenda for the different photographic situations presented in the session, and defines the specific aspects of their work that can be discussed, evaluated, advised, and so on. This is because the goal of the session is to be observed and to receive help on a specific aspect of teaching practice that concerns and interests the teacher, who will therefore only accept interventions involving this topic. The role of the rest of the participating group is to listen and, if necessary, ask questions to gather more information or further details on the situation already described. This will help them complete and understand the discourse of the teacher who took the photograph and requested the session. Therefore, the intention behind this type of situation is not to create a space for evaluative judgement where the teacher's overall work is subjected to public criticism.

Procedure B: Session Requested by One of the External Observers or Other Teachers from the School in Order to Explore Some Aspect of Life Inside or Outside the School Related to One of the Teachers Undergoing In-Service Education

As in the previous case, this group of photo-elicitation sessions arose from a series of academic research and innovation studies, In this session, the photograph is taken by someone other than the teacher who is the subject of these in-service education situations based on the use of still images. For example, Strickland et al. (2010), Miller (2016), Bautista et al. (2016) and Bautista (2017) have developed photo-elicitation situations involving photographs taken by students and their parents for the purpose of informing and asking their respective teachers about their homework, or about the interaction between a group of families in relation to the school. Other authors, such as Richard and Lahman (2015) and Ruto-Korir and Lubbe-De Beer (2012), in their role as external observers, took photographs of the practice of specific teachers, and subsequently analysed the beliefs and theories underlying this practice.

In all these situations, the person that had taken the photograph spoke first and set the agenda for the session. This group of sessions can also be divided into two subgroups, depending on their purpose.

Subprocedure Ba: Descriptive-Informative Purpose of the Photo-Elicitation Session

Our review of studies on this subject shows cases where external observers, parents or colleagues of a particular teacher have sponsored sessions to ask the teacher their reasons or motivations for engaging in a specific activity, or to enquire about a decision made on the organization of classroom spaces, etc.. In other words, after having taken a photograph related to this teacher and shown it to the group, the author of the photograph takes the floor to describe the content of the image, or the significance the elements have for him or her and, usually continues with a "why", addressed to the teacher, about some aspect of the teaching practice shown in the photograph. Obviously, the teacher in question, the subject of that session, must then speak to clarify their reasons or motives for taking that decision or engaging in that activity. Stockall and Davis (2011), for example, took photographs and gave them to teachers so that, once viewed, they could talk about the significance they gave to the children present in them, and in this way understand and explain their theories and beliefs about childhood that underpin their discourse about the actions of these students captured in the image. This type of session involves procedures that could be identified, with some relevant differences, with the criticised micro-teaching sessions, with respect to the proposal made in this chapter to facilitate the emergence of teachers' contradictions and inconsistencies, and not the acquisition of routines in environments outside the classroom and school.

Subprocedure Bb: Interrogative-Informative Purpose of the Photo-Elicitation Session

Finally, the last of the four groups of situations included in the analysis carried out is the most ground-breaking - the one that follows non-traditional revealing formats, the one in which the specific purpose is to interrogate a specific teacher to reveal contradictions and inconsistencies in their work (Walker, Ballet and Kuntz, 2012), or to make demands on the personal and professional identity of an educator (Kearns, 2012), and with it, change their theories, beliefs or practices in order to restore their professional stability to its previous level. As mentioned above, an external observer takes photographs of events involving a colleague in the school and, after the group has viewed each of these images, takes the floor to ask about something that he or she sees as an inconsistency. This is expressed using verbal structures such as "why …, if …", or "if …, why …", for example, "If you intend to develop the creative thinking of your students, why do you propose single-response activities?".

The presence or absence of the teacher in question - the subject of in-service education in a particular session - in the photograph discussed by the participants, requires this teacher to speak at some point in the process. This is because the participants need to know his or her intentions in respect of the activities photographed, and to be able to contrast this explanation with the interpretations made by the other external observers. In the sphere of university teaching, Raven (2015) suggests that all subjects present in the image, students, other teachers, etc., should speak in order to enhance the revealing function of the verbal elements used to interpret the content of the photograph.

Having presented, and partly analysed, the different elements of the four structural procedures of photo-elicitation, in the next section we will discuss and argue that the latter is the one that best reveals the contradictions between theories, between beliefs, or the inconsistencies between the aims and the practices of a certain teacher. This discussion is needed because it is not always possible to obtain the elements that make up the photo-elicitation situations described above. Similarly, as described, not all sessions follow the same order of intervention or type of relationship. Therefore, it is best to analyse the different possibilities and value them according to their suitability for invoking, revealing, and raising the teacher's awareness of the potential contradictions and inconsistencies in their practice.

Structure of Photo-Elicitation Sessions Aimed at Revealing Contradictions

To glimpse a contradiction between certain ideas, beliefs, etc. we first need determine the contradictory situations. Similarly, to perceive an inconsistency between two related elements, such as theory and practice, there has to be a moment when the logical relationship initially linking these elements ceases to exist. To reveal contradictions and inconsistencies, therefore, we need to represent both moments, each of the contradictory situations, in a continuous photo-elicitation session where at least both situations take place. This is possible because these two moments occur in a training evaluation session that includes at least two situations, one for each projection, evocation and analysis of the content of a photograph. Dissonance will emerge in the discourse that attempts to unify the interventions in photo-elicitation situations in a session, because the reality captured in each photograph corresponds to different contexts from the one forming the basis of the teacher's belief, and can be contradictory.

One approach that helps explain the mental processes taking place during the description or the story narrated by a teacher in an in-service education context is narrative inquiry (Atkinson, 2010; Barkhuizen et al., 2014; Clandinin & Connelly, 2000; Harrison, 2002; Huber et al., 2014; Yuan & Lee, 2016; among others). This is based on the notion that every human experience can be understood as a story and, as such, can be told. Specifically, with respect to the subject discussed here, we will focus on photographic narrative inquiry (Bach, 2007; Caine, 2010; Dietz & Davis, 2009; Lemon, 2007; Moss, 2008). In the literature on this subject, most authors agree on including three elements in any narrative inquiry: space, time and the cultural and social context. This justifies the inclusion of photographic narrative inquiry in photo-elicitation in the form of narrative inquiry sessions involving various photo-elicitation situations. This technique is used to encourage teachers to give narrative explanations and make it possible to raise questions that allow them to become aware of a possible contradiction that they will later have to resolve in order to restore their professional and personal stability.

The presence of space and time in any narrative inquiry will require a list of photographs arranged in a certain order to trigger the inquiry process. In this work environment, each image is considered an opening into both its past and its future (Lemon, 2007), where the connection between them is narrated by the participating teacher, drawing on the content investigated by observing the photographs taken of their work by an outside observer. Both the meaning given to each of the images and the motivations that justify the meaning given to the connections made between them are fed and sustained by, among other factors, the teacher's beliefs and opinions of the activities and relationships taking place in the school.

In this way, the external observer who acts as inquirer-evaluator in this photo-elicitation narrative inquiry procedure held to question the work of a particular teacher, will choose photographs showing the professional practice of that teacher over several days, selecting those that represent tasks that are inconsistent with their educational views. For example, when the teacher in question tries to encourage their students to engage in creative or collaborative thinking, but nevertheless one of the images shows them engaging in repetitive tasks copied from the blackboard, and another shows each student working individually at their table, isolated from other class members. Similarly, using various situations/photographs in a single photo-elicitation inquiry session so that the teacher appearing in them expresses the mental processes that step-by-step or situation/photograph-by-situation/photograph lead him or her to make sense of the content of all the images presented, forces the teacher to describe and interpret them, to compare and combine them in order to unify them using a consistent, well-structured story. But to do so, the teacher necessarily has to bear in mind the space–time, social and educational context of each situation photographed, and will then inevitably have to confront any inconsistencies and contradictions that emerge in the narrative. The photograph used in each photo-elicitation situation can remain on the table throughout the session to form a collage of all the previous images and facilitate comparison by placing them side by side.

The foregoing shows the need for a temporal continuum during an inquiry session by accumulating different photo-elicitation situations to bring out the contradictions and inconsistencies between a teacher's beliefs or between their approach to education. However, it will not reveal all the teacher's shortcomings, because this type of continuity is contemplated in the four types of situations described in the preceding section. What is missing, and which of the four best fills that gap?

First, we have already argued that it should be one of the procedures where the photo-elicitation session is requested by an external observer. This person is responsible for taking the photographs, and once they have been displayed will be the first to speak and describe, interpret and argue their content, and eventually point out the possible contradictions and incongruities. Secondly, of the two types that involve an external agent as an informant of the teacher's work, based on the literature on this subject, the most suitable type of situation is the one that interrogates the teacher "under review" using words such as " if …, why …". Specifically, according to Stockall and Davis (2011), the questions used to initiate and maintain a dialogue are sufficient to reveal the teacher's beliefs. However, an opposing argument is needed to bring about a change in these beliefs. Golombek and Johnson (2017), for their part, observed the richness of the reflective processes generated by teachers when an external observer is inserted into their teaching space, above all, when they are questioned or when elements evoked when reporting and analysing the actions in their classrooms and schools are challenged. This line of questioning shows the teacher the meaninglessness of some of their practices, and encourages them to change their underlying motivations, which include their beliefs about education. This kind of change is fundamental in in-service teacher education, because, in the words of King (2003), "we live stories that give our life meaning or negate it with meaninglessness. If we change the stories we live by, quite possibly we change our lives" (2003, p. 153).

Therefore, the questions or doubts that illustrate the teacher's contradictions will be better presented by incorporating the temporal dimension into the description of the elements of the space contained in an image. To do this, several school moments must be captured in photographs to be laid out in a particular order and analysed in a photo-elicitation situation. In this regard, the time gap between the photograph of one situation and another will evidence the changes, contrasts, confirmations and contradictions between the beliefs, theories and educational practices of the teachers featured in the narratives. This is because these elements are more easily represented in a continuum.

Configuration of a Teacher Inquiry and Evaluation Ritual That Promotes the Emergence of Contradictions: Elements and Structure of a Photo-Elicitation Session

To end this chapter, we present a procedure designed to promote in-service teacher education by showing the inconsistencies in their beliefs and the contradictions between their educational goals and the practical work they set their students. This procedure is based on the foregoing arguments regarding the role of the intervening subjects and the procedure to be followed in an inquiry session involving photo-elicitation situations.

One way of implementing this type of in-service teacher inquiry and evaluation is to consider them as part of a training programme approved in the school. This, following Van Gennep (1986), will be taken to be a rite of passage between the two mental states of the teachers undergoing the photo-elicitation session. The latter, with fewer contradictions and inconsistencies due to the knowledge acquired during the ritual. This ritual will involve a symbolic transaction by which the teacher sacrifices themselves on the altar of public evaluation, and in exchange receives knowledge that will enable them to improve their teaching practice. Within the rites of passage, teachers will undergo what Turner (1988) calls a life-crisis brought on by the humiliation at having their professional contradictions and inconsistencies exposed in public; humiliation, according to Turner, is common in the sacrificial victim, in this case, the teacher under evaluation.

A photo-elicitation session taken to be a rite of passage will be more easily understood and have greater social and institutional significance, because the material elements, participants and organized interactions between them will act as signs that will give social and institutional meaning to the process of in-service education in that school. These ritualized sessions will be a temporary parenthesis in a particular space in the institution. Repeating them at regular intervals, or from time to time, will make them part of school life, and although a different teacher will be the focus of each session, the forms and procedures will remain part of the educational rite of passage organized using that space–time structure.

A.   The Participants in the Educational Inquiry and Evaluation Rite of Passage

The human elements involved in the teacher inquiry and evaluation sessions included in the photo-elicitation rituals include the observer, the teacher/subject, participants and witnesses. Officiators include:

A1.   The master of ceremonies. This will be a colleague (teacher) of the subject of the rite of passage. Their role is to coordinate the inquiry-evaluation ritual, and they will also be responsible for appointing an external observer to evaluate the session using a procedure established in the school, for example, random assignation.

A2.   The evaluator. This role will be filled by an external observer who will act as prosecutor. Their duties are to question and present photographic evidence of examples of some of the contradictions and inconsistencies exhibited by the teacher undergoing the evaluation. As the educational rite of passage is sponsored by the school and the contradictions are critically formulated by an external observer, possible tensions and susceptibilities in the relationship between evaluator and subject of evaluation, that is, between the prosecutor and the victim, are avoided. In other words, the school is performing the evaluation, and not a colleague of the teacher under evaluation. The external observer declares his or her intention to help the victim see the concerns that his or her work raises in those who have other interpretive references, in observers who are not influenced by the routines or actions considered common sense in that particular school.

A3.   The subject of evaluation. This is the teacher whose work is the subject of public inquiry and evaluation in that session. As a victim, his or her function is to speak when asked to do so by the master of ceremonies and to anchor the meaning of the photograph in which he or she is present, explaining the intention of the action photographed. In this way, the teacher specifies the meaning of the action and qualifies the interpretation made by the evaluator.

     Finally, the remaining participants or witnesses to this ritual will be colleagues of the teacher evaluated, their students and their students' families, and other observers from outside the school, other than the master of ceremonies, who are invited to attend the session.

B.   The Procedure

B1.   Announcement. The process is started by the master of ceremonies, who announces that the inquiry-evaluation session is to be held on the premises of the school. The master of ceremonies, in accordance with his or her role, chooses a subject or teacher to evaluate and an external observer as evaluator. The evaluator observes and analyses the nature and type of actions carried out by the teacher, who plays the role of victim in this session and, at the same time, shows photographs of the essence of these practices. Similarly, the evaluator analyses the theories, beliefs and educational purposes that guide the teacher's actions. This will allow the evaluator to study and illustrate any contradictions and inconsistencies found and reveal these during the inquiry and evaluation session. The evaluation ritual is held two weeks after the announcement, and the evaluator must complete these tasks within this time.

B2. Conduct of the evaluation ritual.

According to Turner (1988), every rite of passage involves a space and a time where interactions and exchanges take place between the individuals involved, in this case the master of ceremonies, the external evaluator and the teacher being evaluated who is prepared to undergo this ordeal to improve his or her teaching practice. In this space and time, a narrative inquiry session is combined with the content of various photo-elicitation situations, one for each photograph taken and chosen by the evaluator. We will not specify how the participants should be arranged in the space, their clothing, their gestures with regard to the image shown, etc. These details of the rite of passage will be decided based on the historical, social and cultural context of the school. All we will do here is present an outline of how the ritual can be conducted, based on the content of the preceding sections:

B21. The master of ceremonies, as the school representative, speaks first and opens the training session. He or she then gives the floor to the evaluator, who launches the inquiry process by using the relay function of verbal language to ask, question, etc., about the content of the first projected image.

B22. The evaluated teacher is then given the floor so that, using the anchor function, they answer the questions and doubts raised by the evaluator and communicate the intentionality or motivations of the action shown in the photograph.

B23. The foregoing inquiry procedures will be repeated for each of the photographs taken and chosen by the evaluator. The information received will allow the evaluator to validate his or her interpretations and conjectures relating to the possible contradictions and inconsistencies of the evaluated teacher, and then proceed to expose and evaluate these elements. Viewing the photographs as a collage will make it easier to detect possible inconsistencies or contradictions between parts or elements of the entire educational process. In other words, as mentioned at the beginning of the third section of this chapter, several photo-elicitation situations are presented within an inquiry-evaluation session in order to present two apparently contradictory or inconsistent moments in the evaluated teacher's work represented by their corresponding images. These images will facilitate the corresponding photo-elicitation situations.

B24. The evaluator takes the floor again to describe and illustrate the contradictions between beliefs, between theories or, bearing in mind the teacher's approach to education, to show the inconsistencies between the educational goals pursued and the practices proposed by the evaluated teacher.

B25. The master of ceremonies gives the floor to the teacher undergoing the session who, by way of defence, states the intentions and motivations behind the practices shown in the sequence of photographs in order to explain overall meaning of the teaching practice, if applicable.

B26. Finally, the master of ceremony gives the floor to the teacher's colleagues, in their role as witnesses, so that they can contribute their interpretations in light of the opinions voiced by the external evaluator and the teacher undergoing this educational ritual.

The more this educational inquiry-evaluator ritual is systematized and staged, and above all, the more it achieves social consensus as a rite of passage, the better will it become consolidated in the school as a memory, or foundation for change, and as an institutional tradition.

References

Atkinson, B. (2010). Teachers responding to narrative inquiry: An approach to narrative inquiry criticism. *Journal of Educational Research, 103*(2), 91–102.

Bach, H. (2007). Composing a visual narrative inquiry. In D. J. Clandinin (Ed.), *Handbook of narrátive inquiry: Mapping a methodology* (pp. 280–307). SAGE.

Barkhuizen, G., Benson, P., & y Chik, A. (2014). *Narrative inquiry in language teaching and learning research*. Routledge.

Barthes, R. (1994). *El susurro del lenguaje*. Paidós.

Bautista, A. (2017). Comunicación entre familias inmigrantes a través de sesiones de foto-elicitación. *Profesorado. Revista de Currículum y Formación del Profesorado, 21*(3), 327–348.

Bautista, A., Limón, M. R., Oñate, P., & y Rostand, C. (2016). Funciones de la fotografía en las relaciones interculturales entre familias de inmigrantes. *Revista Complutense De Educación., 27*(1), 75–93.

Bautista, A., Rayón, L., & y de las Heras, A. (2018). Imágenes experienciales y foto-elicitación en la formación del profesorado. *Revista Educatio Siglo XXI., 36*(2), 135–162.

Birkeland, A. (2013). Research dilemmas associated with photo elicitation in comparative early childhood education research. *Research in Comparative and International Education, 8*(4), 455–467.

Caine, V. (2010). Visualizing community: Understanding narrative inquiry as action research. *Educational Action Research, 18*(4), 481–496.

Clandinin, D. J., & Connelly, F. M. (2000). *Narratie inquiry: Experience and story in qualitative research*. Josssey-Bass.

Dietz, C. M., & Davis, E. A. (2009). Preservice elementary teachers' reflection on narrative images of inquiry. *Journal of Science Teacher Education, 20*(3), 219–243.

Dockett, S., Einarsdottir, J., & Perry, B. (2017). Photo elicitation: Reflecting on multiple sites of meaning. *International Journal of Early Years Education, 25*(3), 225–240.

Fernández, M. (1988). *La profesionalización del docente*. Escuela Española.

Golombek, P. R., & Johnson, K. E. (2017). Re-conceptualizing teachers' narrative inquiry as professional development. PROFILE: Issues in Teachers' Professional Development, 19(2), 15–28.

Harrison, B. (2002). Photographic visions and narrative inquiry. *Narrative Inquiry, 12*(1), 87–111.

Huber, J., Caine, V., Huber, M., & Steeves, P. (2014). Narrative inquiry as pedagogy in education. The extraordinary potential of living, telling, retelling, and reliving stories of experience. *Review of Research in Education, 37*(1), 212–242.

Kearns, S. (2012). Seeking researcher identity through the co-construction and representation of young people' s narratives of identity. *Educational Action Research., 20*(1), 23–40.

Kennedy, M. M. (2006). Knowledge and vision in teaching. *Journal of Teacher Education., 57*(3), 205–211.

King, T. (2003). *The truth about stories: A native narrative.* House of Anansi Press.

Lefstein, A., & Snell, J. (2011). Professional vision and the politics of teacher learning. *Teaching and Teacher Education, 27*, 505–514.

Lemon, N. (2007). Take a photograph: Teacher reflection through narrative. *Reflective Practice, 8*(2), 177–191.

Mannay, D. (2017). *Métodos visuales, narrativos y creativos en investigación cualitativa.* Narcea.

Miller, K. (2016). Learning about children's school preparation through photographs: The use of photo elicitation interviews with low-income families. *Journal of Early Childhood Research, 14*(3), 261–279.

Moss, J. (2008). Visual narrative and diversity in our classroom: Digital readings of policy. In P. Thomson (Ed.), *Doing visual research with children and young* (pp. 59–73). Routledge.

Panofsky, E. (1972). *Estudios sobre iconología.* Alianza Editorial.

Peirce, Ch. S. (1986). *La ciencia de la semiótica.* Nueva Visión.

Pyle, A. (2013). Engaging young children in research through photo elicitation. *Early Child Development and Care, 183*(11), 1544–1558.

Raven, N. (2015). New perspectives using participatory photography to evaluate widening participation interventions. *Research in Post-Compulsory Education, 20*(4), 470–475.

Richard, V. M., & Lahman, M. K. E. (2015). Photo-elicitation: Reflexivity on method, analysis, and graphic portraits. *International Journal of Research & Method in Education, 38*(1), 3–22.

Rose, G. (2001). *Visual methodologies.* Sage.

Ruto-Korir, R., & Lubbe-De Beer, C. (2012). The potential for using visual elicitation in understanding preschool teachers' beliefs of appropriate educational practices. *South African Journal of Education, 32*(4), 393–405.

Stockall, N., & Davis, S. (2011). Uncovering pre-service teacher beliefs about young children: A photographic elicitation methodology. *Issues in Educational Research, 21*(2), 192–209.

Strickland, M. J., Keat, J. B., & Marinak, B. A. (2010). Connecting worlds: Using photo narrations to connect immigrant children, preschool teachers, and immigrant families. *School Community Journal, 20*(1), 81–102.

Taylor, E. W. (2002). Using still photography in making meaning of adult educators' teaching beliefs. *Studies in the Education of Adults, 34*(2), 123–139.

Torre, D., & Murphy, J. (2015). A different lens: Changing perspectives using photo-elicitation interviews. *Archivos Analíticos De Políticas Educativas/education Policy Analysis Archives, 23*(1), 1–26.

Trott, D. (2013). Means to a meaning: Using photo elicitation to teach a course about workplace spirituality. *International Journal of Pedagogy and Curriculum, 19*(1), 71–84.

Turner, V. (1988). *El proceso ritual.* Taurus.

Van Gennep, A. (1986). *Los ritos de paso.* Taurus.

Walter, K. O., Baller, S. L., & Kuntz, A. M. (2012). Two approaches for using web sharing and photography assignments to increase critical thinking in the health sciences. *International Journal of Teaching and Learning in Higher Education, 24*(3), 383–394.

Yuan, R., & Lee, I. (2016). "I need to be strong and competent": A narrative inquiry of a student-teacher's emotions and identities in teaching practicum. *Teachers and Teaching: Theory and Practice, 22*(7), 819–841.

Chapter 7
The Use of Photo-Elicitation Situations in the Practicum

María Jesús Romera Iruela, Mercedes Blasco Torrejón,
María Rosario Limón Mendizabal, and Antonio Bautista García-Vera

Introduction

This chapter addresses the possibility of using the interrelation processes facilitated by photo-elicitation sessions to interchange the roles initially played by teachers and students in teaching and learning actions in the Practicum. This approach is motivated by the existing literature on the subject and by the formative dimension of the teaching practices described in chapter four. The practicum is a space that combines pre-service and in-service education where tutors and teachers students can develop professionally. The regulations governing the practicum, far from facilitating photo-elicitation sessions in school spaces where the tutor-student relationship occurs, are at times an obstacle to this practice due to the difficulties to use photographic cameras, and the lack of space and time to stage the photograph-mediated exchanges. To this end, in addition to the educational and legal context of the practicum, we will analyse the literature on the subject in order to understand the configuration and evolution of the interactions between school teachers and university students, paying special attention to two case studies on the practicum in pre-school education carried out by the authors of this chapter. In these case studies, we explore the levels of reciprocal

M. J. Romera Iruela (✉) · M. Blasco Torrejón · M. R. Limón Mendizabal ·
A. Bautista García-Vera
Complutense University, Madrid, Spain
e-mail: mjromera@ucm.es

M. Blasco Torrejón
e-mail: cherche@ucm.es

M. R. Limón Mendizabal
e-mail: mrlimonm@ucm.es

A. Bautista García-Vera
e-mail: bautista@ucm.es

A. Bautista García-Vera (ed.), *Photographic Elicitation and Narration in Teachers Education and Development*, Teacher Education, Learning Innovation and Accountability, https://doi.org/10.1007/978-3-031-20164-6_7

complicity, understanding, questioning and mutual improvement emerging between two teachers and two students mediated by photo-elicitation sessions.

Photo-Elicitation in the Pre-service Teacher Practicum

Although photo-elicitation has only recently been introduced in the field of education, it is even more novel, particularly in Spain, in pre-service teacher training. Our review in the principle multidisciplinary and specialised databases shows that, except for some isolated cases, studies on the aforementioned subject have only emerged in the past ten years. In this pre-service training literature we find a notable interest in identifying the potential of photo-elicitation—it has been used to investigate teachers' cognition, their theories, ideas, beliefs and values, providing knowledge that enables awareness and reflection, influencing their development or modification and, consequently, in decision-making in educational action (Bautista, 2016, 2017; Caielli et al., 2018; DiCicco, 2015; Graziano, 2011; Johnson & Smagorinsky, 2013; Mathews & Crew, 2016; McCartney & Harris, 2014; Sinclair & Thornton, 2018; Stockall & Davis, 2011; Varea & Pang, 2018; White & Murray, 2016). Likewise, the teacher's understanding and thinking are enhanced through photo-elicitation, and several studies have reported that this technique has a positive impact on their professional identity (Allen & Labbo, 2001; Bailey & Van Harken, 2014; Da Cunha et al., 2014; Mitchell et al., 2010; Salazar et al., 2016; Savva & Erakleous, 2018; Seow, 2016; Villacanas de Castro, 2017; White & Murray, 2016). This technique has been used in various subjects during pre-service teacher training, but most studies have focussed on Physical education and English (Da Cunha et al., 2014; Langdon et al., 2014; Legge & Smith, 2014; Sinclair & Thornton, 2018; Varea & Pang, 2018; Walker et al., 2017; for the second, Caielli et al., 2018; Dicicco, 2015; Graziano, 2011; Johnson & Smagorinsky, 2013; Villacanas de Castro, 2017; White & Murray, 2016), while two have dealt with photo-elicitation in social studies (Garrett & Matthews, 2014; Mathews & Crew, 2016). The development of visual literacy skills in undergraduate and post-graduate teachers has also been investigated (Bailey & Van Harken, 2014; Sadik, 2011).

In several studies, photo-elicitation was used during the practicum, although in some cases it was part of a course. A number of studies have investigated this technique in undergraduate students, and in others it was part of post-graduate programmes. Pereiro and Páramo (2016) reported the emergent use of photography in the practicum, namely, participatory photography and the techniques of photovoice and photo narration, and have incorporated it and other technologies in an intervention designed for undergraduate students of primary education.

Several studies have focussed on the intercultural training of teachers. Allen and Labbo (2001), based on their exploration of literacy courses in undergraduate teacher training that include a four-week practicum, have described the strategy they follow for culturally committed teaching, which combines photography and narrative with the creation of cultural memories to enable future teachers to explore themselves as cultural beings.

Brown's (2005) study focused on an alternative secondary school teacher qualification pathway aimed at increasing intercultural sensitivity. The programme, divided into three phases—the second consisting of six weeks of practicum—used photography as a self-examination tool to reveal subconscious beliefs and overcome problems of resistance to inter-cultural concepts, and to address the lack of knowledge of and sensitivity to such concepts in future candidates. Based on the foregoing study, and with the aim of providing teacher trainers with strategies, instead of indicators, to improve inter-cultural awareness among future teachers, this study by Brown shows that prior cross-cultural experiences are more significant factors than residency status among future teachers, and that self-photography can be effective in aiding this training process.

Mitchell et al. (2010) carried out several alternative pre-service teacher education projects that used photographic images to encourage reflection. In one such project, a group of teachers was given the opportunity to live together in a local lodge and undergo their four-week practicum in a rural setting. Photographs not only document the process and contribute to their teaching portfolios, but can also serve as photovoice to show a thoughtful approach to "seeing for ourselves" more publicly. One result of this proyect has been an exhibition of the teacher's photographs at a national conference. The study also shows ways in which teacher educators can use visual tools to examine and interrogate teacher education practices.

McCartney and Harris (2014) explored the experience of international practicum in a master's program participated by pre-school and primary school trainee teachers. Using photovoice, these teachers photographed different teaching, living contexts and people that were meaningful to them. During subsequent focus groups, they shared their images and the stories they evoked to continue exploring those contexts, people, and experiences that were personally meaningful. The study describes the changes observed in photographs taken by these pre-service teachers of children and of themselves as teachers.

Wolfenden and Buckler (2015) explored both the challenges and the potential use of photography in inter-cultural research in an undergraduate teacher training program in Sudan, in which many students lack prior qualifications. The analysis and discussion of the images evidenced the physical and symbolic spaces where the teachers' values change, their action is improved, and their capacities and practices are developed. The study gave the teachers the opportunity to reflect on and dialogue about their practice. Along with this, the authors suggest that the potential of reflective photography might not lie in the technique itself, but in the opportunity it gives teachers to engage in critical dialogue with supervisors and researchers.

Case studies by Mathews and Crew (2016) have used photo-elicitation to help their students, all pre-service teachers, to first think critically about the communities around them, and then about those where they might potentially teach, thus strengthening their own concepts on a course in social study methodology. In one of the case studies, which consisted of an equity audit project, these teachers examined and represented the resources and inequity found in their practicum schools and their surrounding areas. This project used photovoice, combining photography with reflection, praxis, and community mapping.

The teaching innovation project headed by Bautista (2017) has shown that photo-elicitation and audio-visual narration sessions held in schools with socio-culturally diverse students can help practicum students achieve effective inclusive and intercultural education.

Photo-elicitation has been used to evaluate the teacher training curriculum. For example, the study by Legge and Smith (2014) used visual ethnography, consisting of photography and layered narrative analysis, to critically analyse their experience of initial teacher training in bush camps, which were one of four outdoor education experiences for undergraduate physical education teachers. The authors found that photo-elicitation was an effective method for reflectively expressing pedagogy in outdoor education.

Finally, in a postgraduate degree course to train teachers working with deaf children in which teaching practices were carried out in two different settings, McCracken (2015) explored the use of photo-elicitation to develop skills in critical reflection. The session started by selecting photographs that would help these students think about their perspectives, and continued with a framing activity, which is an important extension of the image and is of considerable importance for future practice. There are more studies that, like some of the foregoing, present training post-graduate training programmes or include teaching practice for in-service teachers; these will be discussed in the corresponding chapter.

Observing the findings of the above review, it is interesting to highlight some important factors related to the use of photography in initial teacher training. First, the scant attention paid to the analysis of the relationship between practicum student and their school tutors, and the role of photography in these relationships. Second, no mention is made of the possibility of exchanging roles, and in this way making it possible for undergraduate students—the teachers of the future—to develop a role other than that of students taught, while practicum school tutors could relinquish their role as advisor and example of good practice in the classroom and allow themselves to be questioned, interrogated, etc. This, as argued in the preceding chapter, will contribute to their in-service education. Both absences justify the inclusion of this topic in this chapter, and the relevance to investigate which practicum-related elements and situations will help clarify the two aforementioned absences in study subjects. Specifically, we will discuss the role of photography in the regulatory and training frameworks of the practicum.

The Practicum and Its Regulatory Framework

The practicum is a crucial stage between the academic world and the job world—a period of training in which students work in their future professional settings: factories, companies, services, etc. It is an opportunity for students to learn outside the university, working with professionals in their sector in real work environments

(Zabalza, 2003, p. 45), in which the transversal, generic and emotional competences essential to life must be acquired. In this sense, the adaptation of undergraduate degrees in pre-school and primary school teaching to the European Higher Education Area (EHEA) has highlighted the importance of the practicum and given this subject a greater role in university education (González-Garzón & Laorden, 2012; Sepúlveda et al., 2017).

Although the practicum, as an opportunity for real-world training, has always been considered important, both universities and practicum centres did not always ensure the implementation of adequate quality control mechanisms to guarantee successful completion of this subject. Following the implementation of the new EHEA academic model, in which teaching has become student-centred and teachers have taken a more guiding role, the education authorities have specified the competencies to be acquired and tasks to be performed by all agents participating in this subject. The aim is to offer quality work experience that will facilitate the insertion of future teachers in the job market.

In this chapter, we argue that this is made possible when the practicum combines initial pre-service teacher training with the in-service education of practicum centre tutors. This is because it is not enough for future teachers to simply apply the lessons learned in the university to the school classroom—they need to bring a spirit of inquiry to the real problems that arise in their setting. For this, the classroom tutor needs to be a reflective teacher (Schön, 1989), who constantly rethinks his or her own practice, who is in contact with other colleagues to share experiences, participate in projects and apply research results.

Evidence has shown the need for direct collaboration between the university and practicum centres to train highly qualified future teachers based on the acquisition of professional skills (Artime & Riaño, 2012; Cohen et al., 2013). Studies into university-school relationships show that collaboration benefits all those involved, not least classroom tutors in their in-service education and university lecturers who put into practice their experimental theories and draw real-world conclusions. One of these lines of research analyses relationship procedures based on the use of photographs to promote analysis, reflection and deliberation about school and classroom life among future teachers and their practicum tutors. This reflection and deliberation is aimed at mutual learning and permanent teacher development.

In this context, the study carried out by the authors of this chapter tool place in the classrooms of pre-school and primary schools in Madrid with a high percentage of immigrant students. We used photograph-based action-research loops involving undergraduate pre-school and primary school teachers undergoing their practicum training. The objective was to promote permanent inquiry, self-criticism and reflection on their own educational practice that would allow them to break away from their habitual practice. Following the methodology established, Practicum III students took photographs on their mobile phones of moments that caught their attention, either because they found the situations puzzling, or because they thought that some were inconsistent with other actions undertaken by the classroom teacher.

As mentioned in previous chapters, photo-elicitation is a procedure that, among other purposes, uses photographs to establish communication between the viewer, the photographer, and the researcher, producing an array of meanings (Banks, 2007). This leads to a dialogue or narration concerning the different interpretations that each viewer makes of the photograph. Sometimes, hidden beliefs are evoked and laid on the table. These help to understand the motivations behind the actors' intent. This technique allows participants to see events from the perspective of the other person viewing the photograph, thus expanding the interpretations that are often due to different cultural factors.

Photo-elicitation turns its informants (practicum students, tutors and external observers from the university, in our case) into active participants who contextualize and fill the images with meaning. These are then analysed as part of the participants' life stories, but also as a recurrence or isolated event in the investigation to assemble a panorama of significant events (Arias, 2011, p. 181).

The foregoing considerations and arguments reveal the formative dimension of the practicum. However, to conduct these studies during work experience in schools, we have to take into account the regulatory framework governing the practicum as well as the document establishing it as a subject in undergraduate pre-school and primary school teacher training. This is because conducting these studies during the practicum period required a number of administrative formalities. First, we had to contact the school principle and classroom tutors to explain the aim of the study and obtain their authorization and collaboration. We then held meetings with practicum students in these schools to outline the study and encourage them to participate, explaining that this type of research would enrich their professional practice.

We also had to take into consideration ethical-legal issues, which required us to obtain prior authorization from the school principle and the pupils' parents to take photographs in the classroom. For this purpose, the research team prepared a document outlining the aims of the study involving the selected group of pupils, and each parent was asked for permission to take photographs that were considered of interest in during classes. Of course, the photographs would be used solely for research purposes. The study only began once all authorisations had been obtained.

The study protocol also had to take into account the school's rules regarding the use of spaces and school time. For example, the practicum students had to take photographs outside of class time and present them to their corresponding tutors in the photo-elicitation sessions in order to try to understand and resolve the issues that prompted each photograph. Later, out of teaching hours, the pupils, their tutors and the research team held periodic meetings to engage in narrations and deep reflections on the choice of the moment, the motivations behind each photograph, and the meaning, emotion, situation, etc. that they intended capture and represent. Using questions, answers, and more questions, the theories and beliefs of future teachers, classroom tutors, and university lecturers were laid on the table. The dialogues were at times knowledge builders that led the classroom tutors to rethink their practice. These sessions were recorded on mobile phones to be later transcribed and encoded for study.

This regulatory framework is important insofar as it can either help or hinder the use of photography to enable pupils and tutors achieve the goals of the practicum. Because of this, we need to dwell on some regulatory aspects, especially on the competences that students must achieve. For example, we outline here competencies included in Practicum III in order to see the extent to which they can be achieved using photo-elicitation.

Specifically, Practicum III of Pre-School Education includes the following transversal competences, among others:

CT4 Know interaction and communication processes and apply them in different social and educational contexts.
CT8 Know and address school situations in multicultural contexts.
CT9 Display social skills in order to understand families and make yourself understood by them.
CT16 Promote democratic civic education, and the practice of critical social thought.
CMP2 Know about interaction and communication processes in the classroom, and have a command of the necessary social skills and abilities to encourage a climate that facilitates learning and coexistence.
CMP4 Relate theory and practice with the reality of the classroom and pre-school educational centre.
CMP5 Participate in teaching activities and acquire know-how, acting and reflecting from practice.

And for the Practicum III of Primary Education:

CT4 Know interaction and communication processes and apply them in different social and educational contexts.
CT5 Promote and collaborate in social actions, particularly those with an impact on civic education.
CT6 Value the importance of leadership, entrepreneurial spirit, creativity and innovation in professional performance.
CT8 Know and approach school situations in multicultural contexts.
CT9 Show social skills in order to understand families and be understood by them.
CT16 Promote democratic education for all and the practice of critical social thinking.
CMP2 Know about interaction and communication processes in the classroom, and have a command of the necessary social skills and abilities to encourage a climate that facilitates learning and coexistence.
CMP4 Relate theory and practice with the reality of the classroom and the school.
CMP7 Regulate the interaction and communication processes in groups of pupils aged 6–12 years.

Based on the foregoing and on our arguments presented so far, we believe that photo-elicitation is a technique that can:

– teach communication strategies, because this medium allows the practicum student to value and acquire communicative, narrative and expressive skills by using photography as a tool for transmitting subjectivities.

– create a climate that encourages communication and manifestation of beliefs that promote learning. This is because the different observations made of the photographs shown in the classroom by the researcher open channels of communication between the members of the classroom, who can then express their opinions and thoughts of the images displayed. Their feelings emerge from the memories evoked by the photographs. This establishes emotional education channels based on empathy, on mutual understanding, on knowing how to listen and address other people's problems, leading to a better coexistence.

– facilitate understanding between families from different cultural backgrounds by understanding different points of view and creating a climate of coexistence in the classroom and the neighbourhood. Good relations with immigrant families is essential and will prevent the creation of ghettos in the neighbourhood surrounding the school. Families provide photographs of their members and of the customs of their respective countries of origin. They interpret what is seen in the image and thus explain actions that others have not hitherto understood.

– provide information to promote critical thinking, since the analysis of the photograph by one or more members can lead to discussion, to decide what is best, to see what is wrong, to correct mistakes. Critical thinking, reasoning and decision-making are developed through the presentation of an image that has been chosen or taken.

– create a climate of cultural enrichment, because the description of cultural aspects in the photographs provided by the author or the contributor allow all participants the share their experience. Learning from other cultures is a mutually enriching experience.

– promote innovation in professional performance, because photographs create situations that can be analysed in depth. It also encourages critical appraisal of the photographic image.

– align theories with social reality, because photographs allow us to see social reality, understand problems and different actions. In short, photo-elicitation provides a space for practicum students and school tutors to bring together the theory and practice of education.

– reveal participants' personal experience through their reflections and narrations, making them co-researchers.

The results of our study, some of which are presented at the end of this chapter, have shown that the practicum students have undertaken interventions that have facilitated the acquisition of several competences: professional, educational, disciplinary, intercultural and linguistic, in the observation, implementation and evaluation phases. The practicum, therefore, is necessary for the acquisition of competencies that prepare future teachers for their professional practice. Photo-elicitation situations can encourage pre-service teachers to acquire these competences. It can also be used in pre-school or primary school classrooms with a high proportion of immigrants, and gives both university lecturers and in-service teachers to chance to further their professional development, thereby encouraging undergraduates to do the same. Although practicum guidelines and reports in most universities do not include the use of photography, the legal framework governing schools is flexible enough to accept this medium, thereby allowing teachers to acquire the skills to use photography as an educational tool.

But, how can photography, in the form of photo-elicitation sessions, benefit the teaching staff of participating schools?

Photo-Elicitation-Mediated Reciprocal Training Between School Tutors and Practicum Students

In the final part of this chapter on the contributions of photo-elicitation situations to the practicum, we will analyse reciprocal training, or shared personal and professional development between in-service teachers and practicum students in the school, institutional, training and legal contexts described above. Our review of the literature has shown that most authors agree that it is beneficial to create situations in which all those involved in the practicum can work together; specifically, school teachers, university lecturers and practicum students and, sometimes, external observers (Bautista, 2009; Toledo Fierro & Mauri, 2018; Zabalza, 2011, among others). In addition to forums, many studies point to the need to provide, for this purpose, the foregoing agents with photographic and communication media through which ideas can be pooled, such as practicum diaries, portfolios, recordings, etc. (Cebrián, 2011; Meek & Buckley, 2011; Sierra et al., 2017; Soto et al., 2010; among others).

In all these studies, teaching and learning are educational components in which those involved have clearly defined functions, specifically, teachers and lecturers teach; school children and practicum students learn. We will challenge this idea, and argue for the functional ambivalence of both roles, in other words, we suggest that students and teachers can play each other's role in certain situations of reciprocal knowledge and help.

The feasibility of this reciprocal training and development has been shown in a teaching innovation project carried out by the authors of this chapter. One of the aims of the project has been to investigate the level of reciprocal involvement and complicity between two practicum students and their respective practicum tutors during photo-elicitation situations. For the purposes of the study, the 4th year undergraduate pre-school teachers from the Complutense University of Madrid were given cameras to enable them to take photographs of particular scenarios involving pupils or teachers in the classroom and the school that they found unusual or unexpected. Every two weeks, the practicum students, school tutors and two university lecturers acting as external observers attended photo-elicitation sessions to analyse and discuss the photographs. Audio recordings were made of the sessions and later transcribed.

What changes were observed in the photo-elicitation sessions held during the 3-month practicum period? The data collected showed that the process that triggered the change of roles and functions of the school tutors and practicum students has been called progressive *complicity and mutual support* between teachers and university students. This classroom complicity refers to the relationship between the protagonists when engaging in tasks with a common goal. Mutual support refers to actions where each one is present. Both, complicity and mutual support have been observed in the following six indicators found in photo-elicitation processes.

(a) Referring to the other.
(b) Confirming what was said or done by the other.
(c) Contributing to the other's previous intervention.
(d) Giving the same answers simultaneously.
(e) Asking each other questions.
(f) Correcting the other.

The first of the indicators is observed in the transcribed text when one of the teachers or students mentions the other to add credence to what they are going to say or to justify a particular decision or classroom activity. For example, student A1 referred to her tutor T1 thus:

A1: if in the end it's as T1 says, you find yourself repeating 25 times a day the issue of the answer of what I do with the marker that's dry

A1: I liked T1's solution of putting our hands between our knees and reading with our eyes. (Session held on 30 March 2017)

Or this tutor in the presence of student A1:

Tutor 1 (T1): A1 and I were talking about this, and asking ourselves how can we show this in a photo? (Session held on 25 May 2017).

Regarding the second indicator, we have identified Confirming what was said or done by the other in the content of the transcribed sessions when both intervene consecutively and one ratifies what was previously stated by the other. The following are some examples of confirmations between classroom 2 tutor (T2) and her practicum student (A2):

T2: (The boy comes) from Pakistan and doesn't understand Spanish.

A2: Not a word … (Session held on 15 March 2018).

A2: anyone can get hooked (reading a story)

T2: yes, it's easy to get hooked on stories. (Session held on 25 March 2018)

With regard to the third indicator of the level of complicity and support between tutor and student, called "contribution", it differs from the previous ones in that one of them intervenes to contribute some idea, information or argument that helps to understand the content analysed or the activity described. For example:

T2: D is a very immature boy.

A2: Yes, it's not about doing it well, it's about being able to take hold of the pencil, and well, in the photo you can see that he can't. (Session held on 15 March 2018).

T2: (Looking at a photograph of a child taking the roll call..) those that haven't come, we put them in the little house, and then count them.

A2: You can see a big house that's the school, then there are the photos of all the children, and then there's another smaller house that represents their house, so when roll is called, those who have not come to school go to the house and, when we finish, they're counted. (Session held on 26 April 2018)

Simultaneity, the fourth indicator, expresses the complicity between the student and the tutor when they simultaneously give the same answer to a comment made by an external observer. For example:

OE2: (Looking at the photograph of a group of children in the corner of the house)… there's no rule that says I have to play here with these toys, and I can't get up unless I've picked them up.

T2 and A2: Right, right. (Session held on 15 March 2018)

The fifth indicator of the reciprocal help and understanding between both protagonists refers to the questions they are asked. For example:

A2: (Looking at a photograph of the assembly during roll call)… there was one thing that caught my attention, that I didn't understand at the beginning of the practicum, and I asked T2 why the children counted, for example 3,… (Session held on 24 May 2018).

Finally, the sixth indicator of complicity occurs when the student or the tutor corrects the other by putting forward an argument or providing evidence. For example:

A2: (Talking about a child) was not.

T2: He was in the corner, yes… (Session held on 24 May 2018)

Apart from the particular way each students refers to their respective tutors or the frequency of their interventions, the analysis of the transcription shows evidence of a change in the relationship between student and tutor. A trend comparison shows that the same changes occur in both cases or classrooms, and suggests that a relationship of complicity and mutual support has been built up during the photo-elicitation processes. Specifically, more than twice as many reciprocal references occur in the last photo-elicitation session compared to the first. The number of confirmations is reduced by more than half, while contributions more than double. The number of simultaneous responses remains the same. Finally, while there was only one instance where the tutor corrected her practicum student, the number of questions students asked their tutors increased progressively during the last month of the practicum.

The *complicity* between both pairs of tutors and students was established and gradually built up during successive photo-elicitation sessions. The decrease in confirming responses, which led to an increase in contributing responses, is an indicator of the good understanding and mutual assistance between tutors and students, because they were mostly responsible for this change in response. Specifically, one decreased from 42 to 7 confirming statements, and the other from 12 to 5. In turn, both increased their contributing responses from 4 to 12. The confidence gained from the training received in the climate of complicity created in the photo-elicitation sessions helped them understand that their role was to contribute ideas to the discourse created in these sessions instead of merely confirming what their respective tutors had said.

This relationship of complicity gradually eroded the borderline between the teaching and learning roles that each had assumed at the start of the practicum, because the smooth flow of questions and answers between the tutor and the student showed their proximity. In the last four weeks, the climate of understanding, complicity and mutual help gave way to questioning the reasons for some of the actions or decisions taken, which obliged them to specify their motivations and, sometimes, made them aware of the beliefs or theories that underlie them. With respect to the types of photo-elicitation situation described in the previous chapter, in this teaching innovation study, the sessions with a descriptive-informative function were requested by external observers, students and university lecturers involved in the practicum. The questions that emerged during the sessions involved teaching situations that led to learning. The function was performed by both tutors and students, insofar as they described and analysed the content of the photographs at the same time, and over the course of the three-month practicum questions emerged about the content of some of the photographs taken by undergraduate pre-school teachers. The tutors themselves stated at some point that these questions raised doubts in their minds about why they did things in a certain way out of habit, and this prompted them to learn or reflect on their practice.

Finally, it is important to mention that this process was interspersed by exchange situations involving the content of some photographs of situations considered natural or typical of communities of practice (Wenger, 2001; Raposo & Zabalza, 2011), because the educational and legal contexts provided promote these mutual teaching and learning processes between teachers and students.

References

Allen, J. B., & Labbo, L. (2001). Giving it a second thought: Making culturally engaged teaching culturally engaging. *Language Arts, 79*(1), 40–52.

Arias, D. (2011). El co-relato de la imagen fotográfica: la arqueología visual como metodología en la exploración de la memoria etnohistórica. *QuAderns-e, 16*(1–2), 181.

Artime, I. H., & Riaño, X. A. G. (2012). El Practicum de los estudios universitarios de pedagogía: visión y aportaciones de los tutores. *Revista Iberoamericana de educación, 59*(2). ISSN 1681-5653.

Bailey, N. M., & Van Harken, E. M. (2014). Visual images as tools of teacher inquiry. *Journal of Teacher Education, 65*(3), 241–260.

Banks, J. A. (2007). *Educating citizens in a multicultural society* (2nd ed.). Teachers College Press.

Bautista, A. (Ed.). (2009). *Practicum y campus virtual*. Davinci.

Bautista, A. (Dir.). (2016). *La formación del alumnado del* Grado *de Maestro de Educación Primaria mediante sesiones de fotoelicitación en el Practicum* (Teaching innovation project, PIE2016-23). Universidad Complutense, Madrid.

Bautista, A. (Dir.). (2017). *Incorporación de la narración audiovisual, soportada en la foto-elicitación y centrada en la diversidad sociocultural de los escolares, en el Practicum de los grados de maestro* (Teaching innovation project, PIE2017-41). Universidad Complutense, Madrid.

Brown, E. L. (2005). Using photography to explore hidden realities and raise cross-cultural sensitivity in future teachers. *Urban Review, 37*(2), 149–171. https://doi.org/10.1007/s11256-005-0003-5

Caielli, E., Regueira, A. L., & Williams, J. (Eds.). (2018). La foto-elicitación como instrumento para explorar la cognición docente. En J. Aguirre & M. C. Rojas (Comps.), *Pedagogía, formación docente y narrativas: IV Jornadas de Investigadorxs, Grupos y Proyectos de Investigación en Educación* (pp. 306–316). Mar del Plata: Universidad Nacional de Mar del Plata.

Cebrián, M. (2011). Los ePortafolios en la supervisión del Practicum: modelos pedagógicos y soportes tecnológicos. *Profesorado: Revista de curriculum y formación del profesorado, 15*(1), 91–107.

Cohen, E., Hoz, R., & Kaplan, H. (2013). The practicum in preservice teacher education: A review of empirical studies. *Teaching Education, 24*(4), 345–380. http://eric.ed.gov/?id=EJ1022363

Da Cunha, M. A., Batista, P., & Graça, A. (2014). Pre-service physical education teachers' discourses on learning how to become a teacher: [Re]constructing a professional identity based on visual evidence. *Open Sports Sciences Journal, 7*, 141–171. https://doi.org/10.2174/1875399X01407010141

Dicicco, M. (2015). *Picturing the reader: English education pre-service teachers' beliefs about reading using photovoice* (Ph.D. dissertation). Department of Secondary Education, College of Education, University of South Florida.

Garrett, J. H., & Matthews, S. (2014). Containing pedagogical complexity through the assignment of photography: Two case presentations. *Curriculum Inquiry, 44*(3), 332–357.

González-Garzón, Mª. L., & Laorden, C. (2012). El Practicum en la formación inicial de los Maestros en las nuevas titulaciones de Educación Infantil y Primaria. El punto de vista de profesores y estudiantes. *Revista Pulso, 35*, 131–154. ISSN 1577-0338.

Graziano, K. J. (2011). Working with English language learners: Preservice teachers and photovoice. *International Journal of Multicultural Education, 13*(1), 1–19.

Johnson, L. L., & Smagorinsky, P. (2013). Writing remixed: Mapping the multimodal composition of one preservice English education teacher. In R. E. Ferdig & K. E. Pytash (Eds.), *Exploring multimodal composition and digital writing* (pp. 262–280). Ringgold Inc. https://doi.org/10.4018/978-1-4666-4345-1.ch016

Langdon, J. L., Walker, A., Colquitt, G., & Pritchard, T. (2014). Using photovoice to determine preservice teachers' preparedness to teach. *Journal of Physical Education, Recreation & Dance, 85*(1), 22–27.

Legge, M. F., & Smith, W. (2014). Teacher education and experiential learning: A visual ethnography. *Australian Journal of Teacher Education, 39* (12), 94–109. https://doi.org/10.14221/ajte.2014v39n12.7

Mathews, S. A., & Crew, E. (Ed.). (2016). Examining community with pre-service teachers through the use of participatory photography projects. In A. R. Crowe & A. Cuenca (Eds.), *Rethinking social studies teacher education in the twenty-first century* (pp. 295–319). Springer. https://doi.org/10.1007/978-3-319-22939-3

McCartney, H., & Harris, T. (2014). The image of the child constructed and transformed by preservice teachers in international contexts. *Action in Teacher Education, 36*(4), 264–282.

McCracken, W. (2015). Framing and its role in promoting reflective practice among trainee teachers of deaf children in the UK. In S. Miles & A. Howes (Eds.), *Photography in educational research. Critical reflections from diverse contexts* (pp. 128–136). Routledge.

Meek, B., & Buckley, P. (2011). Using digital photographs to stimulate a group portfolio learning journey. *Contemporary Issues in Technology and Teacher Education (CITE Journal), 11*(4), 420–442.

Mitchell, C., Dillon, D., Strong-Wilson, T., Pithouse, K., Islam, F., O'Connor, K., Rudd, C., Staniforth, P., & Cole, A. (2010). Things fall apart and come together: Using the visual for reflection in alternative teacher education programmes. *Changing English: Studies in Culture and Education, 17*(1), 45–55.

Pereiro, M. C., & Páramo, M. B. (2016). Tecnologías tradicionales y emergentes al servicio del prácticum en el grado de educación primaria: Una propuesta de intervención educativa. *Tendencias Pedagógicas, 28*, 81–98.

Raposo, M., & Zabalza, M. A. (2011). La formación práctica de estudiantes universitarios: repensando el Practicum. *Revista de Educación, 354*, 21–43. Enero-Abril.

Sadik, A. (2011). Improving pre-service teachers' visual literacy through online photo-sharing applications. *International Journal of Emerging Technologies in Learning, 6*(1), 31–36. https://doi.org/10.3991/ijet.v6i1.1360

Salazar, M., Ruiz, M., & Mora, E. (2016). Black feminist photovoice: Fostering critical awareness of diverse families and communities in early childhood teacher education. *Journal of Early Childhood Teacher Education, 37*(1), 41–60. https://doi.org/10.1080/10901027.2015.1131209

Savva, A., & Erakleous, V. (2018). Play-based art activities in early years: Teachers' thinking and practice. *International Journal of Early Years Education, 26*(1), 56–74. https://doi.org/10.1080/09669760.2017.1372272

Schön, D. (1989). *La formación de profesionales reflexivos*. Paidós-MEC.

Seow, T. (2016). Reconciling discourse about geography and teaching geography: The case of Singapore pre-service teachers. *International Research in Geographical and Environmental Education, 25*(2), 151–165. https://doi.org/10.1080/10382046.2016.1149342

Sepúlveda, Mª P., Gallardo, M., Mayorga, Mª J., & Madrid, D. (2017). La evaluación del Practicum: un proceso clave en la construcción y reconstrucción del pensamiento práctico. Revista ENSAYOS, 32-1, 93-110. ISSN 2171-9098.

Sierra, J. E., Caparrós, E., Molina, D., & Blanco, N. (2017). Aprender a través de la escritura. Los diarios de prácticas y el desarrollo de saberes experienciales. *Revista Complutense de Educación, 28*(3), 673–688.

Sinclair, C., & Thornton, L. J. (2018). Exploring preservice teachers' conceptions after 'living a hybrid curriculum.' *European Physical Education Review, 24*(2), 133–151. https://doi.org/10.1177/1356336X16669331

Soto, E., Serván, M. J., & Pérez, A. I. (2010). La evaluación como aprendizaje en el practicum de secundaria. In A. I. Pérez Gómez (Ed.), *Aprender a enseñar en la práctica: Procesos de innovación y prácticas de formación en educación secundaria* (pp. 165–182). Graó.

Stockall, N., & Davis, S. (2011). Uncovering pre-service teacher beliefs about young children: A photographic elicitation methodology. *Issues in Educational Research, 21*(2), 192–209.

Toledo Fierro, B. C., & Mauri, T. (2018). Formas de participación durante el prácticum en una comunidad de aula como oportunidades de aprendizaje de la profesión de maestro. *Revista Practicum, 3*(1), 20–33.

Varea, V., & Pang, B. (2018). Using visual methodologies to understand pre-service health and physical education teachers' subjectivities of bodies. *Sport, Education and Society, 23*(5), 394–406. https://doi.org/10.1080/13573322.2016.1228625

Villacanas de Castro, L. S. (2017). We are more than EFL teachers—We are educators': Emancipating EFL student-teachers through photovoice. *Educational Action Research, 25*(4), 610–629. https://doi.org/10.1080/09650792.2016.1215930

Walker, A., Langdon, J. L., Colquitt, G., & McCollum, S. (2017). Using photovoice to initiate improvement in a PETE program. *Journal of Teaching in Physical Education, 36*(1), 83–96. https://doi.org/10.1123/jtpe.2015-0092

Wenger, E. (2001). *Comunidades de práctica. Aprendizaje, significado e identidad*. Paidós.

White, L. M., & Murray, J. (2016). Seeing disadvantage in schools: Exploring student teachers' perceptions of poverty and disadvantage using visual pedagogy. *Journal of Education for Teaching: International Research and Pedagogy, 42*(4), 500–515.

Wolfenden, F., & Buckler, A. (2015). Teacher learning in Sudan: Building dialogue around teachers' practices through reflective photography. In S. Miles & A. Howes (Eds.), *Photography in educational research. Critical reflections frim diverse contexts* (pp. 79–94). Routledge.

Zabalza, M. A. (2003). *Competencias docentes del profesorado universitario. Calidad y desarrollo profesional*. Narcea.

Zabalza, M. A. (2011). Estado de la cuestión en torno al practicum. *Revista de Educación, 354*. Enero-Abril, pp. 11–21.

Chapter 8
Photo-Elicitation in Virtual Environments as a Tool for Teachers' In-Service Training

Laura Cayuela Ferrero

Introduction

Our everyday lives are inundated with images and (audio)visual language in advertising, the media, our imagination and new forms of communication in the digital world. The field of education is no exception, and thus images have not only become a teaching resource in the classroom (Motta, 2016; Rigo, 2014), but have also, in recent decades, emerged as a valuable source of research data (Banks, 2010; Bautista & Velasco, 2011; Pink, 2007).

According to the classification proposed by Sarah Pink (2007), there are three different uses of photography in qualitative research: as a visual method of documentation, in collaborative photography and in interviews using photographs, known as photo-elicitation. As a visual method of documentation, photography has been used in the social sciences to create catalogues or archives of given aspects in the shape of photographic inventories. Pink indicates that such inventories have generally been based on the assumption that the objects photographed have a finite and unequivocal symbolic meaning, which overlooks the question of the meanings that these objects have for the individuals belonging to the community. Meanwhile, in participatory photography, researchers and informants alike collaborate in various ways to produce photographs. Through this collaborative production process, the images capture the intentions of both and represent the result of negotiating visions and meanings. In this chapter, however, I shall conduct an in-depth examination of photo-elicitation as a tool for collecting information through photographs taken by a group of participants in educational situations, not only for research purposes (providing answers to questions or hypotheses) but also for student education and teachers' in-service training.

L. Cayuela Ferrero (✉)
Complutense University, Madrid, Spain
e-mail: lauracayuela@ucm.es

A. Bautista García-Vera (ed.), *Photographic Elicitation and Narration in Teachers Education and Development*, Teacher Education, Learning Innovation and Accountability, https://doi.org/10.1007/978-3-031-20164-6_8

As some of the arguments presented here are based on the results of field work in virtual teaching environments, I shall summarise the corresponding research context below. The project in question, which was launched in 2016, was conducted with tutors of the AVE Global online Spanish as a Foreign Language courses designed and delivered by the Cervantes Institute. AVE Global offers a total of sixteen online courses that can be accessed via a range of electronic devices, including computers, tablets and mobile phones. The courses cover levels A1 to C1 of the Common European Framework of Reference and each course is divided into three thematic blocks. Besides hosting activities corresponding to the different topics, the platform provides various communication and work spaces, including a chat room, a blog, a forum and a wiki.

The course referred to here corresponded to level A1.1 and included the following topics: "Meeting people, greetings and personal information", "Family and friends. Physical appearance and emotions" and "Food". The tutored course comprised a total of 40 h divided into 30 h of individual work and 10 h of group tutorials. Of these latter, 6 h were devoted to asynchronous work and 4 h to oral work in groups via videoconferencing, with one videoconference session at the end of each topic and a final review session at the end of the course. The Cervantes Institute centre responsible for teaching this course is located in Sao Paulo and it was delivered between 13 August and 12 November 2018.

The study aims were: to determine the online tutors' level of intercultural communication competence; to identify the factors favouring or hindering acquisition of this competence; and to explore, in collaboration with the tutors, the most effective strategies for incorporating work on intercultural skills and attitudes into online courses. As can be seen, the project drew on three thematic areas of research: interculturality; teachers' in-service training; and online teaching. Furthermore, not only did it explore online language teaching, but the research itself was mainly conducted in a virtual environment following Hine's principles of virtual ethnography (2004).

When designing the photo-elicitation sessions, a series of questions arose which merit reflection, since the literature identified to date solely discusses use of this method in face-to-face contexts. These questions were as follows. Can the benefits of photo-elicitation be transferred to virtual contexts? Is it necessary to modify the design or procedure of photo-elicitation sessions when these are carried out online? In what ways can photo-elicitation be used in online in-service training for teachers? This chapter will attempt to answer these questions.

Photography as an Act of Communication

Before analysing the design and procedure of photo-elicitation sessions in virtual environments, it will be helpful to discuss the very concept of photography and the photographic act as an act of communication. First, it is necessary to deconstruct the positivist notion of photography as the mimetic—and therefore objective and neutral—reproduction of reality, in which the value of photography is considered to reside solely in its documentary function, either as an illustration of given events or as a photographic catalogue or archive of particular events or communities. On the contrary, photographs are never neutral, because they are taken by a particular individual with a specific intention, using consciously selected framing or lighting.

In opposition to this traditional stance of viewing a photograph as a mirror of reality, that is to say, as a symbol, Marzal (2015, p. 61) suggests that it should considered an "impression of reality" in which external reality is mediated by the particular gaze of the person taking the shot. Photography thus becomes an interpretation of reality, an ideologically and culturally codified construction—a symbol (Marzal, 2015)—that can also represent emotions (Barthes, 1989). This process of mediation is present not only in the production of the communicative act, but also in its reception, as the viewer interprets the photographic text. Photographs acquire meaning under the subjective gaze of those viewing them; thus, individuals construct their own meanings by relating an image to their personal experiences, their previous knowledge and their cultural frames of reference (Pink, 2007).

The photographic act also implies a transformation of reality that operates on the coordinates of time and space. With regard to time, it is worth mentioning that when we take a photograph, we "cut" a fraction of a second in time. Thus, that particular moment is destined to last. As Marzal says, it is a moment that ceases to elapse, an instant that is preserved forever (2015, p. 78). Not only is time stopped, but also the event that occurred is perpetuated, enabling the individual to evoke and recall in the present something that was experienced in the past. Photographic time and chronological time are therefore different, and this is an important factor to consider when selecting images for photo-elicitation sessions and also when sequencing, analysing and interpreting them during research. The chronological order in which photographs were taken is a valid method of categorising them, but unlike in traditional or positivist approaches, from a critical qualitative approach it is not the only one that is valid. Visual elements can be organised according to other parameters such as theme or argument, researcher-imposed categories or research goals, among others (Pink, 2007).

Turning to photographic space, we can see that here too, a "cut" occurs when a photograph is taken, as there is a relationship between what is represented within the photographic field and what remains outside it. As noted in earlier chapters, photographic space is defined by the framing and composition of the image, which enables analysis of the spatial arrangement of the elements in the photograph. Marzal (2015) identifies a third level of photographic space where representation of the space contained within the image is related to the external space in the moment it is perceived by the receiver.

Marzal's (2015, p. 99) adaptation of Laswell's well-known model of communication to the field of photography is enlightening. According to this model, all acts of communication contain the following elements:

- The sender or producer: the person who creates the message, in this case the photographer.
- The message: in our case contained in the photographic text.

- The receiver: the person who receives, decodes and interprets the message.
- The communication channel: that is, the medium or space in which the photograph is located, for example an exhibition, a billboard, a book, a digital newspaper or the internet. The channel determines the way in which the message is received, as well as the techniques and technologies used to produce it.
- The sociological, historical and cultural context: this affects all the above-mentioned elements, from the production of the photographic text to its interpretation.

In conclusion, as Correa (2011) has said:

> Audiovisual productions surround us and shape us; not only do we interpret them, but we also construct them and create them. They form part of our cultural process, constitute our symbolic universe and are part of our internal reality, shaping our subjectivity. In one way or another, audiovisual narratives help us to represent, explain and experience the world. Images exert real effects on our social relations and on our own identities. (p. 54)

Photo-Elicitation in Teachers' In-Service Training

There is a substantial body of literature on the importance of reflection in teachers' in-service training aimed at improving their teaching practice (Imbernón, 2007; Schön, 1989; Segovia, 1997). Schön (1989) distinguishes between two types of reflection, namely: reflection *in* action, and reflection *on* action. The first takes place while an action is happening, without interrupting it, and therefore we can still change the situation that is occurring. Meanwhile, reflection on action occurs once the action is over and we have time to reflect on the changes we made while it was in progress (in the case that we engaged in reflection in action), or on how we should have acted, trying to unravel the beliefs, attitudes, theories or values that informed our decision-making. Along these lines, Vaillant and Marcelo (2015) and other authors in the preceding chapters indicate that one of the principles that should guide teachers' in-service training is that of generating opportunities to improve understanding of the theories, previous experiences and beliefs that act as a filter in teaching practice. Photo-elicitation therefore presented an excellent means to generate such opportunities and thus to encourage reflection on the teaching practice of the AVE Global tutors with whom we worked in order to identify solutions to the problems, contradictions or conflicts that were detected.

Elliott (1997) has defined the reflection processes necessary to improve teaching practice as action-research loops consisting of three stages. The first of these is lesson planning (determining the objectives, content and materials that teachers will require for a period of time). The second is implementation of the lesson plan and recording information on what happened. In our case, this took the form of recording Skype sessions held during the course (four in total) and of capturing images of the materials and communication spaces hosted on the virtual platform. The third and last stage is analysis and reflection on what was recorded in the previous step, for which we used photo-elicitation.

As indicated at the beginning of this chapter, photo-elicitation consists of using an image in research and training situations to elicit information from participants. One of the foundations of this procedure is the response we give through and to different systems of representation. As we know, photography supports three levels of meaning, namely: the denotative, the connotative and the Barthesian *punctum*. Images have more power than verbal language to evoke lived experience because in evolutionary terms, the parts of the brain that process visual information are older than those that process verbal language, and also because exchanges based solely on words employ less brain capacity than those where the brain must process both images and words (Harper, 2002, p. 13). Consequently, photo-elicitation is not aimed at accessing a greater quantity of information, but rather, by using photographs during interviews, at obtaining a different quality of information (Harper, 2002; Pink, 2007) related to tacit aspects such as ideas, intentions, values and affects.

In those observing the image, photo-elicitation can provoke a reaction, evoke or call to mind experiences or generate a dialogue with others. It is precisely this dialogue with others, where meanings are negotiated and the experiential world and cultural frameworks of others are explored, that has enabled successful use of photo-elicitation to strengthen intercultural relations in various educational contexts (Bautista et al., 2012; Rayón & De las Heras, 2011; Ruiz, 2017). Thanks to the evocative power of the image and the inquiry processes generated during photo-elicitation sessions, this procedure provides a valuable means to render explicit the beliefs or theories underlying teachers' practice, and based on reflection, to implement changes that improve teaching practice or that resolve conflicts or dilemmas arising from that practice (Bautista, 2017; Bautista et al., 2016).

If we start from an approach where photography is considered a visual text through which people reference aspects of their experiences and knowledge, then certain questions must be taken into account when designing and planning photo-elicitation sessions. In line with the arguments advanced in Chapter 6, it should be stressed that photo-elicitation is a flexible procedure where the different elements that come into play will inevitably vary from one situation to another. Any prescriptive position on this issue is therefore best avoided, as it is the participants and researchers who are best aware of the specific needs of their training or research context. Nonetheless, it is possible to outline some of the decisions that must be taken in the design of photo-elicitation sessions.

First, one must decide whether the images to be used during the discussion should be taken by the researcher, the interviewee or previously by a third party; they can even be photographs from the participant's personal collection or family album. Pink (2007) stresses that photographs taken by the informants themselves have value on two different levels: on the one hand, the images were taken at moments that were significant for them and reflect their own narrative of events, while on the other, when informants talk about these photographs they place them in a new narrative and give them a renewed meaning (2007, p. 91). However, other researchers such as Clark-Ibáñez highlight the use of images taken by the researchers as an excellent means "to capture aspects that participants take for granted about their lives or community, in order to promote discussion" (2004, p. 1509). Ultimately, the decision will depend on the objectives of the sessions and on the desire, confidence and/or availability of the actors involved to take the images or not.

Another question to consider is the device used to take the photographs. Depending on context, this could be a digital camera, an analogue camera, a webcam or a mobile phone with a camera. In addition, the photographs to be used in the sessions may be originals or copies, or could even be photographs of photographs or digital images. Furthermore, the photographs could also be edited, digitally retouched or not. Bearing in mind the arguments advanced in Chapter 6, it is also necessary to decide the order in which participants intervene when narrating and interpreting the meanings contained in the photographs.

Transferring Photo-Elicitation to Virtual Contexts

Having considered the elements involved in photo-elicitation and identified the necessary decisions, our next step was to meet the challenge of transferring this procedure to an online environment. Given the lack of literature on the use of photo-elicitation in virtual environments, we set out to design the sessions based on other examples of its use in teachers' in-service education in face-to-face contexts (Bautista & Velasco, 2011; Bautista, 2017; Bautista et al., 2018). In this initial design, it was agreed with the tutor that she would be responsible for taking screenshots throughout the course of any aspect that drew her attention, generated questions about her teaching practice or that for whatever other reason she wanted to share during the sessions. However, after several email and Skype exchanges, it became apparent that the tutor felt uncomfortable taking the pictures. As we know, it is impossible in qualitative research to foresee all the situations that may arise once the study has begun, and consequently the design of these sessions must be flexible and open to modification. Thus, it was decided to modify the initial approach and it was agreed that the researcher would be responsible for taking screenshots and selecting the images for subsequent use in the discussion.

This change had important implications for how the sessions were conducted and the roles assumed by the researcher and tutor. As explained earlier, a photograph reflects the intentions and the particular gaze of the person who took it. We were aware that our previous experiences, knowledge and interests would mediate and filter our perception of course delivery: another observer of the same events would probably have taken different images. Therefore, it was agreed that the researcher would select and present the images and the tutor would have to try to discern the intentionality behind the photographs thus presented, taking into account the research topics under study, namely the treatment of interculturality in teaching Spanish as a foreign language, teachers' in-service training and online teaching. We hoped that her inquiry into our intentions would prompt the tutor to elaborate and make explicit the theories or beliefs that had informed her decisions during the course. Thus, she had to reinterpret certain practices or moments during the course in a new light that might either agree with or question her principles and beliefs. We wanted to generate a dialogical process between the researcher and the tutor in which impressions, beliefs and theories were reinterpreted in a process of co-construction of new meanings in the discussion generated by the photographic content. Far from being a disadvantage, we believe that recognition of this dynamic placed us in a strong position to apply the principles of reflexivity to data interpretation (Hine, 2004; Pink, 2007).

On the other hand, the shift in responsibility for taking screenshots implied that the researcher assumed an active role as a producer, with the consequent danger that the power relations between tutor and researcher would change. One way to disrupt this power dynamic between observer and observed is to place the researcher under the scrutiny of the camera as well, using it as a democratising element (Pink, 2007). Consequently, the researcher activated her camera during the Skype sessions and was recorded together with the tutor and the students; on another occasion, in a videoconference session held during one of the units on the family and descriptions of physical appearance and personality, the tutor shared a photograph of her family (Image 8.1) with the group and the researcher subsequently posted a photograph of her own family (Image 8.2) in the forum thread opened for this purpose.

Having analysed the producer and receiver of the photographic text, the dynamics established in the photo-elicitation sessions and the reasons that led to these decisions, it is helpful to examine the medium used to take the photographs. Since this was a virtual teaching-learning environment, we decided to use a digital tool (the Snipping tool included in Windows) to take screenshots of course delivery, since a camera

Image 8.1 Tutor's family. Image used in a photo-elicitation session

Image 8.2 Researcher's family

did not seem an appropriate device for obtaining high resolution images of what was happening on the screen. As indicated when describing the elements of the communicative act, the context and the channel have an impact on the other elements.

A person taking screenshots is necessarily limited to what happens on the screen, reducing his or her capacity for action compared to someone taking a photograph in a face-to-face context with a camera, because in the latter case, the producer can select fundamental aspects of the image such as the camera angle or position, whereas in our case, the element over which we had most control was the frame, as we could only choose between capturing the whole screen or a specific part of the elements displayed. As regards recordings of the Skype sessions (used to answer queries and provide speaking practice), these also reflected solely what appeared on the screen, albeit this was influenced by the position of each user's webcam and even by his or her decision to turn the camera on or not.

As we can see, the very conception of space varies depending on whether we are in a face-to-face educational situation that takes place in three dimensions in a shared space, usually a school that is simultaneously hosting the different actors (teachers, students, researchers), or a virtual environment, where the course materials and the various learning areas (e.g. forum, chat room or wiki) are accessed via a screen, which is a two-dimensional space that is not necessarily occupied simultaneously by the various actors. These are important differences that should be considered in the design and implementation of photo-elicitation sessions, especially if both the sessions themselves and the teaching practices they reflect are conducted online (Image 8.3).

As noted above, the procedure employed during the photo-elicitation sessions was as follows: the researcher took the screenshots and recorded the videoconferencing sessions. She then selected some of the images and noted her reasons for choosing

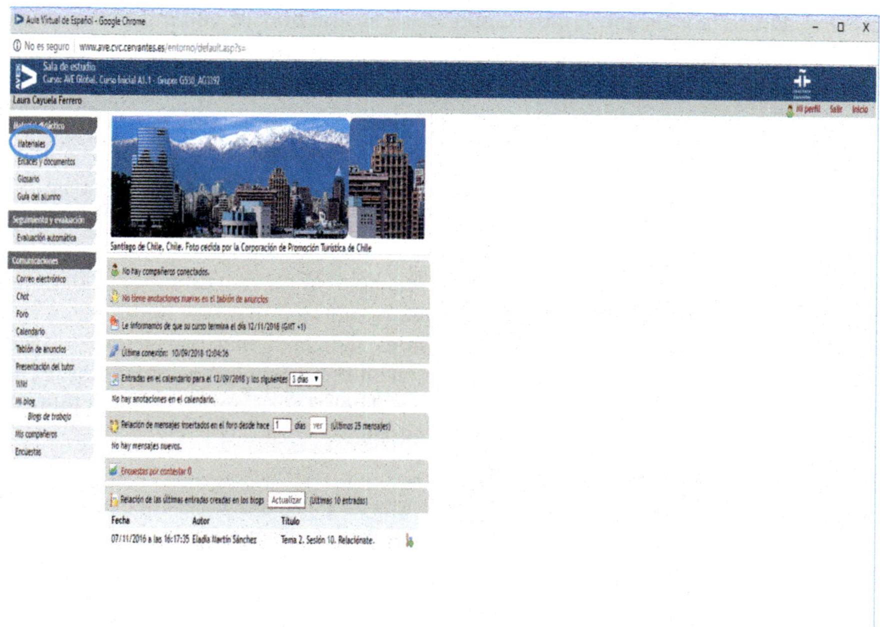

Image 8.3 Course study room. Image used in a photo-elicitation session

them, rendering her intentions explicit. By way of illustration, the notes taken in the field diary for Images 8.1, 8.3 and 8.4 are given below:

- Image 8.1—Tutor's family: "Chosen for its intercultural value and intent to forge a connection with the other. Also, because I believe this activity contributed to narrowing the divide that may have existed between teachers and students and to generating a good atmosphere in the group. This connection with the other is forged on a more micro level, without taking it to the level of the family in Spain or Brazil, but rather focusing on the personal and experiential reality of each one. Find out why she chose this photograph".

- Image 8.3—Study room: "I have highlighted the materials section due to its specific importance in delivering the annual programme. My impression is that the teacher's power to act in this type of course is much more limited than it would be in a face-to-face class, where, even if a textbook is the key element in the teaching-learning process, it is usually possible to select which activities from the book to do and which can done as a group, or to use other additional materials. What role(s) do you play as an online tutor for the AVE Global courses and is it consistent with your roles as a face-to-face teacher?"

- Image 8.4—AVE Global A1.1 course activity: "Selected to reflect on activities that try to include interculturality but remain the student's personal reflection without being shared with the group, which means that this opportunity to interact with peers and reflect on the relativisation and construction of cultural practices is lost. Also as an example of the concept of culture being equated with national culture (of the nation state) at country level. One of the things that the intercultural paradigm promotes is to go beyond the question of what something is like in your country, since this homogenises cultural diversity".

Subsequently, a day and time was agreed to proceed to the discussion stage by videoconference. In this session, the tutor had to try to identify the intentionality behind the selection of images, bearing in mind the topics of study in the research project (interculturality, online teaching and teachers' in-service training), and it was expected that she would reinterpret the moments captured in a new light.

An initial analysis of these virtual sessions indicated that, as in face-to-face contexts, photo-elicitation proved an appropriate tool for rendering explicit the theories underlying the decisions taken in practice. Thus, for example, commenting on the first image, the following intervention took place:

> Tutor So I don't know if other tutors do this, but I think that the question of affectivity, and creating a connection, is very important in the classroom, whether you're a tutor or a teacher. So by bringing something personal, right, you get much closer. Of course, I selected this image very consciously. When I started teaching I was very much against revealing anything personal, but it works very well. I've had to... learn that it works well. So the idea of bringing a personal photograph was a little bit for that reason because I could have used an internet photograph of a family, period. I don't know if that was what attracted your attention, that it was a real photograph, a personal photograph in, in...

As we can see, the tutor explained that she had shown a photograph of her own family because she was interested in issues related to affectivity in the classroom. Believing that it is positive to establish a connection with students in order to promote a favourable affective atmosphere, she decided to use a personal photograph. But this was not the only reason:

> Researcher And why did you choose this particular one?
>
> Tutor I have, I have two actually and I alternate them. This one because there are a lot of people, right, and there are various generations and different types, right, and the other one I have is of a wedding, right? And of a wedding, well, with all the possible clichés. It's there because of the number and, well that, because of the physical differences too and between young people and people... and here for example when we talk about age there is also a lot... they get very confused because here is my older brother and my younger brother, so I wanted there to be different generations because of that. So it was also partly for the practical side that I chose it.

We can see that the act of bringing a photograph of her family into the classroom to carry out a given activity was not accidental, but rather that her decision stemmed from her belief in the importance of the affective dimension in language teaching and the need to provide students with a sample of language tailored to the grammatical and lexical structures being studied in the unit (the family and descriptions of physical appearance and personality). Unlike the other two photographs presented, the tutor had seen this image before and it represented a significant moment for her. However,

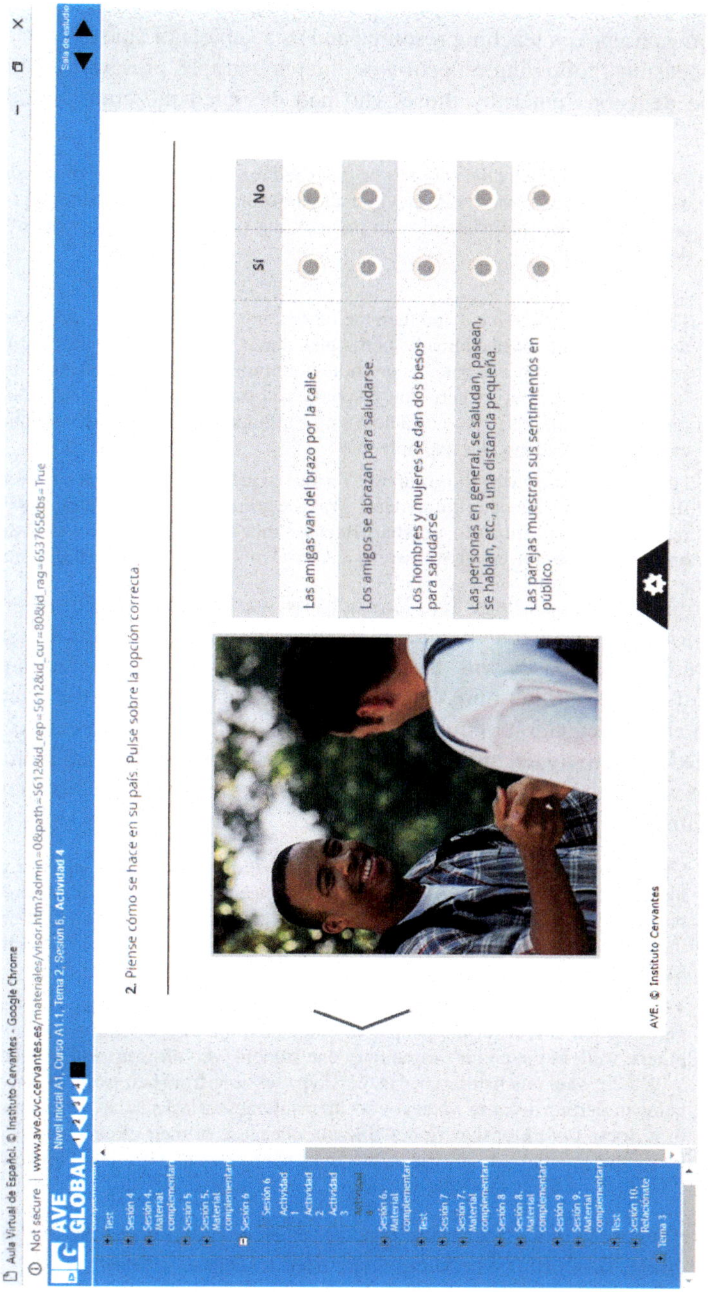

Image 8.4   AVE Global A1.1 course activity used in a photo-elicitation session

its use in the photo-elicitation session gave the image a new narrative and a renewed meaning (Pink, 2007). No longer simply a personal family photograph, the image acquired new meanings as a teaching resource and as a subject of study.

On other occasions, following reflection on the photographs presented, the tutor questioned the decisions made by those who had designed the courses and the platform:

Tutor	No, I don't know why the people who designed the materials used these particular generalities. Where did they get this information? Why did they put it there? What was their intention in transmitting this kind of...information? I don't know...
	[...]
Researcher	That was on the one hand and then the other... my idea behind this screenshot was a little what we had already mentioned, that it's perhaps a very interesting activity to open up a debate, to promote communication and interaction, but in fact it's an activity where you respond, you make a somewhat individual reflection, and that's it, isn't it? There's no continuity or you can't see what has enriched the students, for example.
Tutor	I don't really know why the group was formed, you know? If then you have very little interaction between the students. Was the group created for administrative reasons, for a question of... or what? Because they could be one-to-one classes and one-to-one conversation sessions... And it wouldn't make much difference.

The conversation concerned Image 8.4. This activity was aimed at exploring socio-cultural behaviours, but through individual work without offering students the opportunity to share their responses with their peers and thus promote interaction and knowledge of the other. Furthermore, the material was addressed from the stance of generalisation and the equation of culture with national culture. As we can see, the tutor questioned the activity design and the intentions of the authors when including this content, as well as the very organisation of the students into groups. This question resurfaced again later:

Researcher	Of course, maybe when carrying out the activities, it's like you say, you go through them, you go... everyone at their own pace, right? There's a schedule, but we all know that in the end we do what we can in the time available, and the times when I really got to know the others, the other students, was in the Skype sessions.
Tutor	Yes, basically... [...] also, your group was one of the best in terms of forum participation and of, of the people who attended the Skype sessions because others, well, in the end it's often only one student who turns up and so, like I said, there's not much difference in the Skype sessions from being one-to-one to being in a group because when you set them interaction tasks... they're reluctant or it doesn't work or they're not able uh... because of their circumstances or their work, right, to do it. And in the end I have to wrap it up, I end up doing it for them in the next Skype session.

Concerns therefore arose that affected her practice as an online tutor of these courses, and faced with these concerns or problems, she tried to find solutions:

Tutor	For example, it would be great if when you were taking the screenshots, the forum or a chat room was open to one side, right, because that's where queries arise and

> you could have that interaction. Of course it wouldn't be in real time because it isn't always the same students or the same tutors who are connected, but it would be much more dynamic and easier to respond to. Or, for example, like now, that the Skype session or other types of platform were integrated within the platform.

In this case, the discussion concerned the third image, corresponding to the study room, and the fact that students spent most of their time in the materials section, which hosts the course activities. Faced with the problem of the lack of interaction between students and between students and teachers, a solution was proposed; however, its implementation did not depend on the tutor, as it would involve changing the design and functionalities of the online platform.

This analysis shows that the images served as a catalyst to access the theories or beliefs that mediated the tutor's decision-making (e.g. in the discussion generated around Image 8.1), to question approaches or the design of materials (as in the case of Image 8.4) or to work on finding solutions to previously identified problems (as in the example of Image 8.3). Although preliminary, the results to date seem to be in agreement with those reported in other, similar studies (Bautista et al., 2018; Bautista et al., 2016) where photo-elicitation was used in face-to-face in-service training for teachers.

By Way of an Epilogue

Returning to the questions posed at the beginning of this chapter, I am now in a position to answer the first one in the affirmative. The benefits of photo-elicitation can indeed be transferred to virtual contexts, but as has been argued, and in relation to the second question, design and implementation of photo-elicitation sessions must take into account the particular characteristics of the context of image production and reception, as well as the research context. The person taking the images is necessarily limited to what happens on the screen, and his or her capacity for action is therefore reduced in terms of deciding aspects such as camera position. In fact, in the present case, the medium used to take the images was not a camera at all, but the Snipping tool that enables the user to select which part of the screen to capture.

Lastly, I asked in what ways photo-elicitation could be used in virtual in-service training for teachers. I wish to stress that there is no single way to implement photo-elicitation. Consequently, far from proposing rigid prescriptions or guidelines to be followed, I have posed a series of questions to be taken into account in the design of the sessions (for example, who should take the images, the order in which the participants should intervene in the discussion, or the type of device to be used to take the photographs) and I have reported my own experience, illustrating the flexibility of this technique and outlining the decisions the research team made in response to the situations that arose. I believe that beyond the results, the novelty of this chapter lies in the challenge, given the lack of previous experience in this area, of bringing photo-elicitation into the digital context. Therefore, I have provided various arguments intended to encourage the reader to embark on the exciting challenge of using photo-elicitation in virtual teaching and learning communities.

References

Banks, M. (2010). *Los datos visuales en investigación cualitativa*. Morata.

Barthes, R. (1989). *La cámara lúcida*. Paidós.

Bautista, A. (2017). La foto-elicitación en la formación permanente de maestros de educación primaria. *Alteridad, 12*(2), 202–214.

Bautista, A. et al. (2016). La foto-elicitación en la formación permanente del profesorado. Published in *Libro de actas CIMIE16 Educational Research with Social Impact*. http://amieedu.org/actasc imie16/.

Bautista, A., Rayón, L., & De las Heras, A. (2012). Valor de los registros audiovisuales en educación intercultural. *Comunicar, 39*(20), 169–176. https://doi.org/10.3916/C39-2012-03-07.

Bautista, A., Rayón, L., & De las Heras, A. (2018). Imágenes experienciales y foto-elicitación en la formación del profesorado. *Educatio Siglo XXI, 36*(2), 135–162.

Bautista, A., & Velasco, H. (Eds.). (2011). *Antropología Audiovisual: medios e investigación en educación*. Trotta.

Clark-Ibáñez, M. (2004). Framing the social world with photo-elicitation interviews. *American Behavioral Scientist, 47*(12), 1507–1527.

Correa, J. M. (2011). Antropología audiovisual y tecnología educativa. En A. Bautista García Vera, & H. Velasco Maillo (Coords.), *Antropología Audiovisual: medios e investigación en educación* (pp. 53–67). Trotta.

Elliott, J. (1997). *La investigación-acción en educación*. Morata.

Harper, D. (2002). Talking about pictures: A case for photo elicitation. *Visual Studies, 17*(1), 13–26.

Hine, C. (2004). *Etnografía virtual*. Editorial UOC.

Imbernón, F. (2007). *10 ideas clave. La formación permanente del profesorado: Nuevas ideas para formar en la innovación y el cambio*. Graó.

Marzal, J. (2015). *Cómo se lee una fotografía: Interpretaciones de la mirada*. Cátedra.

Motta, L. D. (2016). La imagen y su función didáctica en la educación artística. *Cuadernos del Centro de Estudios en Diseño y Comunicación. Ensayos, 56*, 1–10.

Pink, S. (2007). *Doing visual ethnography*. SAGE.

Rayón, L., & De las Heras, A. (2011). Etnografía, conocimiento y relaciones interculturales. In A. Bautista García Vera & H. Velasco Maillo (Eds.), *Antropología Audiovisual: medios e investigación en educación* (pp. 68–97). Trotta.

Rigo, D. Y. (2014, April). Aprender y enseñar a través de imágenes. Desafío Educativo. *ASRI: Arte y Sociedad. Revista de Investigación* [online], N°6. Retrieved from: http://asri.eumed.net/6/edu cacion-imagenes.html [3 January 2019].

Ruiz, B. (2017). *La foto-elicitación como procedimiento para el fomento del conocimiento del Otro/a y el aprendizaje de la segunda lengua. Estudio de caso con un grupo de adultos migrantes de la clase de español del CEPA Villaverde (Madrid)* (unpublished doctoral thesis), Universidad Complutense de Madrid, Madrid (Spain).

Schön, D. (1989). *La formación de profesionales reflexivos*. Paidós-MEC.

Segovia, J. (1997). *Investigación educativa y formación del profesorado*. Escuela española.

Vaillant, D., & Marcelo, C. (2015). *El ABC y D de la formación docente*. Narcea.

Part III
Photographic Storytelling in Teacher Training

Chapter 9
A Brief Story About Stories

Javier Mariscal Ariza

Introduction

Ever since the dawn of humanity, our existence has been sustained by the air we breathe, the food we eat and the stories we tell ourselves. The transmission of information has been fundamental for the evolution of our species, an evolution that has also transformed the use we make of our capacity for narrative. This capacity is evidenced from the cave art that can be found throughout the world, through all kinds of tribal songs, myths and legends, folk tales and rituals dedicated to a multitude of deities, to the current concept of creative communication via literature, painting, sculpture, music, radio and film. In the end, everything we create tells our story. Through an infinite variety of narrative customs and forms, we proclaim who we are, where we come from and, to a large extent, where we are going.

J. Mariscal Ariza (✉)
Los Barrios (Cádiz), Spain
e-mail: jmariscalariza@gmail.es

© The Author(s) 2023
A. Bautista García-Vera (ed.), *Photographic Elicitation and Narration in Teachers Education and Development*, Teacher Education, Learning Innovation and Accountability, https://doi.org/10.1007/978-3-031-20164-6_9

Megaloceros painted in Lascaux cave (public domain).

As social beings, we do not just narrate. In most cases, when we need and manage to communicate, we do so with the expectation of receiving a response. For better or worse, it is this ability to connect with each other that has brought us here. "I will tell men my life so that they will tell me who I am", wrote León Felipe in his poem *Who Am I?* Narrative is similar, a reciprocal exchange between individuals who need each other in order to be human, to know who they are and to continue to have something to say.

Narrative, then, could be defined as our ability to tell our version of something, to explain what it is like or how it happened. There are infinite forms of expression, just as there are countless things to tell. Hence the success of platforms such as WhatsApp, Facebook and Instagram, applications that enable us to tell all the world what we want, in the simplest way possible, with the aim of receiving direct and immediate interaction. We do this by means of texts, voice messages and, above all, videos and photographs, which in most cases we create using ever more affordable and accessible mobile devices. The sheer quantity of images that we take every day sometimes poses an obstacle between us and the true power of photographic narrative. From the instant we take a photograph until the moment we analyse what it tells us, we need to set it apart from the rest and endow it with a special meaning.

Beautiful photographs, such as those we see in fashion magazines, are not challenging. Instead, they tend to reinforce stereotypes and tell us things we already know. This approach to photography is harmless, but it does not represent who or what we really are.[1] We must nurture humanity's innate tendency to sift through reality and turn it into a story to be told, putting this capacity to good use so that it does not become diluted in the bewilderment of a host of images that we are unable to store safely or decipher in a meaningful or coherent manner. Having said that, the use of narrative in education and, more specifically, as a tool for teachers' in-service training, seems to me to be essential, primarily because of our natural fascination with

---

[1] Carrol (2015, p. 36).

photography as a tool for discovery, for storytelling, for growth and development, but also because of its potential for application in all kinds of educational, learning and research contexts. Narrative provides us with the means to know ourselves and to know others in an accessible, affordable and up-to-date way that also allows us to explore, know and connect with the world based on the questions and answers that the world asks us.

Photographer Toni Frissell, sitting, holding a camera on her lap, with several children standing around her, somewhere in Europe in 1945 (public domain).

The Photographic Narrative

Photographs have been used as a tool for communication, especially in the press and advertising, since the nineteenth century, but documentary photography did not come into its own until the 1930s and the advent of new, easy to use cameras that provided sharp, quality images for newspapers and magazines. Photography's success was due to its capacity to connect with the disillusioned public of the inter-war period. For readers, photographic narrative became the most reliable and credible way of reading the news. The more and better the images printed on paper, the more convincing and exciting the stories appeared. This credibility is no longer the main reason for today's massive exchange of photographs and videos, which are now easily manipulated, but nevertheless images have retained the capacity to depict and to a large extent explain reality.

The attraction exerted by photographs is based on the classic narrative formula, the essence of the art of storytelling. From classical Greece to the present day, anyone who has tried to make effective use of narrative knows that engaging the audience's attention is essential. This is why the film industry pays millions of dollars for some scripts but discards most of them: some stories use narrative tension successfully, but others do not. The three-act structure can be simply summarised as introduction, plot and denouement. Some say it is carved into our DNA.[2] Throughout what follows, I shall discuss how to tell stories better through photography.

Photography as a Response

Humanity's delight in stories stems from our ability to question things and our need to obtain an answer to each of these questions. The classic three-act narrative structure gratifies our inherent compulsion to decipher the world, endowing it with a clear and creative order by providing answers. This is why most stories start by introducing the characters and contextualising the plot, which is simply answering the questions of where the story happens and who forms part of what is being told. Then, as the plot unfolds, all sorts of questions might arise, which may be answered, or not, in various ways until reaching the denouement. The closer stories adhere to this basic structure, the better they work.[3]

Photographic narrative can be used to ask and answer questions, and images can be used to tell our version of something. Since the golden age of photojournalism (1930–1950), photographic narrative has been used as a dialogue between various photographs, transforming an unspecified number of images into a photo essay. There is no other goal, because photographic narrative speaks of the capacity to tell a story through several photographs. What is really important is to determine how these relate to each other in our story and what role we give to each of them.

Therefore, we must know what types of image we can create in order to answer the questions we want to ask, via different stories told through photographs. We can experiment with ordering them in different ways, explore the world globally or concentrate on details, portray the people around us showing, according to our vision, who they are, and portray ourselves so that we know, according to their vision, who we are. We can use photographs to reflect, make decisions, talk about tolerance, inclusion and equality, concentrate and evade. Images can be used to describe tasks, explain the history of spaces and, in short, creatively decipher the world.

---

[2] Freeman (2010, p. 12).
[3] Freeman (2010, p. 13).

Narrative Structures

Since time immemorial, humanity has studied the best way to tell a story. From Aristotle to any present-day YouTuber, all of us who at some point have had something to tell and have tried to tell it have encountered the enormous quantity of options that exist to explain, narrate or convince our audience.

Later on, I shall write about visual variety and the need we have as documentary photographers to answer diverse questions through different types of image, because not all images answer these questions in the same way. We can choose between a portrait or a detail, we can select a general shot to explain where we are before showing a decisive moment, or we can simply choose not to do so. To compose our stories, we photographers show our intentions, make decisions and make good our shortcomings, because in most cases, when we start to structure a report, we become aware that we must put together a puzzle without having all the pieces.

Hence, it is crucial to understand reportage as a global concept rather than a random collection of photographs. The simplest thing would be to compose our visual stories using the classic narrative structure. To facilitate understanding, the three-act structure can be summarised as an introduction, development to the decisive moment and closure. Documentary photographers use this magic formula that we all understand to better explain their vision, and this is perhaps the most feasible way of working on a photo essay.

Examining our own work and that of our colleagues helps us to identify what we are doing well and also to pinpoint our weaknesses. Perhaps the best way to put our reports in context is to realise that we did not take a general shot to explain where our essay takes place, right after we printed our photographs and showed them to others. This would help us understand that we will take better portraits if we get close enough; that we have to provide ample detail to obtain unique stories, especially if we do so by examining our own work when deciding whether we are good portraitists or if in the end we have captured the detail we originally aspired to do. We must learn from our mistakes in order to implement this training process in the narration of teachers' diaries and life stories, for our personal and professional development and as a communication tool applied to education, research and knowledge.

Narrative in the Photo Gallery

When a project is completed, the next logical step is give it physical form so that it can be shown to and shared with the rest of the world.[4] Interesting work, which always provokes a multitude of debates and reflections, spurs us to print our images and examine them from different points of view, moving away from formal work based on the classic narrative structure. Once we have printed several images from our respective photo galleries, we could share them with others to try together to

---

[4] Vázquez (2017, p. 205).

structure them and seek different ways to reach different narratives. The various possible options include ordering them chronologically or by type, theme, colour or location, furthering our intention to recount something understandable, or not. It is possible to analyse the power of photographic narrative to tell several stories from the same photographs. Images by various photographers may be combined to seek a coherent discourse or a random structure may be used to understand that, beyond their different uses or combinations, photographs always end up narrating something.

In the photographic tradition, the portfolio is viewed as a collection of images that identify its creator, from different points of view, through the deliberate selection and organisation of his or her work to communicate an artistic discourse. Nowadays, due to the vast number of photographs we take, our mobile devices, social media sites and multiple applications related to photography organise our images using folder structures that we can order according to different parameters, such as the date they were taken, the place where they were taken or the people who appear in them. Thus, the analysis and study of a photo gallery can be considered a contemporary concept in photographic discourse, through the selection and reorganisation of our files with the deliberate intention of telling a story better, or by printing some of the photographs to give our photographic discourse physical form in a medium that is easier to touch, share and rearrange.

Photo galleries are a reflection of the photographer who takes them whether we view them on a computer screen in their original state or in a gallery following a complex workflow. Similarly, when a reporter takes photographs at an event, without doing anything to his or her portfolios the very order of events marks an identity, a vision, a battery of decisions that tell something through the photographs that were taken and those that were not. However, there is no doubt that when we examine our photographs, when we order them and seek coherence, when we work on our own narrative and visual harmony, this is when we are our best as photographers and tell our best stories.

We can work on the dimensions of our images, zooming in or out from whatever we considered interesting when taking the photographs. We can take pictures as if we were explorers, capturing small details and highlighting them for our audience. We can introduce ourselves into our stories while taking our photographs and gaining the trust of our subjects, interacting with them, without forgetting that we must analyse them with perspective and observe them from outside, through our general shots, in order to understand where we are and who they are, just before showing them in powerful and startling images, or offering a conclusion faithful to our message with images that invite reflection and convey our idea of the world to our audience.

This method, this intention that the photographer pursues to deploy the power of photographic narrative consistently, marks the difference between a predictable and harmless portfolio and a gallery brimming with possibilities. It is crucial to plan before taking photographs in order to obtain a collection of images that enable you to relate your vision of something and to do so as a professional would.

Narrative in the Photo-Book

Recent years have witnessed growing interest in photo-books as a form of artistic or documentary expression for both amateur and professional photographers alike. Fairs and congresses abound where all kinds of publishers exhibit their new works in paper format, and growing numbers of authors are turning to desktop publishing thanks to affordable print-on-demand prices and the increasing sophistication and affordability of digital printers. However, the photo-book is a complex medium. Its visual unit is the double spread, and the sequence of double spreads is what endows the story in images with its narrative and dynamic flow. From a photographic point of view, knowing that the final product will be made up of a series of images brings with it new demands but also probably relieves the pressure of having to capture a single photograph that summarises an entire event.[5]

Although this chapter is not the place to delve into the exciting world of graphic publishing and editorial design, I nevertheless believe it is helpful to analyse the different options for combining photographs in a double spread or for unfolding our stories over the course of a book. Such information may serve as a starting point for editing a publication containing the photographic narrative projects that the present book is intended to encourage. First, we must subtly transform our vision as photographers into that of graphic editors of our own work, in order to analyse our photographs simply on the basis of the use we wish to make of them in our publishing project, rather than as works in themselves.

For a graphic editor, there are four options for using images in a double spread in a book. The first is to use a single image, however we like, for the double spread, to give it pride of place and dwell on its meaning. Alternatively, we can consider juxtaposition or pairing, which is the art of combining two images to establish a tension between them, in most cases seeking a simple and logical relationship: two people looking at each other, or near-far, before-after or portrait-detail contrasts. We can also seek contrast through dimension, deciding whether to make the photographs larger or smaller in our design, or by studying how they are related in the narrative, based on colour, composition or their emotional, aesthetic and artistic qualities.

Sequencing is used to create movement and rhythm by placing different images that recount the performance of a task, usually taking great care to achieve coherence in the composition and the point of view and thus convey an appropriate sensation of intensity and rhythm, as Eadweard Muybridge did with the subjects of his studies that we shall examine later. The mosaic, the last possible combination of our images in a double spread, presents a collection of small photographs arranged in a block. In this case, the effect of the whole is more important than that of the individual images.[6]

It is important to remember that the aim of the graphic editor is to create a connection between the reader and the work through the turning of pages and the relationship between the different double spreads. It is essential to create a rhythm and tension

---

[5] Freeman (2008, p. 180).

[6] Freeman (2010, p. 147).

between our images throughout the book if the publishing project is to be consistent, and we must accept the idea that our publications must be entertaining while at the same time being offered in a logical and coherent way to our audience.

A good way to create this tension is to structure our images in the planning stage, providing a balanced visual variety until the photographic narrative achieves the desired coherence and abounds with patterns that render it easy to read and understand. For example, we might impose an order on the presentation of our stories through our different double spreads, first presenting a general shot and then juxtaposing a portrait and a detail that, through their pairing, speak to us about who the subject is and how he or she feels. On the next page, we might include a sequence in which the subject performs a task that defines him or her, and conclude with a mosaic in which we make a more or less extensive selection of the theme, perhaps supported by a text in which we explain who the author of the photographs is and what process was used to create the story, until we obtain a coherent vision of something concrete. If we follow this same method, or any other, throughout the book, we will have created a template, which is the best tool that graphic editors have to achieve coherence in their publications.

Visual Variety

Photographs are something of a talisman, a treasure. The ease with which we can create images today using all kinds of devices has diluted the previously exceptional nature of the process of using a camera to explain the world by capturing a moment in time and preserving it forever in an archive. This moment may be a memory, a place, a person or a feeling. Everything can be used by photographic language to order the complexity of all that passes through our minds every day. The photographer Richard Misrach once said that "beauty can be a very powerful conveyor of difficult ideas" because it "engages people when they might otherwise look away".[7] Thus, we talk about photography, and we talk with photographs. Let's see how.

The editors of magazines such as Picture Post, Paris Match, Sports Illustrated and LIFE achieved unprecedented commercial success in photojournalism through their photo essays, which they used to improve their reporting on a wide range of subjects. For each new commission, they sent their photographers what has become known as a technical script, which the photographers used as a guide on what photographs to take to support the stories the journalists wished to write. They discovered that the dialogue between photographs was more powerful and constructive the greater the balance between certain types of image. This formula for creating good photographic stories through visual variety has prevailed to this day and continues to be the best way to use photographic narrative.

---

[7] Carrol (2018, p. 39).

The Technical Script

Photographic narrative works with the inherent communicative power of images alone, above all when they are combined effectively. Images can be classified according to type, and we can use this classification as a guide to make good use of this power. However, before listing the types, I would like to propose a game that can serve as a tool to encourage better storytelling through photographs, using the concept of the technical script in a comprehensible manner in teachers' in-service education and in subsequent application to teaching, research or any area of knowledge and communication.

Real stories are a good starting point for encouraging people to talk about their photographs. Choosing a subject and explaining it in words is the easiest way to begin composing photo essays, because no work really speaks for itself. Humans want to know where things come from, how they were made and by whom. The stories you tell about your work have an enormous influence on how people respond, how they feel about it and what they understand about it, and what people feel and understand about your work affects their appreciation of it.[8]

In my workshops for professional photographers, I encourage my students to tell me their photo essays as if they were a story. I ask them to tell me these stories in words. They can tell me any story they have ever told, or intend to tell through their photographs in the future. Once they have verbally answered the most relevant questions about their photo story, I invite them to substitute each sentence with an image and so on until reaching the end of the essay. In this way, the technical script is written organically, learning from the processes established by the documentary photographer when selecting the photographs that best tell his or her photographic stories. The technical script, therefore, is a kind of wish list specifying the images that the photographer believes his or her story needs. Some are very general and others are very specific, and it is best to use the script as a working document that can be modified during the process.[9]

The use of photographic narrative in training scenarios and of this simple game around the concept of technical script elicits many suitable topics. We may start the proposed essays on our own, introspectively, or in conjunction with a colleague. However, explaining who we are may perhaps be a more complex task than explaining who the people around us are, where they live, how they relate and what their routines or spaces are, using words to describe their reality, their life and their world, selecting a series of photographs that speak of that reality, translating that life into visual images and explaining that world with photographs.

The objective is none other than to continuously answer all the questions we may ask ourselves through a balanced combination of the kinds of images that I shall list below, which we may work on separately or in relation to each other, using this method as a process in continuous evolution, as a resource, as a game, to nurture our creativity and in no case to limit it.

---

[8] Kleon (2016, p. 93).

[9] Freeman (2010, p. 106).

The General Shot

General shots can be used to open our reports, as an introduction to our essay and as an answer to where our story takes place. In this case, the sense of place and the narrative go hand in hand. We are talking about a definition of the medium as a formula for research and reflection on time, history and space. The fleeting nature inherent in the evolution of spaces connects with the idea of human intervention in the world and our relationship with everything around us.

Ansel Adams. The Tetons—Snake River, Grand Teton National Park, Wyoming, in 1942 (public domain).

General landscape shots require an active commitment on the part of the viewer,[10] who can analyse the image in general and then investigate connections between the different elements in the photograph, go into detail and highlight them as outstanding features.

In photographs of spaces, however, the relationship between humans and the space portrayed acquires greater importance, because the latter's architectural motifs, textures and capacity to evolve all speak of those who built and inhabited it,[11] of how the different elements in the image determine personality and meaning, analysing types of behaviour or activities and delving into concepts such as volume and form, presence and absence, or memory and the passage of time.

---

[10] Lowe (2017, p. 44).

[11] Lowe (2017, p. 70).

Walker Evans. General store interior. Moundville, Alabama. Summer 1936 (public domain).

We could focus on the relationship we all have with places, on our capacity to intervene in them and turn them into something different, and on how these in turn have the power to suggest different emotions through context and use. We could start with our own professional spaces, in each of their corners, and then go outside and study what can be seen through a classroom window or on our way home, or we could start by analysing the places we walk through every day without paying too much attention to detail.

For years, I have been studying the evolution of spaces over time, taking the same picture in the same places at different times of the day and on different days. General shots have this capacity for suggestion. Landscapes or photographs of different spaces based on the multitude of elements of which they are composed always bring surprises thanks to the capacity of photographic narrative to connect us with the world and to evolve with it.

Close-Ups and Interaction

With close-ups and interaction, we reveal what is going on by focusing on a group or an activity and using our lens to seek people interacting. This process is nurtured by our research capacity and our ability to capture the relationship between various people, with the same intention as the documentary photographer. We could investigate social, cultural or political trends, or focus on their aesthetic or ethnographic nature by taking a spontaneous photograph of a purely chance moment.

Dorothea Lange. Migrant agricultural worker's family. Seven hungry children. Mother aged thirty-two. Father is native Californian. Nipomo, California. February or March 1936 (public domain).

For years, Dorothea Lange answered questions about "Migrant Mother", her most popular photograph, and about the close-up process that led her to portray a starving woman accompanied by two of her children with breathtaking naturalness. She always answered with patience and honesty about what her job as a reporter entailed, saying that often, it was sufficient just to stay in one place, instead of walking in and out in a cloud of dust; it was enough to sit on the floor with people and let their children touch her camera with their grubby little hands and put their fingers on the lens. She allowed them to do this because she knew that if she behaved with generosity, the world was likely to be generous in return.[12]

Close-up photography, then, makes more sense when a balance is found between the photographer's invisibility and his or her approach to the subject matter, which can be gradual and treated as a method for finding a connection with the people photographed. The goal is to portray them using the power of naturalness, without altering their nature or psychology, amplifying their documentary value and the spirit of the image as a representation of reality. This echoes the analysis presented in Chap. 6 on the importance of the participant in rituals who takes the photograph or photographs, the content of which is subject to assessment. Thus, close-ups also allow us to position ourselves within our stories, to analyse our role as photographers and to gain the trust of the people around us before trying to photograph them naturally, or hoping that they will allow us to take a portrait that really defines them, just as the migrant mother and her starving children did in Nipomo, California, in February 1936, when Dorothea Lange took her famous portrait of them.

---

[12] Walther (1992, p. 21).

Dorothea Lange—Destitute pea pickers in California. Mother of seven children (migrant mother). Age thirty-two. Nipomo, California, February 1936 (public domain).

The photographic narrative speaks of a photograph's capacity to connect with its viewer, and it can be interesting to analyse how a spontaneous image of different people interacting draws us into a private, almost intimate space, or how an unimportant moment can become a document that invites us to reflect and debate. We might even explore how can we turn that spontaneous moment into a sequence over time, accompanying the people who interacted in the hope that that first image could become the beginning of the subsequent performance of a task, keeping ever-present our documentary intention and the narrative value we can transmit to our photographs by presenting the ordinary in an extraordinary way.[13]

Sequences or Micro-Stories

Sequences or micro-stories explain the performance of a task through several photographs, and are used in photojournalism reports to provide movement and rhythm. This continuity relates a sequence of images, allowing the photographic narrative to recount how something happened from start to finish, or with a documentary intent to provide all the necessary information for the viewer to perceive our stories and draw his or her own conclusions, because an image contains an internal story based on its interaction with others. Just as a historian, the photographer takes these fragmentary testimonies and works with them to build a story or argument.[14]

We could begin our analysis of temporality with simple tasks, reducing the photographic narrative to very easy to understand communicative games. We could use a photograph taken earlier which connects with another that we have yet to take, or we could create stories based on the juxtaposition of two images, for example, an image of a teacher listening and another of students talking. As in cinema, the combination

---

[13] Walther (1992, p. 21).
[14] Lowe (2017, p. 209).

of shot and countershot is used to give rhythm and depth to such basic activities as a simple conversation.

From this analysis of the performance of small tasks, we can redirect our sequences to the investigation of more complex essays. However, it might be advisable to start by telling small micro-stories through two, three, four or five images, building up gradually, so that in the very process of narrating we can analyse the concept of quantity, ellipsis and movement. Since its inception, photography has investigated how objects move from an aesthetic and organic point of view, as in the studies by Eadweard Muybridge, one of the great precursors of cinematography.[15] Taking different pictures of a horse while it gallops, for example, can lead us to a surprisingly large number of narrative works related to the illusion of movement, ordering and disordering the images to reveal how the sequences can be altered by modifying the way we visualise them, and how this intervention can in turn alter the way the animal moves.

Eadweard Muybridge. Animal locomotion—16 frames of racehorse "Annie G." galloping Philadelphia, 1887 (public domain).

We could also write a short script with different events, similar to a scene, to begin to explore our ability to create sequences that speak of our lives. Even the evolution of spaces and their relationship with the passage of time could be revisited based on sequences that speak of how these places change according to time, light or context.

Decisive Moment

Images of a decisive moment tell a story in themselves, recounting a fleeting moment and an emotion that brings the essence of our story together in a single photograph.

---

[15] IBI, p. 163.

Here, the choice of moment is everything and relies on the photographer's ability to capture it just before it sinks beneath the flow of events, to rescue it from oblivion and the passage of time.[16] An example would be Robert Capa's famous photograph taken during the Spanish Civil War at the precise moment when Federico Borrel fell to the ground after being hit by the bullet that killed him.

Robert Capa. The falling soldier. 5 September 1936 (public domain).

Professional photographers have always shown great interest in images of this type because they create such a strong impression on the audience, who view them as if they were treasures, like jewels that illuminate us with their brightness and open the door to a world full of mystery and information. They form part of the visual diary of our lives, because historically they have been chosen above all others for the front pages of newspapers, for gallery exhibitions or to hang in our homes. It should be added that such exceptional photographs of a decisive moment are nearly always the result of chance. Recall that the precise moment when Robert Capa took "The falling soldier" was a decisive moment that brought us closer to the devastating experience of men and war, but the small events that happen every day in the street, in school corridors or in the intimacy of any educational event can be equally decisive.

A photograph of my son blowing out the candles on his first birthday cake is therefore a decisive moment. However, it could be argued that photography's unique capacity to portray great moments in history is being devalued by technology in our information society. Mobile devices enable us to blithely take vast numbers of photographs at all times in any circumstances, to accumulate them without selection and to share them massively and immediately without any consciousness of the use of the image as a memory or an object in itself, based on the decisive choice of some images over others, of their printing on paper, of their protection as an element that

---

[16] Meyerowitz (2018, p. 8).

belongs to us and that speaks to us about who we are, accompanying us over the years to give an account of the passing of time and thus preserve our memory.

Thousands of photographs and videos are taken every day without awareness of the photographic act or of the concept of the lived moment. This massive audiovisual consumption is changing our capacity to connect with an image and for that image to tell us things. Consequently, it might be interesting to address the concept of the decisive moment before trying to immortalise such moments in a photograph. We could try highlighting some events over others, analysing this concept from a playful point of view, taking real or imaginary photographs at the precise moment when something happens, photographing patiently, perhaps waiting for days for a singular or exceptional moment that can be preserved thanks to photography, or perhaps avoiding taking that precise photograph so as not to distance ourselves from the moment and be able to rescue it from oblivion simply by having formed part of it. It might be interesting to debate photographs of singular moments we have experienced in the classroom that we did not manage to take, prioritising the transcendent, fleeting moment over the representation that we could have created with a camera.

Detail and Close-Ups

Detail and close-ups help us to highlight elements that provide unique information that more closely reflects what we want to tell. Humanity's attraction to detail is echoed throughout the history of art in the artistic reproduction of a multitude of objects and still lifes. With the birth of photography, this urge to define ourselves by depicting the material objects surrounding us continued. By detailing the material world, we reveal the greatness of the smallest things.

NASA. One of the first steps taken on the Moon, this is an image of Buzz Aldrin's bootprint from the Apollo 11 mission. Neil Armstrong and Buzz Aldrin walked on the Moon on July 20, 1969 (public domain).

The documentary photographer uses this attraction to define the global through the concrete by conducting an exercise in exploration that might begin in our workplace, attempting to create everyday descriptions of the space as a general vessel containing a multitude of small things. First we look, next we explore and then, through our photographs, we direct the viewer's attention to something that would otherwise be ignored, transforming an ordinary artefact into a metaphor or a symbol of something more important.[17]

We can also become aware of photography as a thing in and of itself. We can print different images and then photograph them, or play at retrieving photographs from our family albums to discuss and reflect on the romantic and emotional nature of photography as a valuable act that preserves our past unchanged.

Exploring our belongings as traits of our personalities can also become an exciting task. In examining our belongings as objects that define us, the photographic narrative raises their status from unnoticed elements to things that contain emotional and psychological meaning, endowing the object photographed with the qualities of the person who possesses it.[18]

The logical evolution of the previous activity is to portray different people through their belongings in order to connect the viewer and subject through an object that defines the latter, just as we define John Lennon through his glasses or Charlie Chaplin through his cane and bowler hat.

Portrait and Personalisation

Throughout history, the human face has proved the best window on the subject's identity and the essence of his or her being. Through portraits and personalisation, we obtain spontaneous or posed images of who our subjects are, images that also depict what they look like and how they feel.

The photographer Philippe Halsman became famous for his portraits of political, cultural and entertainment personalities in the act of jumping. He believed that a good photographer was like a psychologist who knew how to extract the truth from a patient. We could begin our dynamics with this same intention, gradually getting closer to spontaneous, natural, more intimate portraits. In order to reveal something about the subject, it is sometimes necessary to maintain control while gaining his or her trust. If we invite subjects to do something fun like jump, doodle or hold their breath, we take their mind off the photographic act, helping to develop a relationship.[19]

---

[17] Lowe (2017, p. 92).

[18] Lowe (2017, p. 93).

[19] Carrol (2015, p. 62).

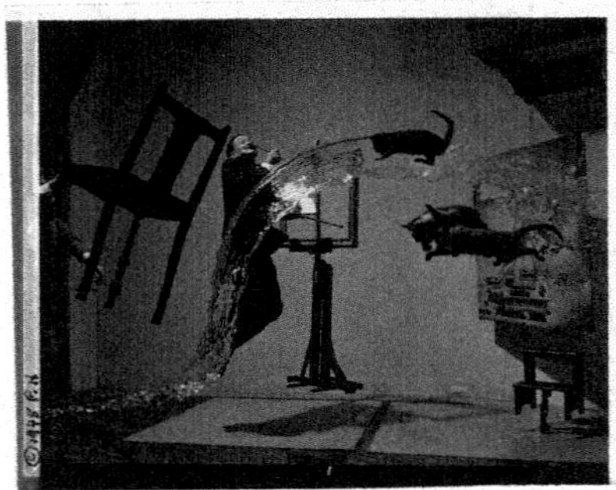

Philippe Halsman. Portrait photograph of Salvador Dali, including objects, cats, and water caught in motion. The photo is similar to Halsman's published photo "Dali Atomicus" before retouching. 1948 (public domain).

The standard portrait, which focuses on the face and physiognomy, tends to highlight some features over others, emphasising the features that establish greater psychological or emotional connection between the viewer and the subject portrayed. The correct use of light is crucial if we want our portraits to reflect what we wish to say about the people we photograph: to isolate them from the world, to portray them in their context or to embellish or dramatise our image. Light is never neutral and always has psychological implications.[20]

The approach that leads to the most telling image of the person portrayed entails observation of their most characteristic details. There are various ways to achieve this. We could take our photograph in front of a window or at a distance from direct light, using the flash or not to control the intensity of our message; we could place our subject in front of a neutral background to detach the person from his or her space, or we could place the subject in a particular place so that his or her world, face and body define it. However, we must never forget that, beyond a study of lines and forms, the portrait forms part of our intention to tell who we are from an emotional, cultural, ethnographic, historical, political or socio-economic point of view. Good portraitists reveal the people around them, exploring and defining them until obtaining a photograph that represents their vision and opinion of their subjects. They are not concerned with taking flattering photographs but with showing the world, and even the subjects themselves, who they really are.

---

[20] Carrol (2015, p. 107).

NASA. On June 3, 1965, Edward H. White II became the first American to step outside his spacecraft and let go, effectively setting himself adrift in the zero gravity of space. For 23 min White floated and manoeuvred himself around the Gemini spacecraft while logging 6,500 miles during his orbital stroll. White was attached to the spacecraft by a 25 foot umbilical line and a 23 foot tether line, both wrapped in gold tape to form one cord. In his right hand, White carries a Hand Held Self Manoeuvring Unit, which is used to move about the weightless environment of space. The visor of his helmet is gold plated to protect him from the unfiltered rays of the sun.

Closing Photographs

Closing photographs are images that serve to conclude our story. They represent a final reflection, a coda, that either supports our message or suggests a contradiction. Within a documentary report, and even more so when published, the closing photograph is usually the last message we transmit to the viewer. Photographers must underscore their narrative intention just before their readers draw their final conclusions.

Throughout "Country Doctor", his famous report for LIFE, W. Eugene Smith presents a rural doctor in relation to his environment and his patients. The report begins with a dark and threatening photograph in which Dr. Ernest Ceriani is walking in a rural setting with black clouds in the background. The photo essay locates him in the midst of frenetic activity in order to depict his demanding, exhausting work. Smith achieves this through numerous images in which Ceriani can be seen in a multitude of spaces attending to all kinds of emergencies and responsibilities. As a hopeful conclusion, the final double spread shows several luminous photographs of the village where Ceriani works, and he too is depicted, exhausted and pensive, with a cup of coffee in his hands, in a place that could well be an operating theatre. Thus, in closing his report on a family doctor, W. Eugene Smith turns the doctor into a modern surgeon. Moreover, his notes for the opening photograph showing the doctor crossing a field contain the instruction to use the darkest ones at the beginning and gradually include the lightest ones later,[21] underlining his clear intention to explain Ceriani's stressful life through the importance of people like him for the development and progress of the most disadvantaged areas.

Thus, closing photographs represent our final chance to show our vision of the world, our discourse on how we understand the things we see and how we believe they should be conveyed to the viewer. It is not so much a surgical quest for truth, but rather a commitment to endow our own way of thinking with authenticity. We can take certain liberties when formulating our stories, since documentary photography is not a precise record of reality, but rather an interpretation of what happens, on which we stamp our own vision and connect with others through agreement or discrepancy. For the professional photographer, this is what the photographic narrative is all about: a path that invites us to make our voices heard. Photographers are always on the lookout for a new photograph that will say something about us. If we go through life wanting to find something to say, sooner or later, we will find it.

The aim is none other than to continually answer all the questions that we may ask ourselves, through a balanced combination of the types of image I have just analysed. We could work on these photographs separately or by relating them to each other, employing the dynamics presented or many others that may arise and that we should attempt if we are to view photography as a journey of experimentation within teachers' in-service training, constantly working on the development of our photo galleries, or printing our photographs so that we can handle them, or creating a photobook that we can show as a reminder of our efforts and our voices as creators, as educators, as people. The photographic narrative must be viewed as part of a process in constant evolution, as a living resource, as an interactive dynamic, to which we turn to nurture —but never to limit— our creativity, to take photographs without fear of making mistakes, without limits, to connect with the world in the conviction that the more things teachers can tell through photography, the better they will become as teachers.

---

[21] Freeman (2010, p. 50).

Dorothea Lange. Toward Los Angeles, California. March 1937 (public domain).

References

Carrol, H. (2015). *Lea este libro si desea fotografiar buenos retratos*. BLUME.
Carrol, H. (2018). *Los fotógrafos hablan sobre fotografía*. BLUME.
Freeman, M. (2008). *El ojo del fotógrafo*. BLUME.
Freeman, M. (2010). *La narración fotográfica*. BLUME.
Kleon, A. (2016). *Aprende a promocionar tu trabajo*. Gustavo Gili.
Lowe, P. (2017). *Maestros de la fotografía*. Gustavo Gili.
Meyerowitz, J. (2018). *¡Mirar!* Gustavo Gili.
Vázquez, R. I. (2017). *El proyecto fotográfico personal*. JdeJ editores.
Walther, P. (1992). *New deal photography USA 1935–1943*. TASCHEN.

Chapter 10
Multimodal Photo-Narration in Initial Teacher Training

Laura Rayón Rumayor and Ana María de las Heras Cuenca

Introduction

If we aspire to a school system that succeeds in its mission to guarantee the right to education and attention to diversity of whatever origin, then we must develop creative, emancipatory approaches in initial teacher training. Trainee teachers must be able to act reflectively and critically against inequalities in order to later build democracy in the classroom. A school system that is fairer, more inclusive and equitable in the transmission of knowledge, that guarantees student learning and participation regardless of personal circumstances and/or characteristics, requires committed teachers who are capable of assuming this responsibility in any educational stage. The methods and strategies used in initial teacher training must be aimed at instilling knowledge that emancipates teachers and empowers them to do the same in turn. If instead such training is based on purely academic goals, interests and strategies aimed at the mechanical reproduction of knowledge, it will contribute to a bias in initial teacher training and the potential failure of the school system. Far from being neutral practices, training strategies can be the means to reproduce an educational model based on segregation and professional practices that are insensitive to inequality. Pérez Gómez (1997, p. 297) suggests an attractive alternative:

> Teachers must engage in the adventure of knowledge, research and critical and reflective inquiry if they wish to instil a love of knowledge and respect for diversity and creativity in the younger generation; they must love democracy and commit themselves to meeting its

L. Rayón Rumayor (✉) · A. M. de las Heras Cuenca
Complutense University, Madrid, Spain
e-mail: larayon@ucm.es

A. M. de las Heras Cuenca
e-mail: delasheras@edu.ucm.es

A. Bautista García-Vera (ed.), *Photographic Elicitation and Narration in Teachers Education and Development*, Teacher Education, Learning Innovation and Accountability, https://doi.org/10.1007/978-3-031-20164-6_10

demand for mutual understanding if they wish to create a climate of supportive relationships and construct a democratic community of learning. To engage in critical culture is to love, propagate and enjoy it as much as it is to apply and recreate it in each discipline, in each problem, in each impression, in each project.

Implementing a part of this alternative in initial teacher training requires two things; one is to promote what Bartolomé (1994) calls "political clarity", the process whereby we identify the possible connections between political, economic and social variables (macro-level) and the academic behaviour of groups in the classroom (micro-level). The second is to foster what she calls "ideological clarity", the process whereby we identify and compare our own explanations with those of the dominant discourses (Bartolomé, 2008). This enables us to understand how our value systems do or do not reflect dominant values, and consequently, how we may be legitimising practices that perpetuate inequality and exclusion.

Students know about today's society, but their understanding of it is fragmented. The implications of certain socio-cultural dynamics for the school system are largely invisible to them. They inhabit local contexts, in a here-and-now in which they experience change and are involved in projects and social relations that are simultaneously localised and de-localised. However, they do so uncritically. They encounter serious difficulties in understanding their experiences in relation to the dynamics of the socio-historical times in which they are living.

Another important issue is that some trainee teachers will not have the same cultural, linguistic and social references as a large part of the student body with whom they will work on a daily basis (Zumwalt & Craig, 2005). Nowadays, the school system comprises a diverse space in which teachers' teaching practice unfortunately reproduces the way they themselves were taught. Trainee teachers must learn how to connect with and intervene in an increasingly wide diversity of cultural, sexual and social identities.

We need aware teachers capable of identifying their beliefs and experiences, of subjecting them to contrasting perspectives and of understanding the contradictory and flawed practices and dynamics that define cultural, economic, work and social life. Only an intelligible and coherent account of the defining features of current society and the resulting changes will enable us to understand education as a series of transformative actions based on equity, social justice, inclusion and the participation of all students. There is no curricular tradition of this in initial teacher training, but nevertheless we must strive to train intellectually and culturally competent teachers so that they can construct more inclusive practices and exercise critical thinking in relation to the established dictates.

If trainee teachers can identify their beliefs about society, analyse how people and differences are embedded in unequal contexts and share, contrast and reconstruct these beliefs, then they will be in a better position to move forwards and assimilate the most inclusive and fairest forms of representation and action with regard to difference in an autonomous, conscious and committed manner.

What practices can we construct that will enable students to identify and above all understand the complexity of the mechanisms of exclusion and rethink their beliefs in order to successfully face the challenges of an inclusive and intercultural education?

How can we create contexts of activity in which trainee teachers can work together to inquire into their particular visions and interpretations of social reality and analyse the educational implications of these?

These challenges and questions serve as an introduction to the subject matter of the present chapter, which explores the use of visual narrative in initial teacher training using photographs. We shall discuss previous studies on the use of photo-narration in different fields of knowledge, paying particular attention to research in education and above all on the use of photography in higher education. We shall then analyse the practical and procedural aspects of employing a photo-narration approach, drawing on several years of practical experience of using this tool in initial teacher training. Our work was the result of a teaching innovation project funded by the Vice-Chancellor's Office for Teaching in the 2016 Call for the promotion of innovation in teaching and learning processes (reference UAH/EV737), entitled "The city as an artistic and pedagogical representation through multimodal narratives" and directed by Laura Rayón.

In this chapter, we analyse how we can use photo-narration in our professional practice to generate varied narrative modalities that together allow us to shape a voice intended to be shared and recreated, as means to enable students to explore reality, endow it with meaning and examine their own views and biases with their peers, while at the same time introducing other ways of thinking and intervening in the school system. The narrative practices that we have explored in initial teacher training revolve around community artistic practices and the concept of "drifting" or wandering in a physical environment. The notion of collaboration in narrative creation and the combined use of photography and elements of visual culture form the backbone of multimodal photo-narration. First, we examine taking photographs individually by students, who once they have specified their reasons and motives for taking a photograph, share the content with their peers through the procedure of photo-elicitation in the classroom. Then, they create a multimodal visual narrative through consensus. We discuss the value of this strategy based on the results obtained, and the possibilities of using this type of narrative to enable trainee teachers to learn to interpret the socio-cultural reality around them and identify unequal and unfair practices.

Photo-Narration and Personal and Social Transformation

Narratives based on photographs taken by participants is a procedure that was initially used in social science research (Banks, 2001; Mannay, 2017; Rose, 2001), but which has now permeated other fields such as health, diagnosis and therapy (Han & Oliffe, 2016; Knowles & Cole, 2008). Narrative supported by photography is considered an exceptional means to access human experiences (Harper, 2012). A photographed act, situation or event can be shared, in the form of a story, by means of photo-elicitation. This method has already been described in detail in the second part of this book, but briefly, the person who took the photograph shows the image and explains his or her reasons for taking it, and others request further information about details in the image or ask the photographer to expand on the meanings it contains. Photography thus becomes a means to generate stories about people's motives, needs and beliefs, paving the way for personal transformation. This approach is used in the fields of health and psychotherapy in order for participants, either individually or in groups, to reflect on their experiences around a variety of topics, such as tobacco addiction, grief for a loved one or mental illness.

Interestingly, these fields emphasise how an event becomes an experience when it is formulated as a story for oneself and/or others, where the narration becomes an act and a new experience which in turn generates new stories. Manrique (2017) has termed this the narrative-experience-action cycle, and it forms the basis for personal transformation. Rodríguez and Manrique (2015) have suggested that film, and by extension other visual languages, can be used in this way in education. They argue that what we consider experience requires a process whereby the person becomes aware through reflection of what is happening in a given moment in space and time. Thus, they claim that narrative using visual languages such as photography and film enables individuals to construct stories in the present about specific moments or situations, and that the subsequent description and interpretation of these stories evokes the past in a reflective and conscious way, enriching the lived experience which is necessarily projected into the future in a different form.

In the field of education, the use of photo-narration has been explored in English-speaking countries by, among others, Lemon (2006), Bach (1998), Leitch and Mitchell (2007) and Thomson (2008). Of particular note is Moss's work on narration using photographs and other visual media to promote the educational inclusion of diverse students (Moss, 2003, 2010, 2011; Moss et al., 2007). Other authors such as Carrington et al. (2007) have analysed how audiovisual narratives enhance the development of an inclusive curriculum and an educational environment that prevents the social exclusion of the most disadvantaged students. The evident desire for change in relationships and improved coexistence locates the use of audiovisual narratives in these works in the principles of equity and social justice that define a democratic education.

In Spain, the work initiated by Bautista (2009, 2011, 2013, 2017) is of particular note. He discusses the potential of narrative using the language of photography to promote understanding of others and the events surrounding the group that is narrating. More specifically, Bautista identifies photo-narration as the basis for an intercultural education in which, through the process of narration, group members, students or families propose stories, discuss opinions about the visual elements to be used, agree on the narrative structure of the photo essay and, above all, are given opportunities to get to know each other and understand their differences, and therefore, begin to appreciate one another.

All these studies evidence the importance of the concept of narrative inquiry, which is based on the idea that an experience can be considered a story, and as such, can be told and shared through the process of photo-elicitation. However, the ultimate goal of narrative inquiry in these studies is social—not just personal—transformation. The value placed on the narrative process itself as a means to promote dialogue, debate and the exchange of opinions between members of culturally diverse groups stems from its capacity to foster mutual understanding between participants. Beyond personal development, narrative inquiry is viewed as a process of participation and exchange between people intended to enhance understanding of other points of view, promote mutual comprehension and improve relations between diverse students experiencing inequality in the school system.

Similar approaches have prompted Bautista (2017) to propose the use of photo-narration in teachers' in-service training. Photography is a means to promote reflection on and knowledge of personal theories and beliefs by questioning teachers about what they do and the decisions they make in their teaching practice based on images of their classrooms taken with a camera. Thus, through inquiry and subsequent reflection, images can be used to transform and improve actions in the classroom (Bautista et al., 2018). Ketelle (2010) has also used photo-narration for teachers' in-service training, working with eight head teachers to investigate the demands that school leadership and management place on teachers. Her goal was to understand the role that each of them played, determine how they perceived themselves professionally and personally and establish a dialogue between them that gave them access to different points of view and enabled them to compare their beliefs in order to improve their work as teachers.

Photography, Narration and Learning

In her interesting study aimed at understanding the learning experience in higher education using photography, Stroud (2014, p. 99) described learning through the combined use of images and narrative, emphasising that photography facilitates access to the internal aspect of learning, which is otherwise difficult for university researchers and teachers to penetrate. Cooper et al. (2017) have used photography as a tool to promote experiential learning and critical dialogue among participants in an undergraduate community health course. Ciolan and Malasian (2017) have employed visual representations with university students to identify learning styles, using photographs to explore the processes of construction and metacognition. In their study, students took photographs and then shared their meaning, generating conversations about how learning occurs and what students think about what and how they are learning.

Another area of research aimed at improving instruction is reported in the studies by Bailey and Van Harken (2014), Christensen (2012), Cook and Buck (2010), Edwards et al. (2012), Leipert and Anderson (2012), Lichty (2013) and Zenkov and Harmon (2009). All of these were aimed at understanding how photography can enhance academic performance by using it to detect errors in learning, thus accessing students' individual interpretations of the products of their learning. Copperman et al. (2007) used photography in a similar manner to investigate the learning process when students attempted to learn a new concept or solve a problem. Other studies on initial teacher training have been oriented towards the use of resources that support the creation of stories (Sadik, 2008), but focusing more on the design of digital applications and environments than on using narration to encourage the exchange of ideas, beliefs and opinions.

Previous research has paid little attention to the function of photography as a representational practice for telling stories in a creative communicative process (Mannay, 2017). However, research is lacking on the use of photography to generate a symbolic space of intersubjectivity through the construction of stories that can be shared in order to promote student participation in university classrooms, in particular in initial teacher training.

As we have seen in the first section of this chapter, cameras can help trainee teachers to express themselves through images as channels for stories and to locate their personal beliefs about and visions of socio-cultural reality in relation to the mechanisms of inequality and its correlates in education. Photo-narration can thus be used to extend and enrich their professional identity. Britzman (2003) has contended that this identity is shaped by individual biographies of family, community, lived learning experiences and social relations, arguing that objects of knowledge are largely absent from teacher training practices. We believe that storytelling supported by photography would permit a transition towards an initial teacher training connected to students' experiences and particular ways of seeing and interpreting reality.

Moss et al. (2007) have suggested that photo-narration disrupts the unidirectional communication dynamics that characterise academic learning in the classroom because it allows students to talk about subjects that concern and affect them. This represents an interesting approach to explore in teacher training. These authors contend that narrative supported by photographs facilitates access to students' individual conditions and circumstances without dissociating them from the environment and the casuistry that condition their lives, and consequently promotes understanding of their lived situations. Photo-narration enables students to learn, reflect and grow from their experiences, and invites change because images can be read and re-read over time, giving them new meanings in a process of semiotic transformation (Leitch, 2008; Lemon, 2006).

Photograph, Narrate and Share: Constructing Other Discourses and Experiences

The course plan developed over the years for students taking teaching degrees at the University of Alcalá is based on a series of values such as creativity and participation, and university classrooms are conceived as a community that shares subjective experiences and interpretations of socio-cultural and educational reality. The medium, photo-narration, focuses on the following aspects:

- Placing cameras in the students' hands for them to give physical form to their experience and create images that provide interpretative references. By means of photo-elicitation, these references become visible and can be contrasted, expanded and elaborated.

- By combining visual images and narration, photography provides new knowledge about how students see reality, whose gazes become socially constructed knowledge.
- Images and narration forge diverse stories which take different forms for communication and sharing.

The use of photo-narration presented here formed part of a project based on two types of process with different approaches to story production. In one, a story was shared verbally through photo-elicitation, and inquiry emerged in response to the students' photographs, while in the other, a story or narration emerged through the creation of a collage mural. However, both approaches employed photo-elicitation as the basis for narrative inquiry, albeit on different levels and in different ways. Below, we describe our work with initial teacher training students in terms of organisation, space, time and procedure.

Wandering, Taking Photographs and Composing Narratives Through a Collage Mural

This project was implemented from October to December 2015 with 17 students, in a workshop called *Transigrafías* ["transigraphs"], a term coined by Albalá (2018) to conceptualise a process of participative work involving collaborative exchange in urban spaces with the aim of exploring, documenting, interpreting and representing journeys through the act of walking and taking photographs. Participants were asked to construct a story based on the photographs taken, which they could combine with written language, drawing or any other object and/or element related to visual and digital culture. Three groups were formed to carry out the following procedure and tasks:

- Prior planning on a map of the route to be taken through the city of Alcalá de Henares. After consulting maps of the city, students planned the routes they would take, indicating the main routes to take (Fig. 10.1) on a given day. They were advised to walk quietly, to observe and to capture moments or situations that attracted their attention. No limits were placed on the number of photographs they could take, nor were any specific themes defined that they should stop and observe or on which they should focus their attention. Each member of the group was instructed to photograph whatever caught their attention that they considered significant, to be shared subsequently with the other members of their group.
- Next, the photographs were printed and brought to class for the groups to analyse, seeking and sharing the meanings supported by the images. At this point, they had to identify a thematic thread with which to construct a visual story that illustrated a problem or situation to be explained, which was then analysed and questioned

by the other groups. The questions "What have we photographed and why?", "What are the meanings of the photographs taken?" and "Why is this photograph important to me?" formed the starting point for students to begin identifying an agreed upon theme that could be narrated in an individual voice. Students exercised full control over which photographs to (Figs. 10.1 and 10.2).

- Representing: by this stage, the students had already defined the theme and content of the story; now, they had to decide how to represent their narrative, using photographs and any other form of representation, written text or visual elements

Fig. 10.1 The narrative creation process (1)

Fig. 10.2 The narrative creation process (2)

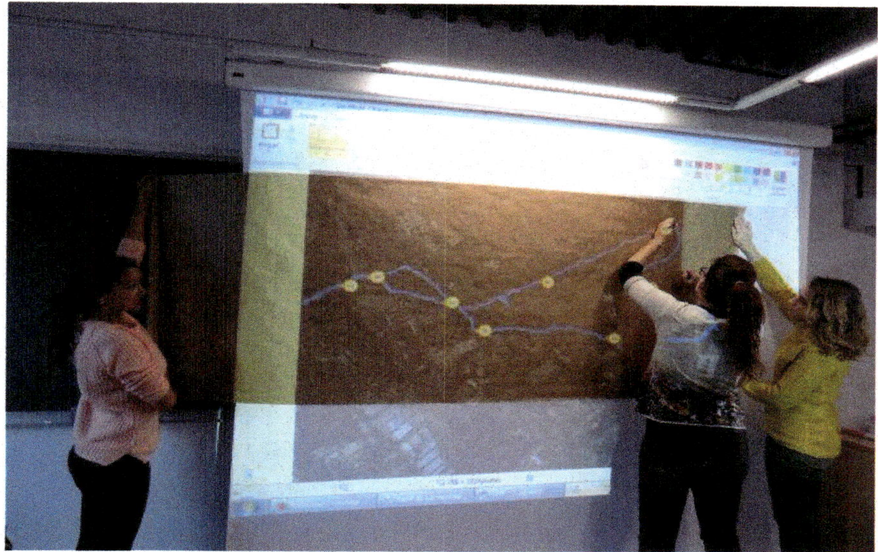

Fig. 10.3 The narrative creation process (3)

they considered appropriate. This was a creative process in which they exercised full control over the physical form of the composition (Figs. 10.3, 10.4 and 10.5).
- Their visual narrations gave rise to a space for representation or a multimodal story: *inequality as a construction of access according to social origin* (Fig. 10.6); *the city centre and periphery* (Fig. 10.7); and *diversity as inequality in different spaces and manifestations* (Fig. 10.8), using photographs, drawings, written text and handcrafted objects to compose stories in a collage mural that covered the walls of the faculty.

Breaking the Frame

As evidenced by the students' productions, visual narratives based on students' photographs support subjectivation and the construction of complex meanings. The transformation of tangible images into visually and conceptually dense narratives formed the basis of the narrative inquiry carried out by groups. This enabled them to move towards a story shaped by a collective voice, albeit not without uncertainty and intensity in the analyses and debates generated in the classroom.

Inquiry into the meanings associated with the photographs taken and their value as regards contributing to a story that was meaningful and relevant for the students formed a powerful cognitive and social process. Photography as an instrument for collecting moments of experience in the city, and as a means for subsequent evocation in the classroom in the photo-elicitation stage, gave rise to participatory knowledge

Fig. 10.4 The narrative creation process (4)

Fig. 10.5 The narrative creation process (5)

Fig. 10.6 Inequality as a construction of access according to social origin

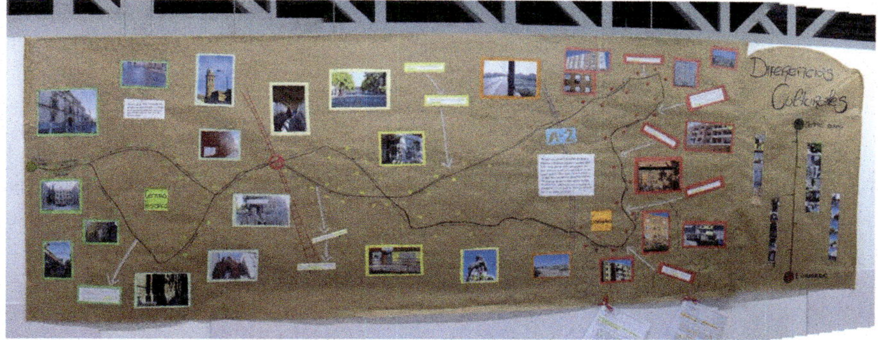

Fig. 10.7 The city centre and periphery

construction, but was not without its difficulties. This stage was characterised by the complexity of constructing a consensual story, and although rich in evocations of the meanings supported by the photographs, it would have been even more enriching if the participants had been provided with a card for each photograph on which to note a title for the photograph, a description of it and the reasons for their choice, as proposed by Moriña (2017) when starting to work with photographs created by participants.

An initial process of semiotic construction was defined in accordance with Leitch (2008, p. 2), who has contended that by themselves, photographs do not narrate. Rather, it is the meaning attributed to them and the voice behind the photograph that allow memories to emerge, evoke the place and the moment and bring the

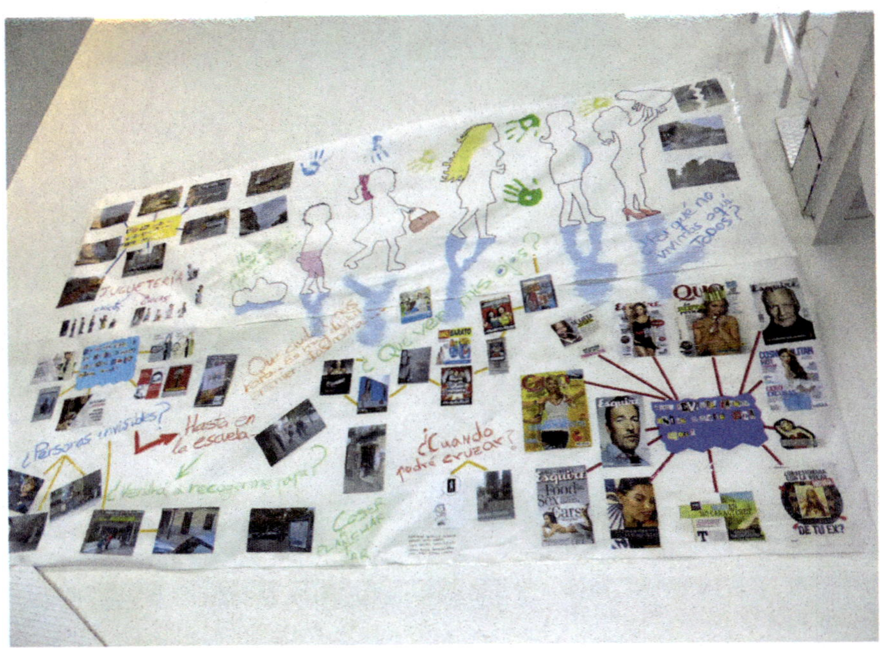

Fig. 10.8 Diversity as inequality in different spaces and manifestations

photographs back to life. Each photograph evoked visible references to the experiential image participants had in the city, and this generated an initial semiotic process of constructing oral stories. Each photograph functioned as a discursive unit. Next, they were placed in relation to other visual references, other photographs, in order to construct the lived experience by assembling a final group of images (Fig. 10.1). These two semiotic construction processes formed the basis for a third stage when the photographs were ordered, sequenced and arranged on the mural (Fig. 10.4), giving rise to a third level of construction of meanings that led participants to place the photographs in relation to other elements of visual culture, written text, drawings or magazine images. The processes of narrative inquiry have an analogy in Russian dolls, the *matryoshka* dolls, in which each doll encases another. In this case, the photograph as discursive unit was the matrix for moving towards a sequence of photographs that defined a thematic and/or temporal order of still images. From there, the story or narration was completed by relating the sequence of images to other systems of representation and to images constructed by others for other purposes (Fig. 10.9).

This process generated multimodal stories based on the sequence and arrangement of the photographs and images, which were not left to chance because they defined a conceptual narrative order. Thus, as can be seen in the first and second multimodal narratives (Figs. 10.6 and 10.7), the students constructed narratives by contrast or antithesis, to create a social representation of inequality according to social class, in the case of the first narrative, and in the second, a representation of the segmented

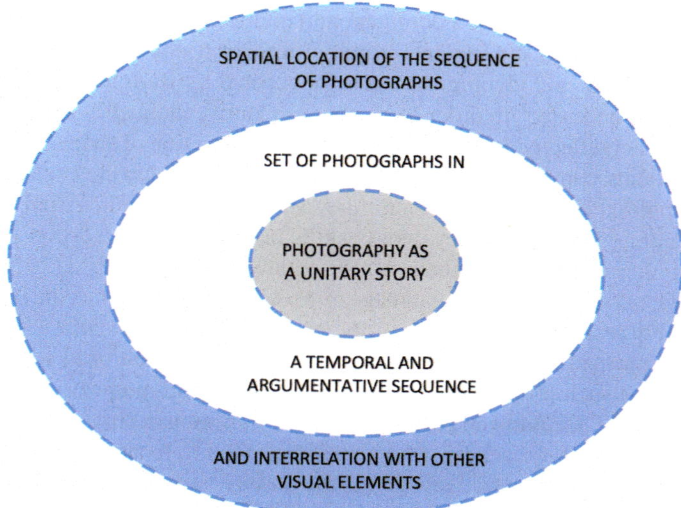

Fig. 10.9 By the authors

urban space formed by the World Heritage city and the city on the outskirts, consisting of working class neighbourhoods and new housing developments.

In the third narrative (Fig. 10.8), this stage was defined by more complex and diverse semiotic processes. By means of discursive units consisting of a sequence of photographs complemented with drawings and magazine images, the participants created micro-stories, in the sense defined in the previous chapter, that all showed diversity as inequality, although gender inequality prevailed as the central theme. In this series of micro-stories, inequality was conceptualised through different ideas and socio-cultural manifestations. Synecdoche and antithesis were intertwined in the visual representations, giving rise to a semiotically multidimensional narrative comprising the experiential image, the photographs and magazine pictures. As with the other two productions, drawing reinforced the organisation and discursive sequences that defined each micro-story.

In this respect, it is worth noting that the photo-narration constructed by assembling various photographs and combining them with other visual elements enriched the conceptualisation and argumentation of the story thus constructed. We consider that this method of using photography in training is richer than if photo-narration had been based on a simple verbal description of the reasons or motives for taking a particular photograph or series of photographs. Identifying, sequencing and arranging photographs as a photo essay is an act of creation in which other elements of visual culture may intervene, giving rise to more complex and richer processes of construction of meanings. Placing photo-narration at the service of multimodal production generates what Butler (2009, p. 12) has termed breaking the frame, in other words questioning a reality that is taken for granted, exposing the resources and discourses used to maintain and legitimise a dominant and interested vision of that reality. This is an essential condition for students in initial teacher training if they are to move towards the political and ideological clarity advocated by Bartolomé (1994, 2008), which in turn is necessary in order to be able to identify inequality and injustice in schools and to act reflectively and critically in the construction of an inclusive school.

When students control the process of creating photographs, they select subjects to photograph that are relevant to them, they shape their voice in visual narratives freely and autonomously and they deploy skills in order to see, question and depict reality through imaginative productions. We believe that, as Bautista (2011, p. 119) has indicated, narration using the language of photography diversifies the intellectual and social options and opportunities of the people narrating, because "audiovisual languages in particular encourage participation when they are used to tell stories collectively (…) such production includes the need for communicative actions that lead to agreement". Defining and delivering photo-narration in university classrooms presents a challenge for teachers, who sometimes need to locate themselves on the margins in order to define practices such as the one we have described and discussed here. However, we should also point out that such processes convert academic spaces into places for the transformation of teaching and learning and the creation and communication of messages based on multimodal literacy processes. In the words of Emilio Lledó: "Orality is the present; while we speak we share a common time, which embraces us".

References

Albalá, C. (2018). *Transigrafías*. https://www.carlosalbala.com/transigrafias/

Bach, H. (1998). *A visual narrative concerning girls, curriculum, photography etc.* QUAL Institute Press.

Bailey, N. M., & Van Harken, E. M. (2014). Visual images as tools of teacher inquiry. *Journal of Teacher Education, 65*, 241–260.

Banks, M. (2001). *Visual methods in social research*. Sage.

Bartolomé, L. I. (1994). Beyond the methods fetish: Toward a humanizing pedagogy. *Harvard Educational Review, 64*(2), 173–194. https://doi.org/10.17763/haer.64.2.58q5m5744t325730

Bartolomé, L. I. (2008). La pedagogía crítica y la educación de los profesores y profesoras: radicalización del profesorado futuro. In Pedagógia crítica: de qué hablamos, dónde estamos (pp. 357–390). Graó.

Bautista, A. (2009). Relaciones interculturales en educación mediadas por narraciones audiovisuales. *Comunicar, 33*, 149–156.

Bautista, A. (2011). Miradas de la antropología audiovisual al estudio de las funciones de las herramientas simbólicas y materiales en educación intercultural. In H. Velasco Maillo & A. Bautista García-Vera (Eds.), *Antropología audiovisual: medios e investigación en educación* (pp. 112–136). Trotta.

Bautista, A. (2013). Indagación Narrativa visual en la práctica educativa. *Educación y Futuro, 29*, 69–79.

Bautista, A. (2017). La foto-elicitación en la formación permanente de maestros de educación primaria. *Alteridad, 12*(2), 202–214. https://doi.org/10.17163/alt.v12n2.2017.06

Bautista, A., Rayón, L., & de las Heras, A. (2018). Imágenes experienciales y foto-elicitación en la formación del profesorado. *Educatio Siglo XXI, 36*(2), 135–162. https://doi.org/10.6018/j/333001

Britzman, D. P. (2003). *Practice makes practice: A critical study of learning to teach.* State University of New York Press.

Butler, J. (2009). *Frames of war: When is life grievable?* Verso.

Carrington, S., Allen, K., & Osmolowski, D. (2007). Visual narrative: A technique to enhance secondary students' contribution to the development of inclusive socially just school environments-lessons from a box of crayons. *Journal of Research in Special Educational Needs, 7*(1), 8–15.

Ciolan, L., & Malasian, L. (2017). Reframing photovoice to boost its potential for learning research. *International Journal of Qualitative Methods, 16*, 1–15.

Cook, K., & Buck, G. (2010). Photovoice: A community-based socioscientific pedagogical tool. *Science Scope, 33*, 35–39.

Cooper, C. H., Sorensen, W., & Yarbrough, S. (2017). Visualising the health of communities: Using photovoice as a pedagogical tool in the college classroom. *Health Educational Journal, 76*(4), 454–466.

Copperman, E., Beeri, C., & Ben-Zvi, N. (2007). Visual modelling of learning processes. *Innovations in Education and Teaching International, 44*, 257–272.

Christensen, J. (2012). Utilizing photovoice as a method to elicit self-reflection in adolescents with developmental disabilities. *Journal of Intellectual Disability Research, 56*, 810–822.

Edwards, M., Perry, B., Janzen, K., & Menzies, C. (2012). Using the artistic pedagogical technology of photovoice to promote interaction in the online post-secondary classroom: The students' perspective. *Electronic Journal of e-Learning, 10*, 32–43.

Han, C. S., & Oliffe, J. L. (2016). Photovoice in mental illness research: A review and recommendations. *Health, 20*(2), 110–126. https://doi.org/10.1177/1363459314567790

Harper, D. (2012). *Visual sociology.* Routledge.

Ketelle, D. (2010). The ground they walk on: Photography and narrative inquiry. *The Qualitative Report, 15*(3), 535–568. https://nsuworks.nova.edu/tqr/vol15/iss3

Knowles, J. G., & Cole, A. L. (2008). *Handbook of the arts in qualitative research: Perspectives, methodologies, examples, and issues.* Sage.

Leipert, B., & Anderson, E. (2012). Rural nursing education: A photovoice perspective. *Rural and Remote Health, 12.* https://www.ncbi.nlm.nih.gov/pubmed/22668083

Leitch, R. (2008). Creatively researching children's narrative through images and drawings. In P. Thompson (Ed.), *Doing visual research with children and young people* (pp. 37–58). Routledge.

Leitch, R., & Mitchell, S. (2007). Caged birds and cloning machines: How student imagery "speaks" to us about cultures of schooling. *Improving Schools, 10*(1), 53–71.

Lemon, N. (2006). *Using visual narratives for reflection.* AARE Conference. http://www.aare.edu.au/06pap/lem06537.

Lichty, L. F. (2013). Photovoice as a pedagogical tool in the community psychology classroom. *Journal of Prevention and Intervention in the Community, 41*, 89–96. https://doi.org/10.1080/10852352.2013.757984

Mannay, D. (2017). *Métodos visuales narrativos y creativos en investigación cualitativa.* Narcea.

Manrique, R. (2017). *Subjetividad en construcción.* Paidós.

Moriña, A. (2017). *Investigación con historias de vida. Metodología Biográfico-Narrativa.* Narcea.

Moss, J. (2003). Picture this: Visual narrative as a source for understanding diversity in our classrooms. *Festival against racism in education.* University of Melbourne.

Moss, J. (2010). Visual methods: The exposure of exclusion and inclusion. In R. Hampe (Ed.), *Multimodalität in den künstlerischen therapien* (pp. 359–370). Frank & Timme.

Moss, J. (2011). Understanding visual and intertextual approaches in pedagogical and curriculum research: A pretext. *International Journal of Inclusive Education, 15*(4), 379–388.

Moss, J., Deppeler, J., Astley, L., & Pattinson, K. (2007). Student researchers in the middle: Using visual images to make sense of inclusive education. *Journal of Research in Special Education Needs, 7*(1), 46–54.

Pérez Gómez, A. I. (1997). *La cultura escolar en la sociedad neoliberal.* Morata.

Rodríguez, C., & Manrique, R. (2015). Perturbando mentes: El cine como herramienta de transformación persona. *Revista Interuniversitaria De Formación Del Profesorado, 29*(1), 109–118.

Rose, G. (2001). *Visual methodologies.* Sage.

Sadik, A. (2008). Digital storytelling: A meaningful technology-integrated approach for engaged student learning. *Education Tech Research Development, 56,* 487–506. https://doi.org/10.1007/s11423-008-9091-8

Stroud, M. (2014). Photovoice as a pedagogical tool: Student engagement in undergraduate introductory chemistry for nonscience majors. *Journal of College Science Teaching, 43,* 98–107.

Thomson, P. (2008). Children and young people. Voices in visual research. In P. Thomson (Ed.), *Doing visual research with children and young people* (pp. 1–20). Routledge. Taylor & Francis Group.

Zenkov, K., & Harmon, J. (2009). Picturing a writing process: Photovoice and teaching writing to urban youth. *Journal of Adolescent and Adult Literacy, 52,* 575–584.

Zumwalt, K., & Craig, E. (2005). Teachers' characteristics: Research on the demographic profile. In M. Cochran-Smith & K. M. Zeichner (Eds.), *Studying teacher education: The report of the AERA panel on research and teacher education* (pp. 111–156). Erlbaum.

Chapter 11
Modes of Photo-Narration by Teachers and Their Effect on Inquiry into Teaching Practice

Joaquín Paredes Labra

Introduction

One of the many ways of examining the relationship between theory and practice in teacher training is inquiry. To inquire is to investigate, generally something that concerns or refers to oneself, one's beliefs, theories, attitudes, values and emotions, and to reflect on how all this informs one's work as a teacher. Inquiry into educational practice therefore entails a multidimensional review of what can generally be called school practices, a mixture of introspection, collaboration, critical thinking and political will to transform the school system (Gutiérrez Cuenca et al., 2009).

Inquiry is often articulated in dense stories told by the teachers themselves. Such stories can be constructed in various languages, including the language of photography. In the field of teacher training, the idea of "mental image" has been used to refer to beliefs (e.g. Clandinin & Connelly, 1988). Below, we shall see how images are involved in each of the components of inquiry.

Inquiry is, first and foremost, introspection, insofar as it establishes connections with the trainee or practising teacher's past as a student when reflecting (Schön, 1998). Sources may include life stories, photographs and recordings of work in the classroom, students' visual diaries, critical incidents in the classroom, teaching experiences and accounts of projects undertaken. Retrieval of autobiographical events enables teachers to examine their preconceptions, to render explicit processes of socialisation and to explore the main building blocks of their identity, critical incidents in their life story, how their demands and expectations have changed and the factors that have influenced their attitudes towards life and the future. Diaries, and public writing in general, are highly useful tools for narrative inquiry. As discussed

J. Paredes Labra (✉)
Autonomous University, Madrid, Spain
e-mail: Joaquin.paredes@uam.es

A. Bautista García-Vera (ed.), *Photographic Elicitation and Narration in Teachers Education and Development*, Teacher Education, Learning Innovation and Accountability, https://doi.org/10.1007/978-3-031-20164-6_11

in the previous chapter, diaries can be constructed not only with words, but also with images.

A second aspect is collaboration (Lieberman & Miller, 2003), which seeks to establish connections with the practices of other professionals with whom to understand and address situations that require transformation in the school. By sharing them, images can be used to forge these connections, and their ambiguity facilitates a margin for consideration by others and dialogue about their evocative content.

A third element is critical thinking about social relations within the school, which have been termed the school grammar (Tyack & Tobin, 1994). This grammar dictates the way things seem to work "naturally" in schools and at some point becomes the organisational or cultural norm, but it can be revised. Particularly in an exercise of memory, images can reveal the fact that schools repeat past organisational formulas or reproduce mass production spaces, which can prompt teachers to consider other forms of organisation that exist in other schools or which their colleagues devise and implement in their classes.

The fourth and final aspect of inquiry is political will. According to Gutiérrez et al. (1998), the aim of educational inquiry is the transformation of schooling, because a profession dependent on the public sector is always subject to change, particularly since the anti-authoritarian movements of the 1960s and 1970s and technocratic reform. Change, moreover, is linked to the ethical nature of the teaching profession, which requires teachers to tailor their educational action to the values to instil in the classroom and achieve what in chapter six has been called educational coherence.

Inquiry has the virtue of provoking a mirror effect in the lives of those who read and analyse these stories (Liston & Zeichner, 1993; Gutiérrez Cuenca et al., 2009), prompting reactions that can lead to their transformation as teachers. Comparing situations and identifying consistencies or drastic changes can cue a reconsideration of what the images reflect. Questions arise that cause teachers to become aware of contradictions and resolve them by changing their theories, beliefs or teaching practices. Inquiry into practice has given rise to a new professional positioning, theoretical and practical knowledge and emotions (Bautista et al., 2018). The use of inquiry in teacher training has the potential to raise awareness of the importance of mental images and illuminate new educational positionings.

In various ways, photography can record and elicit evocations and resonances of what was intended or occurred in class. Therefore, as I shall show, images acquire enormous importance in the construction of inquiry by teachers. In this chapter, my aim is to identify ways in which inquiry emerges through photo-narration, raising trainee and practising teachers' awareness of their practices and generating transformation. I shall also assess how this can be implemented in teacher training.

Prior Technical Considerations

Continuing with the idea advanced in chapter nine concerning photo-narration as a dialogue between several images, it is worth recalling the fundamental role here of the principle or argument that serves as the connecting thread (Freeman, 2010). Now that it is so easy to take pictures with a mobile phone and nearly everybody has one, practically anyone can assemble spontaneous stories from their accumulated bank of photographs. These stories can be re-elaborated and reflected upon.

It should be noted that it is possible to convert these sequences into other audio-visual formats such as comics and videos, and that some narratives can give rise to others, adding specific features of these audiovisual genres. By incorporating these features, narratives acquire new expressive values. Whereas a single photograph captures a space limited by a frame, a photo montage widens the view of the observed spaces. The production of these stories forms part of the process of compiling experiences. The sequence in which ideas are ordered can be likened to a collection of slides. A sequence of images with lead-ins and speech bubbles can be presented as a comic, in analogue or digital format, using specific software.

To create a sequence that can be presented as a single unit, it is only necessary to save the pictures in the tool used for image organisation, which may be electronic presentation software, a video format or a video editor (already installed on many computers or easily downloaded), and then arrange the photographs. Accompanying soundtracks represent additional elements that can evoke an emotion (as has traditionally been the case with audiovisuals set to music), enrich the sequence, endow it with character and guide the plot generated through the production of these materials. Therefore, some aspects of audiovisual or cinematographic language are applicable to the production of photographic material arranged sequentially.

Audiovisuals Are Absent from Teacher Training

The language of cinema is generally a self-taught code which students may acquire in the private sphere, but among whom drawing in the margin of a notebook or book (40% of young people) is far more common than the practice of graffiti or image animation (between 3 and 10%) (Marcellán et al., 2013). Among students taking teaching degrees, the production and analysis of narratives is also infrequent, and is unfortunately associated with a lack of intercultural values (Medina & García-Morís, 2018). Furthermore, teacher training students rarely seem initially tempted to employ the language of cinema beyond their social groups and leisure activities.

For young people, audiovisual media are perhaps confined to the private sphere, in a mixture of seeking, self-affirmation, transgression and entertainment. The reasons for this exclusion are related to the dangers to digital identity arising from simple exposure, and addressing this should be an additional task for schools and teacher training colleges. Unfortunately, audiovisual media do not seem to form part of the stories authorised to students in teacher training colleges, nor are they perceived as a channel for communication, first because of their difficulty and second because of their infrequency.

The production of audiovisual materials is thus transformed into a complex task for students (Fernández-Río, 2018). Audiovisual projects entail several stages, the successful completion of which requires expertise on the part of the group planning and executing them (Ezquerra et al., 2016). It might be added that teachers are not particularly prone to generating audiovisual productions or films. It is as if schools had no time to generate such complex stories and as if the multiplicity of meanings ran counter to teaching practice, which brings to mind the concern for form rather than meaning and the restricted language used by teachers of visible pedagogies according to Berstein (1990).

Students require guidance throughout the process, from the initial idea for a photo-narration, through the documentation required to reconstruct it, to discussion of what is relevant and the final montage or result. This helps them acquire the technical skills necessary to generate photo-narrations. In their analysis of what happens from conceptualisation to production of a photo-narration, Bautista et al. (2018) found that rhetorical figures played an important role, in particular metonymy and the meanings attributed to objects and lived situations. Montage is a second form of writing, adding narrative elements (Bolívar, in Gutiérrez Cuenca et al., 2009) that can be technical, moral, emotional or political.

Social media and the internet can also be leveraged in the production of audiovisual material. Stories can be shared in public spaces that identify communities of practice, which will be discussed later in this chapter. This entails new problems in working with students, such as the right to suppress images of children or the need to protect people's privacy, which is understandable but may become an obstacle given many people's reluctance to maintain a public professional profile on social media. Driven by fear of online harassment and lacking a strong digital culture, some people are unwilling to share anything on the internet that could identify them. This limits the existence of collective spaces for professional development. It is therefore useful to hold class discussions on the importance of the public processes undertaken, the precautions to take to render these compatible with digital identities and their future impact on students' personal and professional lives.

Improving participation in audiovisual culture will help bring school culture and external culture into step, with two important consequences for classroom methodology: a learning relationship between peers will be established and the boundaries between learning, production and distribution will vanish. Perhaps most importantly, images (which may be equivalent to the way we see the world) will not be imposed, but will be owned and shared with others.

Photo-Narration as an Inquiry Practice

Many educational projects conducted in class with teacher training students address some of the features of inquiry practices from an introspective, collaborative, critical and transformative perspective. Some do not include all of these perspectives, while others include new ones, such as the dimension of authorship inherent to production with technology; the pursuit of participation and horizontality in school relations, with shared languages that were previously alien to the educational institution; a new vision of the tools that connect subjects with knowledge; the role of the curriculum as a vehicle rather than an end in itself; or militancy in gender or community perspectives.

In view of the aforementioned barriers to expressing themselves though audiovisual media, for the majority of students their use implies a journey into the unknown, and therefore a journey of trial and error. For some students, several of the techniques may constitute new learning, while for others they might represent inquiry. Still other techniques will teach participation, transforming trainee teachers into authors. It is also possible to address some of the content and delivery of the curriculum itself by working with space and time. As stated in chapter one, a media-based education is fundamental to understanding digital identity (what it is, how to construct it, how to protect it) and the acquisition of sufficient digital media competence to feel comfortable about analysing one's own practice and having it analysed by the teaching communities generated.

Inquiry is the narrative process that leads to the possession of a vehicle for constructing knowledge and culture. In this respect, it is worth recalling the work of Freire and the illustrator Francisco Brenand on "The Favelas Project". As part of this project, in which the community used mobile phones to create images of daily life, Freire asked Brenand to generate a composition with ten images reflecting the life of agricultural workers, for Freire to use in his literacy work. He wanted images that made it clear, through a historical overview from pre-modern agriculture to the most up-to-date techniques, that this activity was the result of a context rather than being a natural state. The images were projected as slides in literacy sessions with the agricultural workers who were learning to read and write, and represented a cultural artefact that changed their lives as they recognised themselves through these media as authors and transformers of culture. Something similar can occur through the use of various techniques with images that speak of teaching practices, seeking to make their authors realise that these are constructed rather than natural, and that they can therefore be changed.

One should start by exploring emotional, creative and recreational proposals, and then introduce more rigorous inquiry procedures, although experience in managing projects in the classroom suggests that students require several pathways—not just one—to achieve any goal the trainer sets.

Types of Narrative for a Variety of Inquiries

The types of photo-narration presented in previous chapters have included portrait-self-portrait, reportage, essays, photo montage or collages, photo diaries or books and landscapes. I shall consider all of these.

Portraits attempt to capture the essence of people (what they are like, how they feel and how they see the world), and portraiture—for which photography is one possible medium—has a long history in the world of art. The value of a portrait is that it makes us stop and look at a person and consider who that individual is and what his or her aspirations and interests are. In education, this activity has been warmly welcomed as a means to humanise others, which can happen just by looking at the photographs on the student cards that teachers compile. There are portraits on the coat racks in infant schools and in end-of-year class photographs, reflecting the students' human, non-objectified nature. They can also be found in teachers' reports on the activities in which students have participated, attempting to reflect, from a close-up to a shot that captures body language, the actual emotion of each student portrayed.

In general, any photograph connected with a school's social and sporting activities can be considered a portrait. Such photographs are taken to preserve a memory of what happened and to promote a sense of belonging. They are testaments to what happened and can provide complementary information about what happens in a classroom or school. During teacher training, students may take portraits of their peers to investigate what they are like, what they feel, what concerns them, what surrounds them, what they perceive and what they expect, as the basis for subsequent dialogue in class. One can inquire into the stories behind the portraits. This can be done on the basis of what the photographer saw when taking the photograph, what the person in question perceived or what the trainee teachers perceive when analysing the images. Such photographs depict the life and teaching aspirations of trainee teachers.

This also entails using the language of stills through the resources of camera position, lighting and colour, reading them and introducing new feelings and emotions. At other times, cultures that have received insufficient attention could be championed by trainee or practising teachers, perhaps through depicting them as part of their own origins, or attempting to capture them purposely by taking the person portrayed in that context or dressing him or her in that way. A variant of this activity is to place oneself in the same spaces depicted in earlier photographs and to reflect on happens to memory, the transformations that have taken place and the present challenges that face the person who occupies this space from the past.

Thus, photographic portraits can form part of projects intended to reflect the aims of humanist photography as represented by photographers such as Henri Cartier Bresson, Robert Doisneau and Sebastião Salgado. These photographers have produced series of photographs with a social and political message. In the case of teachers who follow in their wake, they can reflect the students' diverse expressions and attitudes and the similarities between them that bring them together, as an analysis will confirm.

Similarly, leveraging the principle of juxtaposition discussed in chapter nine, teachers can be encouraged to inquire into their practice through various contrasting photographs and classroom contexts, which may have an emotional or conceptual force whose evocation promotes analysis and reflection. Another possibility is a humanist project with photographs of the community in which trainee or practising teachers live, with similar goals to those indicated above. These may discover that they are surrounded by diverse people who feel and work, and in turn, may generate projects in these contexts and reflect on themes, whether related to schooling or not, that shed light on their present or future students' concerns and difficulties and those of other agents in the community.

Some portraits no longer make sense, such as the school photographs in the teacher's desk, which date back to the 1930s, continued to be taken until the 1970s and may have been the only time a child was portrayed, because at the time, photography was a sophisticated and expensive technique. However, their use in class can provide the opportunity to reflect on what teaching and children's lives were like then. Another idea would be to carry out projects based on performing what is depicted in the photographs or attempting to reproduce what they were intended to convey and express. Such projects could be conducted with trainee teachers to stimulate discussion about the differences between the schooling and contexts depicted in the past and those in the present.

Self-portraiture enables students to reveal themselves to the class and can be a source of inquiry by their peers, helping to create a good relationship in the class and promoting dialogue. At the same time, the activity encourages introspective inquiry because the audiovisual material stimulates internal dialogue. Such representation enables trainee teachers to reorganise their experience, which is essential for critiquing preconceptions about their future teaching practice.

A photo reportage captures an aspect of interest in the life of a school or classroom through a collection of photographs. As discussed in chapter nine, such projects require inquiry to produce a script, as well as planning in order to take the minimum number of photographs with the maximum amount of information. Although photographs entail no material costs thanks to digital technology, revising all the material to assess its value for the projected story may prove costly in time. In schools, reportage can begin spontaneously, but is generally aimed at documenting an activity such as breaks, the beginning of the school day, individual work or lunch times. Other reportage themes that emerge from teachers' inquiry into their practice may include diversity, the environment of school activities, family life, the neighbourhood, work, the status of women and a host of other topics related to the curriculum, with the aim of producing a record that can be analysed and used in education. Teachers can report on what is happening in their schools and neighbourhoods, capturing problems that arise in their communities (e.g. social difficulties or accidents) for subsequent use as the basis for inquiry into these problems and decision-making to improve school life. Reportage concerning activities that involve a process, such as workshops, can provide feedback (and therefore training) for the group involved, or for their successors.

A photo essay is a visual version of the equivalent literary genre: the photographer expounds ideas about a subject or problem through a series of photographs, using a particular style created through shots, angles and lighting. As with multimedia projects, which also require perhaps unaccustomed technical know-how, photo essays should focus on problems that rarely receive attention or aspects where the visual component is of crucial importance. The associated inquiry required of the teachers will yield knowledge that will define the script, and this in turn will give visual support to the series of ideas. Photo essays can be used to generate discussions on complex or rarely analysed problems in education.

As discussed in previous chapters, a photo montage is the result of cutting and gluing several photographs together ("collage" is the French term for "gluing"), and may include texts from newspapers and other lightweight materials such as fabrics. As at its inception one hundred years ago, the inquiry informs the process of photo montage can lead teachers to report, poetise or seek new spaces and times that reconfigure the organisation of the educational institution.

Likewise, a photo diary is a collection of images assembled with a purpose, such as capturing important incidents in the classroom or an issue that concerns the students or the teacher. As with teaching diaries, it constitutes a bank of information for the teacher, an instrument for reflection and reworking in other materials, which is not necessarily made to be read by anyone other than its author. Alternatively, a photo diary may contain life stories for sharing with other teachers. These materials can be shared in the form of photo-books, for inquiry, discussion and explanation with the aim of prompting the author and other trainee teachers to reflect on educational practices.

Lastly, one of the least frequently used forms of narration in education is landscape photography, which involves capturing the space in which we live and work. This is particularly interesting in terms of architecture and lighting, because schools—and educational buildings in general—reflect ideas about order and participation that are indicative of the type of teaching practices implemented, and therefore their analysis is productive.

Other Ideas for Inquiry Using Photo-Narration

Paul McIntosh (2010), who teaches social workers, has proposed familiarising oneself with prospective techniques from the most emotional and least personal point of view as possible. Thus, a group of trainee teachers who had carried out teaching practice were asked to characterise their experience using an artistic image from a bank of figurative paintings provided by the teacher/facilitator, in which one colour predominated. For example, Renoir's painting of a woman sitting beside the sea is full of blues, and to launch the activity, participants were invited to examine the composition, form, tone and space to determine the underlying theme. They were then asked to talk about the tone of the class in which they had participated in their teaching practice (accompanying a tutor, or alone with a group of students younger than themselves), the feelings they had experienced and how the artistic work was connected to what they had felt. According to McIntosh, the exercise enabled students to talk about what had happened during their teaching practice and connect it with other experiences. He contends that art allows us to give shape to confusion, conflict and uncertainty in the light of our own reasoning.

Digital storytelling has been used to evoke trainee teachers' relationship with technology (or any other subject), their previous knowledge, their biases and their initial view of lifelong learning. An example would be a photo-narration that includes images of artefacts, spaces and relationships with technology that are significant for the author. Techno-autobiography means expressing these relationships in different formats, using audiovisual and text resources created by students. The productions are watched by the entire group, stimulating individual and group reflection and constituting an initial diagnosis that provides clues about individual starting points as teachers and students. Through analysis, these can be demystified, revealing their everyday nature and our daily contact with them. The aim is to render the invisible visible and thus trigger the proposed learning process.

Visual maps are productions that inquire into subjects' learning paths (Sefton-Green, 2016). Although they are not strictly photographic sequences, but rather artistic products, the material content the teachers pour into them is equivalent. Graphic representation, in this case usually a handmade poster with cut-outs, colours and whatever other elements participants desire, presents a challenge because most of them will have forgotten the freedom that everyone should allow themselves to create something graphically. The authors comment verbally on their productions in a dialogue with peers and activity facilitators. There may be informal phases of dialogue during creation, and formal stages in a presentation to the group. The works can continue to evolve until this moment of presentation to the group. When asking about the biographical relationship to trainee teachers' learning, the opportunity will hopefully arise to challenge some of their stereotypes about teaching.

Literature is a resource that connects the stories of others with one's own life (Kincheloe, 1999). In describing people's vicissitudes and stereotypes, literature invites us to inquire into other spaces worth exploring and inhabiting. In this literary context, trainee teachers can use series of photographs to talk about their concerns, their training, their analyses of life at school and in the community, their ideas for change and even the concerns, fears and joys that these situations elicit in them. They can tell stories or condemn something.

Photo-dialogue is a technique with a Freirian basis that mixes images and literary creation to engage members of a group in an analysis of situations that enables them to reflect on their past and their present. Originally, it was used with Latina women in literacy classes in the United States with the idea of adding content to a writing task in order to depict each woman's life through a sequence of five images of consecutive moments in her life, and to stimulate discussion while learning as adults to improve their reading and writing. In another training context, young female teachers who had been invited to speak as women within a feminised profession chose artists, athletes, scientists, vocational teachers or their mothers as the vehicle for a freely proposed story (Paredes-Labra, 2014). When they reflected in writing on these visual stories, they become aware of their own trajectories and status as women.

Other ideas for inquiry using photo-narration are based on classroom projects on a relevant subject such as memory. Old photographs can be superimposed on new ones in an attempt to understand what has happened in the space or with the group of people who appear in two similar photographs from two different time periods. This activity raises questions about the spaces and the relationships that occur there. As with time, spaces can also be the subject of a story associated with a meaningful journey for teachers. Spaces are loaded with meaning, and the freedom to travel through them, the memories they bring and the associations they generate are important to understand the lives of trainee teachers.

To launch an activity on space and time, it can be useful to suggest someone other than a trainee teacher as the main character, and to think of a parent, a grandparent, an acquaintance, a fictional character or someone of the opposite sex or another race making that same journey. The journey and the reasons for undertaking it also help raise critical awareness. Another possible subject for projects is daily life affected by personal or community issues. This technique is called photo history (Keremane & McKay, 2011), a participatory research method in which participants photograph their daily lives to inquire into them in focus groups (Bautista et al., 2018; Clandinin et al., 2007).

Other subjects for photo-based inquiry include the organisation of shared spaces, the questions generated by work or the feelings experienced. According to McIntosh (2010), the analysis should be declarative (what appears), symbolic (explaining the symbolism used) and relational (identifying the model of relationships contained in the representation). Later, another analysis can be added, of resonances, referring to the evocations our representation suggests to us and to others. According to Gebhard (1990), these activities can in turn facilitate joint problem-solving between the tutor and the trainee teachers. Notably, these latter have different points of reference for solving the problems they encounter, such as a tutor's guidance, their peers' opinions, their own sources or self-discovery.

Additional Considerations for Analysing Photo-Narration in Teacher Training

Although the procedures and some of the results of inquiry through photo-narration have already been discussed, it will be useful before concluding to explain the functions of the teaching knowledge generated through portfolios. Connected to the class curriculum, students' portfolios are one of the sources of practice that provide visual evidence. Teachers may wish to organise analyses of the productions through comparison and sequencing of portfolio materials, gathering a representative sample from the class, or even its entirety, and ordering this sequence using various criteria and pursuing distinct goals. For example, as part of teachers' continuous training, they can examine how their perceptions of certain teaching practices have changed, through a series of practices ordered using this criterion. They could also analyse the moment during the academic year when these practices occur.

The use of narrative inquiry based on portfolios involves a presentation and a public text open to written comments and responses from facilitators and peers, or viewing in face-to-face sessions followed by focus groups in which the materials are commented on by peers and, in the case of continuing education, by parents and students (Bautista, 2017). The portfolio is a living document, which is unusual in standard educational practices, where a task is generally finished once it has been handed in. Virtual spaces such as forums have also been used to facilitate the formation of communities of practice (Paredes-Labra, 2014; Paredes-Labra et al.,

2013) in relation to work with diaries and public writing, common among teachers in the English-speaking world (for example, Lieberman & Miller, 2003). This has the potential for open learning, communicative interaction and active participation of students in the collaborative production of knowledge. Unfortunately, research by Colas et al. (2018) casts doubt on its empirical value, indicating that further research is required to refine the rigour of its presentation.

Some techniques include successive analyses, focus groups, discussion with the producer, recordings of the sessions for re-analysis and a written presentation of the subject explored, whereas others can be less involved, aimed at training teachers in more complex analysis processes through assessments of a sentence or image that evokes the subject or a song that adds emotion to the analyses.

It should not be forgotten that the productions of students in teaching practice delve into various problems, use different sources and have a very broad framework of interpretation, so that the responses from their peers and from the teacher/facilitator will be complex. Teachers who observe their teaching actions through photo-narration become more reflective and acquire the capacity for self-assessment (Kaneko-Marques, 2016). By conducting a thorough analysis of practice, they identify and understand the complexities of teaching.

When this activity is collaborative, it can be expanded to other situations (e.g. students and parents, other educational institutions, groups and associations) and form the basis for changing the conditions of teaching and the school's community, forging a community of practice with a critical, transformative purpose, which Bautista has called the third stage (1994). The effect on inquiry into practice is that participants become aware of the characteristics of the contexts in which they work, their schools and classrooms, the competencies these require, the actions they take and the political, ethical and collaborative nature of their teaching practices.

References

Bautista, A. (1994). El papel de los intelectuales y la no neutralidad de la tecnología: Razones para un uso crítico de los recursos en la enseñanza. *Revista De Educación, 303*, 243–260.

Bautista, A. (2013). Funciones del vídeo en la formación del profesorado para una educación intercultural. *Educatio Siglo XXI, 31*(1), 255–268.

Bautista, A. (2017). La foto-elicitación en la formación permanente de maestros de educación primaria. *Alteridad, 12*(2), 202–214.

Bautista, A., Rayón, L., & De las Heras, A.M. (2018). Imágenes experienciales y foto-elicitación en la formación del profesorado. *Educatio Siglo XXI, 36*(2), 135–162.

Bernstein, B. (1990). *La estructura del discurso pedagógico.* Morata.

Chatman. (1992). *Historia y discurso. Estructura narrativa en la novela y en el cine.* Taurus.

Clandinin, D. J., & Connelly, F. M. (1988). Conocimiento práctico personal de los profesores: imagen y unidad narrativa. In L.M. Villar. (Ed.), *Conocimiento, creencias y teorías de los profesores* (pp. 39–62). Marfil.

Clandinin, D. J., Pushor, D., & Murray Orr, A. (2007). Navigating Sites for Narrative Inquiry. *Journal of Teacher Education, 58*, 21–35.

Colás, P., De Pablos, J., Reyes de Cozar, S., & Conde, J. (2018). Innovación pedagógica en la formación del profesorado apoyada por videos en red. *Educatio Siglo XXI, 36*(2), 163–186.

Ezquerra, A., Burgos, E., & Manso, J. (2016). Estudio comparativo sobre las estrategias desarrolladas por los futuros docentes de Primaria y Secundaria en la elaboración de audiovisuales educativos. *Revista Eureka Sobre Enseñanza y Divulgación De Las Ciencias, 13*(2), 493–504.

Fernández, S. R., Sosa, M. J., & Valverde, J. (2013). El LipDub como experiencia educativa para la expresión social y la participación de la comunidad universitaria. *Tejuelo: Didáctica de la Lengua y la Literatura. Educación, 8,* 105–122.

Fernández, R. J. (2018). Creación de vídeos educativos en la formación docente: Un estudio de caso. *Revista Electrónica Interuniversitaria De Formación Del Profesorado, 21*(1), 115–127.

Freeman, M. (2010). *La narración fotográfica.* Blume.

Gebhard, J. G. (1990). Models of supervision: Choices. In J. C. Richards & D. Nunan (Eds.), *Second language teacher education* (pp. 156–166). Cambridge University Press.

Gutiérrez Cuenca, L., Correa Gorospe, J. M., de Aberasturi, J., Apraiz, E., & Ibáñez, E. A. (2009). El modelo reflexivo en la formación de maestros y el pensamiento narrativo: Estudio de un caso de innovación educativa en el Practicum de Magisterio. *Revista De Educación, 350,* 493–505.

Gutiérrez, A., Alonso del Corral, A., Bautista, A., Ferguson, R., Gallardo, A., García Matilla, A., de Oliveira, I., Piette, J., Pinto, M., Quin., R., & Villagra, A. (1998). *Formación del Profesorado enla Sociedad de la Información.* Universidad de Valladolid.

Kaneko-Marques, S. M. (2016). Supervisión colaborativa docente a través de clases grabadas en video. *Profile., 17*(2), 63–79.

Keremane, G., & Mckay, J. (2011). Using PhotoStory to capture irrigators' emotions about water policy and sustainable development objectives: A case study in rural Australia. *Action Research, 9*(4), 405–425.

Kincheloe, J. (1999). *Repensar el multiculturalismo.* Octaedro.

Lieberman, A., & Miller, L. (2003). *La indagación como base de la formación del profesorado y la mejora de la educación.* Octaedro.

Liston, D., & Zeichner, K. (1993). *Formación del profesorado y condiciones sociales de escolarización.* Morata.

Marcellán, I., Calvelhe, L., Agirre, I., & Arriaga, A. (2013). Estudio sobre jóvenes productores de cultura visual: Evidencias de la brecha entre la escuela y la juventud. *Arte, Individuo y Sociedad, 25*(3), 525–535.

McIntosh, P. (2010). *Action Research and Reflective Practice: Creative and visual methods to facilitate reflection and learning.* Routledge.

Medina, S., & García-Morís, R. (2018). Multiculturalismo y literacidad visual: Análisis de las narrativas históricas del profesorado de primaria en formación. *Revista De Didácticas Específicas, 18,* 101–117.

Paredes-Labra, J. (2012). Cambiar el panorama de las escuelas. Indagación narrativa, artes visuales y TIC en una escuela activa radical. In *Antropología visual e investigación sobre Tecnología educativa.* Trotta.

Paredes-Labra, J. (2014). Memoria de la escuela y escuela para la comunidad. Análisis de un caso en formación de maestros. *Tendencias Pedagógicas, 24,* 9–22.

Paredes-Labra, J., Herrán, A., & Correa, J. M. (2013). New narratives to learn to discuss teaching in a faculty community of practice. Four case studies. *Action Researcher in Education-Greece., 4,* 122–131.

Schön, D. (1998). *El profesional reflexivo: Cómo piensan los profesionales cuando actúan.* Paidós.

Sefton-Green, J. (2016). Representing learning lives: What does it mean to map learning journeys? *International Journal of Educational Research, 84,* 111–118.

Tyack, D., & Tobin, W. (1994). The "grammar" of schooling: Why has it been so hard to change? *American Educational Research Journal, 31*(3), 453–479.

Chapter 12
The Artist's Book as a Form of Autoethnography for the Teaching Profession

Marián López Fernández-Cao

Reflections on the Photographic Act

Photography both connects and separates us from reality. As Susan Sontag pointed out in her famous *On Photography*, the camera (nowadays, usually a smartphone) is both a bridge and a divide. It unites but also insulates us. Perhaps that is why we take and save photographs of things that unsettle us, to make them our own. Photography is an act of possession, even if we do not know exactly what for and why we appropriate something external. Authors such as Barthes (1989), Thysseron (2002), Sontag (2014), and Berger (2000), have discussed photography and the photographic act from various points of view that all nevertheless refer to an always unfinished and failed understanding of reality, of a reality that is impossible to pin down.

Humans take photographs to know, possess, understand and acquaint themselves with external—albeit possibly familiar—facts, events and realities. Photography renders the familiar strange and the strange familiar. There are a myriad of gazes, ranging from a desire to dominate to a tenacious observation that seeks to understand what is before us, in front of our eyes, through its imaginary capture: from a wide-angle shot looking down, that restores a feeling of domination over reality, to a close-up that reveals the humility of the person observing, of the person seeking to understand and be understood through the photographic act. Rafaèle Genet, who works at the University of Granada Education Faculty, teaches her students to see through new eyes using photography. In her doctoral thesis, "City and Artistic Education in Initial Teacher Training: Educational Research Based on the Visual Arts" (2016), photography becomes an educational medium that renders the commonplace new and connects our gaze to events, emotions, forms and education.

M. López Fernández-Cao (✉)
Complutense University, Madrid, Spain
e-mail: mariaanl@ucm.es

© The Author(s) 2023
A. Bautista García-Vera (ed.), *Photographic Elicitation and Narration in Teachers Education and Development*, Teacher Education, Learning Innovation and Accountability, https://doi.org/10.1007/978-3-031-20164-6_12

Genet, R. (2015). *Enseñar, matemáticas* [Teaching, mathematics]. Photo essay composed of one digital photograph by González, R., one by Chalmers, S., two by Rodríguez, Y., one by Ramón, L. and one by Campos, A.

Genet, R. (2015). *Enseñar, matemáticas* [Teaching, mathematics]. Photo essay composed of one digital photograph by Baltar, E. and another by Lara, N.

Genet, R. (2013). *Detalles significantes I* [significant details I]. Photo essay composed of one digital photograph by Callegari, E., one by Gutíerrez, M. D., one by González, J., one by Callegari, E., one by Lamela, A. and two by Callegari, E. Using a simple and synthetic approach, she teaches students how to observe

Genet, R. (2015). *Procesos de aprendizaje, la ciudad enmarcada II* [learning processes, the city framed II]. Photo essay composed of four digital photographs by Sánchez, J. M.

Migrant Mother, California, 1936

Photography establishes a relationship between ourselves and others. The great photographer Dorothea Lange described "migrant mother" (Nipomo, California 1936), one of her most famous photographs, as follows:

I saw and approached the hungry and desperate mother, as if drawn by a magnet. I do not remember how I explained my presence or my camera to her, but I do remember she asked me no questions. I made five exposures, working closer and closer from the same direction. I did not ask her name or her history. She told me her age, that she was thirty-two. She said that they had been living on frozen vegetables from the surrounding fields, and birds that the children killed. She had just sold the tires from her car to buy food. There she sat in that lean-to tent with her children huddled around her, and seemed to know that my pictures might help her, and so she helped me. There was a sort of equality about it.

Her method of working is best explained in her own words:

My own approach is based upon three considerations: First — hands off! Whenever I photograph I do not molest or tamper with or arrange. Second – a sense of place. I try to picture as part of its surroundings, as having roots. Third – a sense of time. Whatever I photograph, I try to show as having its position in the past or in the present. (in López Fernández Cao, 2015)

Beyond presenting a history of photography that could be related to the profession of teaching, with the ethics of listening, observing, learning and sharing, I believe that to photograph is also to observe, to listen to the world, to stop, to seek connection and to reflect on and arrange what one has seen. Art, and in this case photography, has the capacity to order what is outside and disorder what is inside. This is why art is always an act of restructuring.

Masumi Hayashi

Turning to Masumi Hayashi's work and the juxtaposition of multiple gazes, can the idea of constructionism, of cognitive collage, of fragments of reality, be better expressed in one gaze?

Frances Benjamin Johnston. *Stairway of the Treasurer's Residence: Students at Work*, from the *Hampton* Album, 1899–1900. Moma, NY

Benjamin Johnston's work in general, and this photograph in particular, is extremely attractive. The picture shows six people working on a joint project. They all appear to be utterly absorbed in something that is simultaneously collective and individual, each one working with care and diligence on his part of the project. It reminds me of a Renaissance descent, where dynamism and harmony coexist and complement one another. Could this be the image of a research project? I believe that theorists of art-based research mean something similar to this when they claim that images—non-discursive languages—offer us useful representations for thinking.

Artists' Books

Artists' books are not books of or about art. Rather, they are works of art conceived in book format and often published by the artists themselves. A product of the 1960s, they are the conceptual result of a spirit that rebelled against the elitism of the art world. The images in such works must have an interconnection. An artist's book is conceived as a project with a sequence, a rhythm and a particular cadence, and is related to the idea of photo-book narration discussed in chapter nine. There are few rules about the artist's book because artists are little given to setting rules and more predisposed to independent self-regulation, but it is a work of art in itself, where each and every one of the pieces is necessary for the book's symbolic function. I shall focus on two examples that have perhaps formed the basis of the work I have been doing for many years now with my students. Both books are published by the same house, Mestizo, with which I must share a similar vision.

Through her family album, Ana Casas Broda seeks a shared identity, for being through, for and towards others. Her backwards-looking quest forms a dialogue with her grandmother's diaries that in some way is a communication backwards, forwards and towards herself. The work in *Álbum* pivots around the family relationship as seen through photographs (Casas, 2000). The house and the body are the structural coordinates while photography is the medium that, in her words, allows us to fix our gaze and let others enter it. Through photographs and texts, the book addresses issues such as memory, personal and cultural heritage and photography as a way of exploring identity. *Álbum* was published as a book in 2000 by Mestizo (Spain) and presented in an exhibition that brought together photographs, texts, videos and objects:

My mother took me to Mexico when I was eight years old. I was born in Spain and lived part of my childhood in Vienna, Austria. I worked on *Álbum* for fourteen years. I was drawn to the project by my deep attraction to the photographs that my grandmother took of my early childhood in Vienna. I could not distinguish my memories from her images and felt that they held a mystery that was essential to me. This led me to make a series from some of the photographs of my childhood, which subsequently grew and spurred me to reflect on photography and its relationship to memory and identity. Gradually, *Álbum* became a more in-depth exploration and addressed issues central to family relationships, the history of my ancestors and the construction of the body within the search for identity.

Vienna, 23 July 1996
The house is in its last days. A company is here to take everything away. They have scrapped most of the furniture, smashing it with axes because they say it is worthless. I take pictures of everything so as to save every last detail.

I want to say goodbye with my eyes open.

Vienna, 2 January 1995
Today when I was in the bath, I felt an uneasiness for the first time. A certain sadness in the walls, an air that I hadn't noticed before, crept into me. Something is falling apart. I haven't been able to sleep ever since I arrived. I read until dawn and during the day I wander drowsily around the house. I'm scared.

Vienna, 12 July 1995
I returned to Vienna a few days ago. Omama will have to leave the house this summer; she is eighty-five years old and can no longer live alone. When we call my mother, she is always very nervous and makes plans. Yesterday, she talked about taking her to Mexico. From Omama's tone of voice, I think that she wants to stay.

Vienna, 13 July 1995
Today we went to a home surrounded by huge trees. We were accompanied by my grandmother's sister. They told me that when they were children they had lived only a few streets away, and that there had been a meadow there where they used to play. Omama remembers where every stick of furniture had been in that house, where to stretch out her hand to switch on the light. That was over eighty years ago. I know that she's already decided.

To journey through Ana Casas's *Álbum* is to enter an identity shaped by lost and recovered spaces, by one's own and others' memories, by the bonds that trap and strengthen us. I believe that the meditated construction of her artist's book using the family album and other images that move her represents an exercise that emerged from the awakening of mechanisms beyond the discursive ones, signalling the importance of artistic, poetic and visual resources.

In *Recuperar la luz* (Canal & Ramiro, 2004), Rosa Sánchez Ramiro introduces her book as follows:

> Some time ago I was lucky enough to fall seriously ill. This gave me a wealth of knowledge and life experiences that more than compensated for the danger. That's how I feel. I believe that the way in which I lived the experience of illness was decisive in reaching this clear conviction. I don't know if what happens to us is merely the result of a chain of events or if there is a need that drives everything that happens. What I do know is that from the day when measured time stopped, everything has happened as if it were inevitable.
>
> It all started when, shortly after making my debut as a hospital patient, a peculiar looking man appeared in my room. After introducing himself as my doctor and telling me the chemotherapy treatment I would be given, he let me know in a few words that I was on the other side of the mirror. I haven't made it clear that this man —who was obviously Carlos— was not alone. He was accompanied by a camera, hanging from his neck and resting on his white coat, a Cyclops ready to act as a witness to the challenge I had been given. The idea was to reflect my feelings through photographs during my stay there; we would also photograph my face each time, as a way of not forgetting my identity despite the physical changes that my appearance might undergo during the process. That's how it all started, almost like a game. Every other day, I sought an image in my confined surroundings that would symbolise what was going on inside me. Without having seen the printed result, the image remained like a negative in my mind, until it was eventually revealed in the form of written lines that escaped from my fingers as if the act of pressing the shutter button had unleashed an unstoppable mechanism.
>
> Carlos gave me a new way of looking —photography— and this, almost instinctively, allied itself with my other voice: the written word, providing the tangle of thoughts, fears and concerns that boiled inside me with a "channel" (another coincidence?) through which to flow. The result is in your hands and in the sentences that introduce this text.

Rosa took photographs of her process, of the exterior, but also of herself in order, as she says, not to forget her identity in spite of the physical changes, so as not to lose sight of who she was, who she is and who she can become. It is a moving book that makes us see that illnesses do not exist; rather, there are people who are ill, and over and above being ill, these are people who are unique. Sometimes scared, sometimes desperate, but often hopeful.

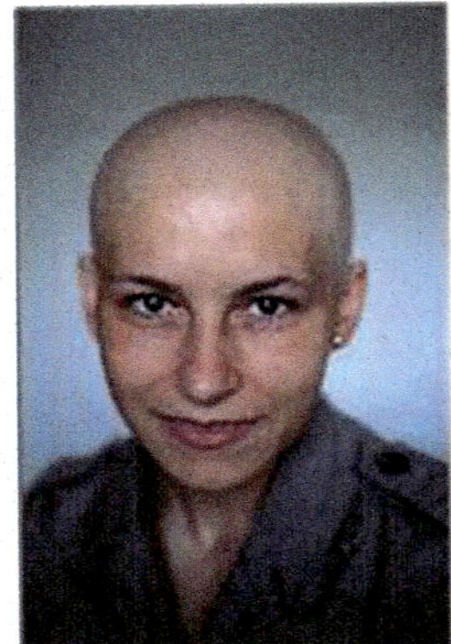
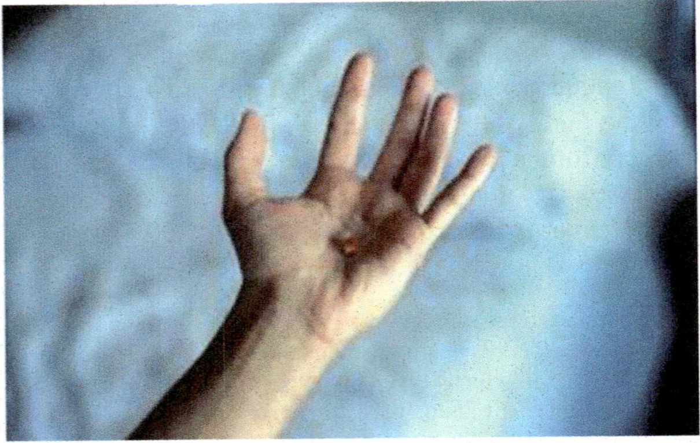

// 19 May 2000 //18. Dos tesoros [two treasures]

ATRA is my great ally: thanks to ATRA, my illness has a very good prognosis. With the help of other drugs, induction therapy with this small two-toned pearl has already achieved complete remission. Not only have my bone marrow cells stabilised, but the molecular alteration of my genes has been corrected. Quite a triumph. But this precious pearl does not float in the air all by itself: it is held aloft in a hand, a left hand, which is meant to represent the importance in healing of factors that are not solely scientific. The emotional help received, the inner journey throughout this time travelled, the ghosts of memory, finally exorcised... a heavy burden without which it has been much easier to swim to the surface and gulp in a deep breath of pure air which, in the form of small two-toned pearls, circulates through my body to restore my health, so that the result of the cellular and molecular analysis of my marrow is a faithful reflection of my being.

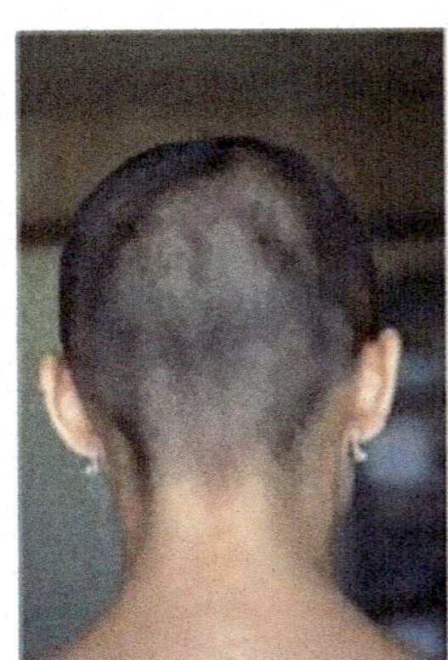

// 4 August 2000 //38. El mirador del centinela [the sentry's lookout]

This place, christened with the same name as the title, after a story I shall keep to myself, is a small hill in the countryside near my home. I often go for a walk in the late afternoon, accompanied by my dogs, my cat and a book. Sitting on a concrete block, I bear witness to the passage of time until nightfall, my attention divided between reading, the smells and sounds of the countryside and the sighting of a rabbit making the most of the last days of the closed season. Bees are also abundant, as there are hives nearby. One of their inhabitants is responsible for the fact that my face is now misshapen thanks to the effects of a sting. You shall therefore allow me, perhaps in a ridiculous gesture of vanity, to hide my face from the camera today. A couple of days ago, when I was at the sentry's lookout watching the sunset and accompanied by my beloved animals, I was flooded by a warm feeling of plenitude. I felt that I had no need to aspire to any more in life, that in that moment I had everything I needed, precisely because I knew that I didn't need anything. At any rate, that's how I try to explain the feeling I was experiencing, because in that moment everything was summed up in one sentence that, out of context, might be difficult to understand. The real title of the photograph that represents that moment is *Ya me puedo morir* [I can die now].

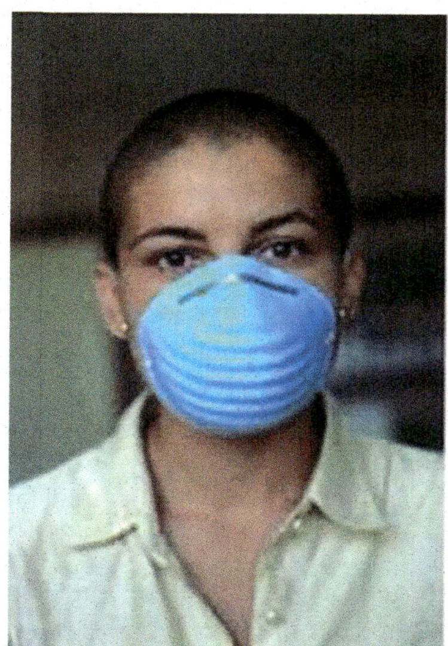

// 28 August 2000 //46. *Casi te puedo tocar* [I can almost touch you]

Today, finally, my neutrophil count is up. The comeback begins. I feel as if I can now see the end of the road, something that until now was always far away. After this, at the very least, the fragile tower will not be demolished again in order to start building another identical one to knock down. It will be a start, but in a new direction: that of normality, which will never be normal again, flowing down the river again, but with new waters. As I advance by stages, everything takes shape and begins to have an overall sense. Today I am aware that I am healing. You are there, very close, if I stretch out my hand I can almost touch you.

Artist's books are proof of the power of the creative process to tell our stories, in an exercise of new lucidity and reconfiguration. They are, therefore, important examples for teaching reflection, since there is nothing like education to connect us with the other, make us responsible for him or her and reconfigure us as beings who accompany the story, the other's story.

Photo-Narration in the Configuration of Teachers

In relation to the above, Connelly and Clandinin (1995) have noted that humans are "storytellers": we inhabit lives that are or should be inserted in a story through which we experience the world. Thus, in line with Mateos and Núñez (2011), narrative is directly related to the representation we construct of the personal and social world in different ways and forms:

- It is a way of ordering our experience of life and giving it meaning: "Through narrative, humans project the interpretation of events, actions and situations and confer meaning and significance to their own experience" (Mateos & Núñez, 2011, p. 121).
- It is involved in the way we experience the world and contains practical knowledge. As Colom and Mèlich (2003) have observed, there is a two-way relationship between narrative and life. On the one hand, narrative refers to life, since the process of creating and composing a story is carried out by the reader. In this sense, reading is a way of living, just as telling and reading stories is to live them in the world of the imagination. On the other hand, life itself refers to narrative insofar as it entails not only biological development, but also the accumulation of a biography, story or tale whose text can be interpreted and experienced in different ways (2003, p. 121). Events or actions must be organised into the plots or arguments of a narrative story with meaning and significance.
- It is an instrument to transmit one's own and other people's experience, acting as a mediator of the education-culture connection. Within oral cultures, narrative plays an important role as the main intellectual and practical tool for the transmission of knowledge (Colom & Mèlich, 2003).

It is from this premise, from the need to tell our stories, that "emancipatory narratives" arise (McEwan, 1997), stories that free our thought from the pressure to conform and from established narrative, providing the means to express and create new meanings that thus become a restructuring and permit a re-reading in other terms.

Starting from this position, narrative allows for deconstruction and constitution, in line with Derrida. A deconstructionist stance activates participants' capacity to subvert the definitions, roles and constructs that society has established. A constitutionalist stance, on the other hand, suggests that lives and identities are constructed from the meanings that people give to the account of their experiences; from the language that they select to express it, together with the vocabulary they use to narrate their lives; and from the position or hierarchy that people occupy in the social structure in which they participate and the power relations that this entails (Carr, 1998).

Reflecting on these three factors—meaning, language and power relations—helps to identify and take apart the subalternities imposed by others that at a given moment have produced isolation or emotional discord.

Similarly, according to White, the methods used in narrative therapy can be very useful in education and therapy when:

- We adopt an advisory position of collaborative co-authorship.
- We help participants to see themselves as separate from their problems by externalising the problem.
- We help participants identify the moments in their lives when they were not oppressed by their problems because they found unique outcomes.
- We reframe our participants' descriptions as action scenarios and awareness scenarios.
- We link unique outcomes to other past events and help extend the story into the future to form an alternative, giving preference to a self-narrative in which the self is seen as more powerful than the problem.
- We invite significant members of the participants' social network to share this new self-narrative.
- We document new knowledge and practices that support the new self-narrative using literary means.
- We allow others, who are also trapped by similar oppressive narratives, to benefit from their new knowledge through feedback (Carr, 1998).

Narrative mobilises aspects that help us to look at ourselves from other perspectives beyond those where we have been located or have unconsciously located ourselves. Thus, photo-biography (Sanz, 2015) helps to extract and exteriorise internal chaos and pain, giving it form through language—whether written, drawn, dramatised or danced—as we see it outside ourselves: organising it using lines, colours, composition or structure, through verbs, adverbs and adjectives, through rhythms, gestures and movements, to reflect on why some and not others. To give them a new meaning, for this to be shared and to communicate it to others.

Autoethnography in the Configuration of the Teaching Profession

In relation to the interpenetration of image and text, Springgay et al. (2005) have described a/r/tography as an approach to interpreting the self by means of living inquiry through art and text. Such inquiry endows our experience with more than a single meaning: loss, shift and rupture are foundational concepts that allow new meanings to emerge, and this double meaning includes the creation of art and words. These are not, therefore, "discourses laid on top of one another in the hopes of transferring meaning from one textual realm to another; rather, they are interconnections that speak in conversation with, in, and through art and text such that encounters are constitutive rather than descriptive" (Springgay et al., 2005, p. 899).

For many years, I have been encouraging my students to construct narratives that bring reflectivity and emancipation into play. I started when I was teaching the optional subject "Intercultural Arts Education" for primary education. Before thinking about how to plan a class of diverse students, I asked them to open their family albums and, in their artist's book, to ask the photographs inside (of their great-grandparents, grandparents, great-aunts and uncles, parents, cousins) where they had been born, where they had lived and why they had moved, what events were depicted, what had been hidden in that mythical image that is the photo album and where they were in the photographs of family celebrations or rather, where they had been placed. In addition, I asked them to map their families' movements throughout Spain, Europe or the world. The result also had to be creative, and in it they had to reflect on why they had chosen to take my course in the Faculty of Education. Furthermore, they would have to show it to their peers. The result was surprising, not only for them, but also for me. Confirming my experiential knowledge, all the autoethnographies (in the sense of autobiographical narratives discussed in the preceding chapters) showed that we are migratory beings driven by hunger, political repression or love. In addition, the students discovered things about their family histories that they would never have known if they had not participated in the activity. Some discovered the pain of grandparents and great-grandparents who had been imprisoned, orphaned or abandoned in a harsh post-war period. Others discovered letters that their relatives had fondly but fearfully kept and now showed to the younger generation. On many occasions, they sat down for the first time with their grandmothers, with the photographs in front of them, and listened to their stories attentively. The activity helped them to know who they were, where they came from, what they were repeating or what they were rebelling against.

Since then, for more than fifteen years I have been repeating this activity with my students, whatever the subject. I ask them who they are and why they are here. I think it is an exercise in professional but also existential identity. In many cases, they are looking back for the first time, to find out where they come from and to think about the expectations that others—generally their parents, but also themselves and society—have of them. Many discovered that they were the first generation in their family to go to university, others that they were the second generation not to have experienced hunger. Almost all of them found there had been loss and grief, and more of them than I had imagined uncovered traces of domestic violence hidden among the most unfathomable secrets.

Two Cases of Autoethnography in Primary School Teacher Training

To complete this text, I wrote to some former students with whom I had worked some years ago, asking their permission to show images from their autoethnographies. Most of them took no more than a few hours to respond, thanking me for the opportunity to show their work: their images were stored not only on their computers, but also in their symbolic memory. I think that reflects meaningful learning. I could show many, but I have chosen two. Thank you Coral Pámpano and Marta Fraile, for letting me share a fragment of your lives. They spent many hours with me on the Master's Degree in Art Therapy and Education for Social Inclusion, at the Complutense University of Madrid Faculty of Education.

Coral Pámpano created an autoethnography entitled *Piola*. She says:

"Piola" is a word that was used, and I hope will continue to be used, in the area where I live to declare time-out during a game: during hide-and-seek or tag, you shouted "Piola!" and you were free to stop the game. This, together with the implicit meaning of returning to my home, to my roots, forms the title for the collection of poems and writings that I have been accumulating. (Pámpano, 2017)

Fragments from *Piola*

Via subtle images delicately placed in a small book and accompanied by poems, she journeys through her life. In a way, returning to the past is to adopt a stance towards the future: clear, self-reflective, with roots. Meaningful.

Marta Fraile created a sphere of images, representing her identity:

To be born again. The first thing I thought of when I wanted to represent my world was definitely a kind of sphere, not closed, of segments and pieces. The sphere is one of the most universal and natural forms. The earth, the sun, the planets, our cells, our atoms or electrons. It's the form that contains all other forms, the "Cosmic Egg", eternity. The cycles, the rhythms and their eternal movement. It is, therefore, totality, integrity and fulfilment. A sphere is made up of circles that close in on themselves and it therefore represents unity, the absolute, perfection. It is a symbol of heaven in relation to earth, of the spiritual in relation to the material. It is related to 'protection'. (Fraile, Autoethnography, 2016)

She writes:

Nowadays, I feel that I am made of bits and pieces, of experiences, of all the people who have passed through my life (…) of summer afternoons in the village, with my grandmother, with my bicycle, of the void of my grandfather. Of endless songs that will always dance to the sound of the August sun and the spotlights of the summer festivities. Of my friends. Of attachment to what one has experienced, which sometimes exceeds the desire to continue living.

Of feeling, of the pain of my illness and the rupture it caused in my life. Of dates that are engraved on my mind, of the pain of absences. Of broken glass. Of you Natalia, my shooting star who left me recently, on 1 July 2015, leaving me speechless, of your courage, strength and will to live in the face of our illness, of the tremendous lesson that your smile gave me in the face of life and death. (Fraile, 2016)

Fragmentos de Autoetnografía. Marta Fraile

Photographic autoethnographies, complex and subtle artist's books, ask questions but only partially answer them, in an uncertainty that helps in the seeking rather than the finding. They plunge into the depths of identity construction, into the story of life, into its whys and wherefores. On this path, the creative action, the creative process, has the virtue of simultaneously opening and structuring, showing and offering a way of thinking that is united to emotion and therefore, dares to think anew: in a body, from a biography, for others.

These autoethnographies, or autobiographical narratives, are based on the assumption that narratives do not represent or reflect identities, lives and problems, but instead construct them (Bruner, 1986, 1987, 1991). The subject authorises his or her "own voice", transforming it into an essential element to articulate information and interpretation. Knowledge thus constructs a form of narration about life, society and the world in general (Rivas, 2010). In accordance with this stance, the process of being once again the "author" of a personal narrative not only reflects but can also help change lives and perceptions of problems and identities, because personal narratives construct identity (Carr, 1998), identity being a forever unfinished, mobile and complex concept. The concept of identity acts as a pivot between the social and the individual, so that it is possible to define it in terms of mutual interaction (Rivas, 2010).

As we saw in the previous chapter, for decades, the narrative approach has also been used to inquire into teaching knowledge that will help teachers improve their practice, employing various methods and tools. An example of this is the case of Father Manjón (1900), the founder of the *Ave Maria Schools*, and the importance he gave to keeping diaries in which teachers and students could record the most important events that happened in the schools (Mateos & Núñez, 2011). According to these authors, narrative "implies entering not only into the terrain of what is happening, from these scenarios, but also into the subjective dimension from which these educational actors give meaning to reality" (Mateos & Núñez, 2011, p. 114). This is so because, as Lisette Model is quoted as saying on the National Gallery of Canada website (2019), "the camera is an instrument of detection. We photograph not only what we know, but also what we don't know".

References

Barthes, R. (1989). *La cámara lúcida. Notas sobre la fotografía*. Paidós.
Berger, J. (2000). *Modos de ver*. Gustavo Gili.
Bruner, J. (1986). *Actual minds, possible worlds*. Harvard University Press.
Bruner, J. (1987). Life as narrative. *Social Research, 54*, 12–32.
Bruner, J. (1991). La autobiografía del yo. *Actos de significado* (pp. 110–115). Alianza.
Canal, C., & Ramiro, R. S. (2004). *Recuperar la luz*. Mestizo.
Carr, M. (1998). White's narrative therapy. *Contemporary Family Therapy, 20*(4), 485–503.
Casas, A. (2000). *Album*. Mestizo.
Colom, A., & Mèlich, J. (2003). Narratividad y educación. In *Otros lenguajes en educación*. ICE de la Universitat de Barcelona.

Connelly, M., & Clandinin, J. (1995). Relatos de Experiencia e Investigación Narrativa. In J. Larrosa, *Déjame que te cuente. Ensayos sobre narrativa y educación* (pp. 11–59). Laertes.

Fraile, M. (2016). *Autoetnografía.* Unpublished (images and texts by courtesy of the author).

Genet, R. (2016). *Ciudad y educación artística en la formación inicial del profesorado: una investigación educativa basada en las artes.* Universidad de Granada.

López Fernández Cao, M. (2015). *Para qué el arte. Apuntes sobre arte y educación en tiempos de crisis.* Fundamentos.

Mateos, T., & Núñez, L. (2011). Narrativa y educación: Indagar la experiencia escolar a través de los relatos. *Teoría de la educación, 23*(2), 111–128.

McEwan, H. (1997). The functions of narrative and research on teaching. *Teaching and Teacher Education, 13*(1), 85–92.

Model, L. (2019). https://www.gallery.ca/collection/artist/lisette-model

Pámpano, C. (2017). *Piola.* Unpublished (images and texts by courtesy of the author).

Rivas, J. I. (2010). Narración, conocimiento y realidad. Un cambio de argumento en la investigación. In J. I. Rivas Flores & D. Herrera Pastor, *Voz y Educación. La narrativa como enfoque de interpretación de la realidad.* Octaedro.

Sanz, F. (2015). *La fotobiografía.* Kairós.

Sontag, S. (2014). *Sobre la fotografía.* De Bolsillo.

Springgay, S., Irwin, R. L., & Kind, S. (2005). A/r/tography as living inquiry through art and text. *Qualitative Inquiry, 11*(6), 897–912.

Thysseron, S. (2002). *El misterio de la cámara lúcida.* Ediciones de la Universidad de Salamanca.

Chapter 13
Training Sahrawi Teachers Using Photo-Narration in School

Ángeles Ariza Núñez

Introduction

The arrival of the internet, technological advances and extreme economic difficulties are just some of the factors that have spurred the need for lifelong learning in Sahrawi society. In a globalised world, the question arises of whether ancestral knowledge related, for example, to calculating birth dates, caring for goats and camels, conducting the tea ritual, using camel skins, understanding natural cycles or reading clouds is compatible with knowledge about biodiversity, social media, sport, climate change, soil fertility and so on, generating diverse and at times paradoxical concepts. Rebuilding Sahrawi community values by promoting a school for all—young and old, men and women—has been the Sahrawis' goal ever since their first day of exile and the beginning of their status as a refugee people.

In response to this situation, this chapter presents two training programmes based on the use of photo-narration in an educational environment, highlighting the utility of this practice and reporting the data obtained in two different contexts in terms of the living conditions and type of concerns of the Sahrawis living in each of them. One of the programmes was a personal and professional development course for teachers based on the use of photo-narration and delivered at the Miyik school in the Liberated Territories of Western Sahara. The second was a teacher and student training programme delivered in Algerian territory, where the Sahrawi refugee camps are located, and promoted by the *Club de la Esperanza* [Club for Hope], which will be discussed in the section on field work at this location. The first directly addressed the issue of education and responsibility as regards landmine prevention in the zone,

Á. Ariza Núñez (✉)
Complutense University, Madrid, Spain
e-mail: gelyariza@yahoo.es

A. Bautista García-Vera (ed.), *Photographic Elicitation and Narration in Teachers Education and Development*, Teacher Education, Learning Innovation and Accountability, https://doi.org/10.1007/978-3-031-20164-6_13

which contains several war fronts. The second was aimed at instructing teachers on the creation and representation of ideas in interaction with their students to help these latter express their concerns and uncertainties.

The Geographical and Human Context

Context 1: Liberated Territories

A journey through the desert forms an interesting introduction to the network of schools coordinated by the Ministry of Education of the Sahrawi Arab Democratic Republic (SADR) in the Liberated Territories, whose headquarters are located in the Rabouni camp. The territories not occupied by Morocco ('abbey' in Hassaniya Arabic) cover approximately 50,000 km^2 and represent 25% of the territory of Western Sahara. They are bordered to the north by the desert plateau of Tindouf, Algeria; to the east and south by the Azufal dunes in Mauritania; and to the west by the wall built by Morocco during the 1980s (Fig. 13.1).

At present, the community's response to schooling in a nomadic context has been to incorporate a sedentary component that also establishes a dynamic connection between families coping with the constant difficulties that arise. These include the

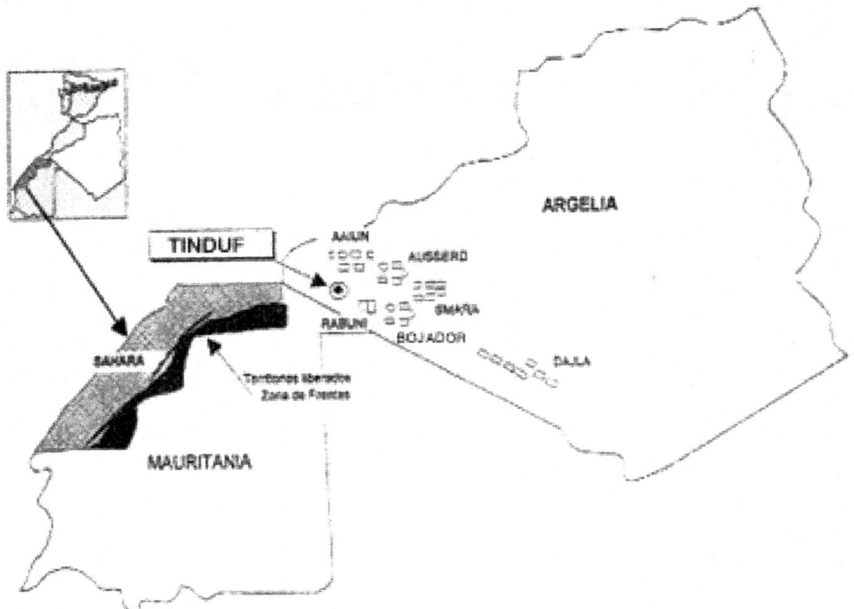

Fig. 13.1 Map of the zone

sirocco wind, water shortages, army alerts, lack of electricity and temperatures of 50 °C.

The Sahrawi people are of Arab-Berber and black African origin. Hassaniya Arabic is their mother tongue and Islam their religion. The ceasefire declared on 6 September 1991 established a United Nations Mission (MINURSO) to preserve the status and designated the Polisario Front as one of the representatives. Teachers today stress that many problems, such as ill health, have become chronic, with students often suffering from dermatological conditions, such as mycosis, pediculosis and scabies, as well as growth disorders due to malnutrition, chronic diarrhoea, parasites or gluten intolerance, which is very common.

Population actions aimed at improving hygiene and access to vaccination programmes, antibiotics and medicines have significantly reduced morbidity and mortality rates in the target population. Nevertheless, many families prefer to live in the Liberated Territories rather than in the refugee camps because these latter form part of the diaspora with no expectation of work and under bureaucratic pressure to regularise or accept the status of occupied territory in their country. In contrast, the Liberated Territories offer a guarantee of employment, and inhabitants engage in activities related to livestock farming or trade with Mauritania, are nomadic depending on the temperature and are guaranteed basic care by the SADR army, which occupies military regions in the zone (Fig. 13.2).

Population	Madrasa [school]
Dougaj Zug	Ahmed Mahmud Mohamed Lamin
Agounit	Larabes Ali Brahim
Mijek	Mulay Haj Sid Brahim
Mheiriz	Labat Selma Mojtar
Bir Tiguisit	Abd Bulahi Mulay
Tifariti	Jalihenna Mohamed Budda
Bir Lehlu	Mohamed Budda

Fig. 13.2 Western Saharan populations under SADR control with *madrasas* (schools) (*Source* by the authors)

Context 2: Sahrawi camps in Algerian Territory

Each Saharawi refugee camp constitutes a *wilayah*, or district, which contains several villages or *dairas*. Named after towns in Western Sahara (Laâyoune, Auserd, Boujdour, Smara and Dakhla), the camps are the primary recipients of international cooperation targeting this population. Accommodation in the *dairas* mainly consists of *jaimas* (Sahrawi tents) with some adobe buildings. The overall population is around 175,000, but the figure varies according to the source and there is no official public census. Some of the inhabitants have been there since 1975 and the youngest are third generation refugees who have never known their home country. The camps are a fertile ground for events, reflections and ideas for cooperation among the nomadic Sahrawi teachers, who create networks as the only possible means to perform their work and assume responsibility for educating people on how to survive.

Storytellers have emerged in the camps as repositories of their people's traditions and knowledge. According to Mahmud Awah (2010), in the land of the Sahrawis, where culture is faithfully preserved in the memory of the people and the libraries are humans, when an old man dies, a library dies with him. One way of leveraging the need to tell stories is to hold cooperative learning sessions so that together, students and teachers can contribute to the transmission and renewal of knowledge, enriching identity and improving survival.

Schooling and Teacher Training as the Collective Construction of Social Responsibility

Trained and considered as artists, Saharawi teachers in both contexts show a social and professional commitment to tackling the historical legacy of their people: personal survival and survival of the essential values that make up their identity. To facilitate this goal, the SADR Ministry of Education created the 9 June Teachers' Centre in order to meet the individual and collective training needs of practising and trainee teachers aged between 19 and 30. Trainee teachers live as weekly boarders (Sunday to Thursday), and 96% are women.

There are different training priorities for teachers with extensive experience of literacy in the trenches and younger ones with a knowledge of languages, social media and so on. Age, gender, expectations and motivation also differ. Schools continue to inspire recognition and respect (including in the study context), are viewed as defenders of identity and employ a traditional teaching model. From the perspective of an occupation within the production system, teachers are not seen merely as caregivers of students while parents work, nor as paid, uncritical transmitters of knowledge.

Saharawi teachers receive a low salary that is not guaranteed and have little time or resources to prepare material, study, meet family needs, attend to visitors, participate in cultural and sports activities, guarantee inclusion or motivate their classes every morning while also supervising attendance, hygiene and nutrition. This creates problems in a State with no guarantee of a sustained civil service, but which needs their involvement and work. Hence, initiatives such as that of the *Club de la Esperanza* [Club of Hope] are welcomed because they make up for acute deficiencies.

The directors of the Saharawi Teachers' Centre are aware of the importance of teaching beliefs and how these influence situations and decision-making throughout the teaching and learning process. Therefore, the Centre's mission is to promote and coordinate training programmes for teachers because at present, a variety of methods are employed. The responsibility of teachers who are starting out in education restricts the power of the school if this is not considered an integral part of life and a learning community. It has been argued that the study of teaching beliefs can render explicit the frameworks of reference that influence how teachers perceive and process information and analyse, make sense of and direct their educational actions (Alarcón et al., 2014). In this respect, the Teachers' Centre promotes quality actions that enable better coordination and participation of teachers and, secondarily, development workers. In class, teachers reinforce the children's cultural identity and raise their critical and active awareness, while recognising that their location and context of a ceasefire puts them in constant danger.

To this end, training programmes are provided aimed at professional and artistic development, using intuitive tools that promote representation and communication of their responsibilities and uncertainties in the spaces of survival where they have sought refuge. Important among these systems of representation is photography, which although simple to use, remains a challenge in this context because not all schools in the refugee camps have electricity and so photography is not always possible.

Two Training Programmes Based on Photo-Narration

The proposed activity using information and communication technologies (ICTs) in schools for the nomadic population and in the Sahrawi refugee camps has generated a space for the creation of photo-narrations based on a language that is familiar, personal and liberating. Images and their accompanying narratives have proved valuable in formal and non-formal education alike as a means to preserve memory, understand the present and ensure survival. History must be considered in relation to a plurality of events that form threads and leave traces across the territory (Gimeno & Robles, 2015). Images are replete with language. We know that images are related to verbal language but they transmit messages that words cannot. Jai (1993) has argued that one cannot write without evoking images. When a group of teachers and students consider and discuss an emotion or sensation represented by several projected photographs, this provides an important opportunity for learning what is presented (e.g. affects, meanings) and enables the values of participation and understanding to emerge and contribute intentions and interpretations of the image content (Bautista, 2013). Sahrawi culture is based on its members' memories rather than on written works. Sahrawi oral narrative, composed almost entirely of stories, is anonymous. Stories in Sahrawi society are generally transmitted within the family, usually from grandparents to grandchildren (Mahmud Awah, 2010). In this respect and in both contexts, photo-narration serving as support for the verbal language of Saharawi teachers formed the basis of the training programmes for the survival of all in general and the improvement of teaching practice in particular, through reflection and debate on their work.

1. Field Work in the Nomadic Area

Salka Salem is a teacher in the Liberated Territories. Every day, she waits for the children to gather round the flag outside the school. Their families are nomads who, for reasons of health, livestock or travel, have pitched their tent in the area, and the children come from miles around to the simple school building named after Sahrawi heroes fallen in war. Her willingness and ability to dialogue with the children who attend reflect a professional teaching experience that includes looking, listening, recreating and constructing knowledge. As an artist in progress, she needs ideas for her classes, but also for the logistics and management of food and safety, for example, and for seeking support to maintain the school. Optimising resources reflects well on the school with its students, their families and the institutions, and helps ensure that the school remains open in the community. It was at such a location that the idea emerged to implement an innovative teaching improvement programme using photo-narration at a school staffed by six teachers and a director.

We proposed to present poster images concerning landmine prevention, based on material and advice sent previously by officials of the Saharawi Ministry of Education, which could be used for prevention education. The structural and organisational rules of these schools do not differ from those found in the refugee camps in terms of assessment, curriculum, subject timetables, inspection visits or assessment criteria. Part of the timetable is devoted to teaching Islam, especially in the first years of schooling, but language (Arabic and Spanish) and mathematics are the fundamental areas (Ariza, 2016). We asked participants to take photographs that when shared with the group would promote reflection on the part of the teachers, while at the same time describing and analysing their goals in relation to their involvement as teachers in terms of strategies for qualitative improvement in their educational community and their commitment to cooperate in the eradication of mines.

Thus, photo-narration supported by verbal narrative served two core purposes in the study: as a means to improve teaching, critical and communicative skills, and as a channel for social advocacy, warning and prevention. In this context, posters were selected that would have a direct impact on children but would also contain a message about responsibility for teachers, the military, parents and relatives. Meetings were held with teachers and students alike, to learn their thoughts about the benefits of this training plan and how it would affect them (Fig. 13.3).

Fig. 13.3 One of the posters proposed to stimulate discussion

Participants were asked to comment on the posters and then, in a subsequent session, to bring personal images for photo-narration sessions from whatever perspective they liked. The knowledge thus generated would be used to plan action templates with these intervention models. The aim was to take photographs with mobile phones and then to present the images. Previously, we confirmed that the images shown at the photo-narration session would depict details of the surroundings that presented elements of identity and concerns about safety and the future. The participants produced texts and images related to the school building, the classroom, the flag, the blackboard, landscapes and a nearby tent. Narratives were presented at both sessions, and those in Hassaniya Arabic (their first language) were translated. Their work corresponded more to their struggle as a people than to any individual concerns, although anxieties about work and family were also expressed. In this session, the authors of the images were asked to explain their selection before narrating the experiences and beliefs depicted. It proved largely unnecessary to moderate the session. Unlike the other photo-elicitation and photo-narration sessions in teacher training contexts described in previous chapters, the debate generated here fundamentally concerned how to resolve the conflict and find ways to ensure survival, rather than inquiry into the value of the situations, processes and teaching triggered.

Aspects that would improve working conditions and gratitude for participating in the teacher training programme were frequent in the first sessions. In all instances, the images had an explicit and an implicit motive. The reason for selecting the image might be that it was the one with the best light, and from there the discussion would move on to the elements that reminded participants of family situations in which the parents still lived and how they lived honourably, Saharan proverbs, religious principles, praise of the army and so on. Congratulations, thanks and courtesies gave way to recognition of the situation and even proposals for joint school actions in remembrance practices. Hence, we could classify the interventions according to whether they were courtesies related to the visit or the training programme, explanations of the image, emotional expression or professional practice. Of all these topics, the one that consumed most discussion time was the vindication of their rights. The procedure employed in the photo-narration session using posters led to a description of the conflict, politics or management and the role of the European powers and the UN, supported by images as a context for prevention and collaboration in actions aimed at protection and security. The use of images, aesthetic composition and so on were briefly discussed in a mixture of Hassaniya Arabic and Spanish.

The participative photo-narration sessions also contributed to literacy in the language of photography and questioning of the value of the representations of reality presented. The teachers saw their role not only as teachers, but also as members of the community and as such, expressed their opinions accordingly. In subsequent sessions, consideration was given to the need to include parents and development workers and to allocate time to work on first aid. At the same time, second-hand mobile phones were obtained so that the students could take photographs and participate in literacy classes on visual language. Participants also requested more innovative proposals for classroom work. Through the creation, revision and analysis of the posters during meetings, the message was established through joint observation and reflection, the central core of the images was assessed and the context and its ethical and aesthetic perspective were included (Fig. 13.4).

This type of participative work in a training programme for nomadic Saharawi teachers proved important as a means to transform theory into practice, given the effect that the strength of their representation and verbalisation of conflicts had on their self-image and on their practice as teachers. They may not have been familiar with the public speaking required by photo-narration, but they were committed to defending their rights. Teachers located in the Liberated Territories are required to discuss, exchange and develop teaching practice with barely any resources. Consequently, sharing narratives offers a useful dialogical strategy to consolidate identity, prepare for and prevent unanticipated emergencies and improve their practice in a hyper-mediatised global culture and where immediacy has become a social pressure.

The other aspect of the teacher training programme supported by photo-narration was that, as desert nomads, the teachers working in the Liberated Territories then implemented the sessions with their students, encouraging them

Fig. 13.4 Pictures of the school in the nomadic area, taken by the group of teachers

to select and sequence some of the photographs they had taken. To this end, the teachers raised these questions and suggestions with them:

How will you explain to your family what you have seen? Say it with an image. We are waiting to hear what you have to say. Describe what you learnt today. Don't forget that where you live is the entire setting, and you decide on the characters and theme. Tell us how it tastes, smells, sounds or feels on the way to school, or when you play around the tent, when you are looking after the animals, if the goats escape, or when you find water or couscous is waiting for you at home.

The specific details of their photo-narrations shed light on what is happening. They said whether the posters helped provide a better knowledge of the terrain or what to do in an emergency, such as discovering a mine on the path (Fig. 13.5).

Fig. 13.5 Image of the outside of the school in the nomadic area, at the start of a new day. Illustration of the texts compiled when pooling images from the posters. Taken by the group of teachers

2.   Field Work in the Refugee Camps

The second Saharawi teacher training programme based on photo-narration was delivered in the Saharawi refugee camp of Smara, with the help of Mohamed Moulud, a photographer by training and one of the founding members, together with Ahmed Buyema, of the *Club de la Esperanza* [Club of Hope]. This association was launched in 2016 with activities and workshops for children to promote creativity, imagination, self-esteem, social skills and abilities (https://www.facebook.com/El-club-dela-esperanza-2993134671188715/). Through its connection with the SADR Teachers' Centre, a theoretical and practical training programme was drawn up aimed at teachers and students in the seventh grade or first year of secondary school. The purpose of the programme was to assess the value of participative photography, highlighting its potential for communication and consolidation of identity and the improvement that this knowledge brings when planning teaching work. To this end, children were encouraged to reflect on their relationship with their surroundings, on themselves and on others in an informal educational context but one endowed with the resources of formal education and the cooperation of the Abda Mohamed school management and its teachers, in the *wilayah* of Smara.

In line with the training programme, workshops were based on descriptions, portraits and mini photo-narrations, and the aspects that the teachers assessed most positively were enthusiasm, innovative knowledge, motivation and social impact. Aware of the interest shown by associations of friends of the Saharawi people in Spain, the teachers collaborated by sending them requests for support, enabling them to participate in the campaign by collecting mobile phones. They also engaged in the project, because as one of the teachers said: "We've discovered that it's good for coexistence between colleagues, that you can learn outside, work cooperatively, go and see new realities together, even if they're as close by as the next dune". In addition, Mohamed Moulud considered that it was a valuable means to detect problems, from family difficulties to conflicts between children or weaknesses in learning, which were then transmitted to the teachers for further resolution. The workshops were held outside on the sand or indoors in a classroom when the goal was to deliver theoretical knowledge, and they were always held in the afternoon, after school, as a voluntary activity. Besides the teachers, there were never fewer than ten other attendees, all aged between twelve and thirteen (Fig. 13.6).

The same flexibility as that described for photo-elicitation in earlier chapters was applied in these sessions aimed at perception, analysis, reflection and debate prompted by the different forms of photo-narration. In these training workshops, it was the students who took the photographs and used them to create stories with important characters: the teachers at the school hosting this training programme.

As Mohamed Moulud observed, the children who attended were able to describe how they lived through photography. We always started with a few minutes devoted to simple technical aspects before moving on to a common subject. For example, as the children leave after school, situations arise such as the ones captured in the photographs shown in Fig. 13.7, taken by Hamdi Mohamed, Wali Salem and Jalil Said, among other students. These photographs create the opportunity for subsequently discussing with their teachers why they run as they leave, feeling lonely in the absence of friends, or the distribution of sandwiches. Values, ideas and emotions are transmitted via the images. The possibility of having a recycled mobile phone allowed participants to construct their own photographic discourse: being able to make as many mistakes as they liked formed the basis for creative activity, because as with a blackboard and chalk, there was no great cost or waste of energy involved in keeping something. In addition, the teachers acquired the knowledge to analyse, discuss and, if they considered it necessary, redirect their teaching practice in the classroom and the school.

It is difficult to eradicate dominant gender role stereotypes, and in the workshop, it was fundamental for boys and girls to work together. Nevertheless,

Fig. 13.6 Poster for mobile phone collection, for the *Club de la Esperanza* [Club of Hope] Photography workshop

raising awareness in the educational community of the need for girls to partic-ipate outside school hours and in contexts other than school remain challenges to be overcome (Fig. 13.8).

In their assessment of this training programme in the Sahrawi camps, the participating teachers, students and their families considered it positive for the children to be creating their own images rather than always being portrayed as refugees. The work of production, but not of reproduction, is that of educating the gaze, which subsequently facilitates awareness through the narration of what is represented in a particular way using the language of photography. The gaze can connect practice and narration. We believe that the imagination, determination and commitment of these teachers in terms of inquiry into their practice not only improved school outcomes but also revitalised the curriculum of the Saharawi people. In this case, technology was not the biggest obstacle.

Fig. 13.7 Activity proposed in the workshop: children leaving school after the distribution of sandwiches

Supporting the School of Resistance

What have these training programmes given to the participating teachers? Among other perceptions, teachers felt encouraged to remain at the school where they worked. At the end of the course, one of the teachers said "It has been a good experience to be able to talk and communicate through the photographs we took and in doing so, to feel that what we talked about while looking at the images was very important to others. This gives us the strength to keep doing what we do, and for other teachers in these remote areas to feel that telling stories with photographs is like a bucket for getting water from the well. It's not just that we lack material things; often we feel burnt out with no ideas. We welcome ideas that help us move forwards without rejecting our culture and our resistance". Another teacher assessed the training as follows: "It's necessary to talk together to share and analyse what

Fig. 13.8 Practical workshop session (*Source* Mohamed Moulud)

we do, and that's why I liked sequencing the photographs while saying why I did it that way. I also liked it because training for the teachers here shouldn't just be about technological specialisation or language courses, but should require each and every one of us to think together. The photo-narration sessions and the trips to the Teachers' Centre were fundamental, as was experiencing these initiatives in which personal and joint effort brings new perspectives that will last for a long time".

These two assessments refer to both training programmes using photo-narration to promote inquiry into and reflection on teaching in order to improve the participants' teaching practice under the difficult conditions in which they find themselves. The collaborative production of images has proved a fundamental tool to stimulate discussion of conflict and generate answers particular to a population in need of an education for survival. We have developed an approach that combines photography with the accumulated verbal legacy of the history of the Saharawi people, using photo-narration as a tool to document and acquire information and raise awareness of risks. From a dialogical perspective, these training narratives have heightened interest in the preventive aspect of education, in the communication of oneself to others and in the associated element of creativity in contexts of uncertainty. In sum, this chapter has sought to contribute to the recognition of photo-narration and its critical and expressive potential in educational environments in extreme situations, to explore ways of seeing in teacher training, to disseminate the participants' efforts, to continue the work in this school of resistance and to express our hope that it may be well received in other contexts to promote a culture of peace.

References

Alarcón, P., et al. (2014). Conceptualizaciones metafóricas sobre el rol del profesor en estudiantes de pedagogía. *Estudios Pedagógicos, 40*(2), 29–37.

Ariza, A. (2016). *Educación y cooperación en situaciones extremas de vida: el caso de los refugiados saharauis.* SICOE. Universidad de Málaga. file:///C:/Users/InforPC11/Downloads/Libro%20de%20Actas%20SICOE_2016.pdf

Bautista, A. (2013). Indagación Narrativa visual en la práctica educativa. *Educación y Futuro, 29,* 69–79.

Gimeno, J. C., & Robles, J. I. (2015). Hacia una contrahistoria del Sahara Occidental. *Les Cahiers d'EMAM, 82,* 24–25.

Jai, M. (1993). Ojos abatidos. Akal.

Mahmud Awah, B. (2010). Literatura oral y transmisión en el Sáhara. *Quaderns De La Mediterrània, 13,* 207–210.

Proyecto Almadaras. (2019). https://prensahara.org/cooperacion-con-el-parlamento-de-andalucia/

Printed by Printforce, United Kingdom